Scientific Writing Techniques and Project Management in Biotechnology

Scientific Writing Techniques and Project Management in Biotechnology

By

Dr. Simmi Kharb
Associate Professor
Medical Biochemistry
Pt. B.D. Sharma PGIMS
Rohtak, Haryana

UNIVERSITY SCIENCE PRESS

(An Imprint of Laxmi Publications Pvt. Ltd.)

BANGALORE • CHENNAI • COCHIN • GUWAHATI • HYDERABAD
JALANDHAR • KOLKATA • LUCKNOW • MUMBAI • PATNA
RANCHI • NEW DELHI

Published by :

UNIVERSITY SCIENCE PRESS

(An Imprint of Laxmi Publications Pvt. Ltd.)

113, Golden House, Daryaganj,

New Delhi-110002

Phone : 011-43 53 25 00

Fax : 011-43 53 25 28

www.laxmipublications.com

info@laxmipublications.com

First Edition : 2009

OFFICES

✆ **Bangalore**	080-26 75 69 30	✆ **Chennai**	044-24 34 47 26
✆ **Cochin**	0484-237 70 04, 405 13 03	✆ **Guwahati**	0361-251 36 69, 251 38 81
✆ **Hyderabad**	040-24 65 23 33	✆ **Jalandhar**	0181-222 12 72
✆ **Kolkata**	033-22 27 43 84	✆ **Lucknow**	0522-220 99 16
✆ **Mumbai**	022-24 91 54 15, 24 92 78 69	✆ **Patna**	0612-230 00 97
✆ **Ranchi**	0651-221 47 64		

USW-9267-150-SC WRI TEC & PRO MAN IN BIO **C—16081/08/07**

Typeset at : Kalyani Computer Services, New Delhi.

CONTENTS

1. Techniques in Molecular Biology ... 1–40

Introduction	...	1
Techniques in Molecular Biology	...	1
Isolation and Separation of Nucleic Acid	...	2
Restriction of Mapping of DNA Fragments	...	7
Polymerase Chain Reaction (PCR)	...	14
Nucleic Acid Blotting	...	23
Nucleotide Sequencing of DNA	...	24
Gene Probe, Derivation and its Detection	...	30
Microarrays	...	36
Summary	...	39
Review Questions	...	39

2. Techniques in Recombinant DNA Technology ... 41–76

Human Genomic Project	...	41
Recombinant DNA Technology	...	42
DNA Libraries	...	51
Analysing Whole Genome	...	54
Analysing Genes	...	55
Identification of Genes in Cloned DNA	...	58
Analysis of Human Genome Database	...	59
Analysing Gene Expression	...	61
Protein Arrays and Protein Chips	...	73
Summary	...	75
Review Questions	...	75

3. Bioinformatics and Computer Applications ... 77–151

Bioinformatics : Introduction	...	77
Computational Biology	...	95

Gene ... 121
Genomics ... 122
Microarrays ... 133
Molecular Imprints or Protein Chips ... 136
Sequence Analysis of Proteins and Nucleic Acids ... 136
Software Programs for Finding Genes ... 139
Prediction of Structure and Function of Proteins and Genes ... 140
Proteomics ... 143
Summary ... 148
Review Questions ... 148

4. Scientific Writing ... 152–175

Scientific Paper ... 152
Guidelines for Writing a Scientific Paper ... 154
Review Articles ... 156
Reports ... 158
Thesis and Dissertation ... 161
How to Write References Bibliography of Research Paper:
Vancouver Style ... 162
Additional Notes on the Vancouver Style ... 172
A Sample Reference List ... 173
Summary ... 174
Review Questions ... 174

5. Scientific Literature ... 176–184

Writing an Abstract for a Scientific Meeting ... 176
Using the Computer in Research ... 176
The Literature ... 178
Methodology References ... 179
Computer-Based Searches and Other Aids to Literature ... 183
Summary ... 183
Review Questions ... 184

6. Funding Agencies ... 185–190

Science Funding Organizations ... 185
Basis and Technology for Starting a New Project ... 186

Summary ... 189
Review Questions ... 189

7. Preparation of R & D Projects for Funding ... 191–206

Organization of Research Project ... 191
Certain Considerations ... 191
Modern Models of Team Work ... 193
Three Common Characteristics of Successful Team ... 193
Organization of a Research Project ... 194
Research Process ... 195
Criteria for the Selection of a Research Problem ... 200
Types of Research ... 200
Aims and Objectives of Research Projects ... 201
Ethical Issues in Data Collection ... 202
Summary ... 204
Review Questions ... 204

8. Biological Resource Centres & Bioresources ... 207–227

Introduction ... 207
Biological Resources ... 208
The Need for Biological Resource Centres ... 209
National & International BRCs ... 213
Financial Support for BRC ... 217
Responsibilities of BRC ... 220
A Call for Action for Biological Resources ... 226
Summary ... 227
Review Questions ... 227

9. Capital Investment ... 228–235

Commercial Potential of Biotechnology ... 228
Cost Estimation of the Project ... 231
Biotech Product-Based Life Cycle ... 232
Summary ... 235
Review Questions ... 235

10. Marketing Strategies for Biotechnological Products ... 236–246

What is Project Management ... 236
New Product Development ... 237
What should a New Company Have? ... 239
Bioentrepreneur ... 240
Marketing Strategies for Biotechnology Products ... 241
Advertising ... 242
Market Trends ... 242
Summary ... 246
Review Questions ... 246

11. Intellectual Property Rights Concepts and Relevance ... 247–252

Intellectual Property (IP) ... 247
Benefits of IPR ... 248
Categories of IPR ... 248
Management of IPR ... 250
Benefits of IPR ... 251
Problems of IPR ... 251
Summary ... 251
Review Questions ... 251

12. Biotechnological Patents ... 253–263

Introduction ... 253
IPR ... 253
Patent ... 254
Biotechnological Patents ... 257
Patenting of Genes and DNA Sequences ... 259
Broad Patents in Biotechnology ... 260
Indian Response to Patent Upheaval ... 261
Basics of Patent Licensing ... 262
Summary ... 262
Review Questions ... 262

Preface

The book titled 'Scientific Writing Techniques and Project Management in Biotechnology' has been designed to provide a comprehensive basic text for medical and biotechnology students to make them conversant with molecular biology techniques, bioinformatics, art of planning and writing scientific research, issues of ethics and funding that arise while doing a research.

In the past decades, the power of genetic analysis has grown with the introduction of recombinant DNA technology and genomics. Acquiring DNA sequence has become a routine! Deciphering genetic information encoded in DNA sequence requires knowledge of what to look for, algorithms capable of detecting interesting features in sequences and computers to perform such complex analysis, leading to emergence of the new field of **bioinformatics.**

Molecular biology is driven to a great extent by economics and a future researcher/ biotechnologist needs to be conversant with patenting issues; biotech project management and product life cycle and capital investment and marketing, leading to emergence of a specialized subject **biotechnology entrepreneurship.**

The book has separate sections on survey of techniques in molecular biology; research and development of projects; management of projects and marketing of biotechnology inventions; and intellectual property and patenting.

Although every effort has been made to ensure the correctness of the text, the author would be grateful to hear from any reader who discovers possible errors and inadequacies. Constructive suggestions for improvement of the text would be welcomed with due acknowledgement.

—AUTHOR

Chapter 1

TECHNIQUES IN MOLECULAR BIOLOGY

INTRODUCTION

Amazing developments in biotechnology in late twentieth century include—decoding of human genome, cloning, gene therapy, progress in stem cell research and RNA interference.

Many earlier landmark discoveries that unveiled the mysteries of genetics and paved way for modern molecular biology. Beginning with Mendel's experiments with garden peas published in 1866, suggesting concept of genes as discrete units of heredity. Morgan in 1910 revealed chromosomes as units of heredity and Avery in 1944 confirmed through bacterial studies that DNA carried genetic information with Watson Crick's DNA double-helical model of DNA in 1953, Smith demonstrated that DNA can be cleaved by restriction enzymes. This facilitated the subsequent development of RECOMBINANT DNA TECHNOLOGIES.

With construction of genetic map using restricting enzymes by Nathans, Southern Blot was invented in 1975 to detect specific DNA sequences. This led to development of DNA sequencing methodologies and first complete DNA sequence of bacteriophage was discovered. PCR (Polymerase Chain Reaction) was developed by Mullis and Coworkers in 1985. Then, simultaneous interrogation of gene transcripts by DNA microarrays became a reality in 1996. The human genome sequence was completed in 2003.

These great discoveries shaped the modern genetics, molecular biology and biotechnology.

TECHNIQUES IN MOLECULAR BIOLOGY

Almost all the experiments dealing with gene manipulations require pure forms of DNA, RNA or both. Thus, there is need for reliable isolation techniques for nucleic acids.

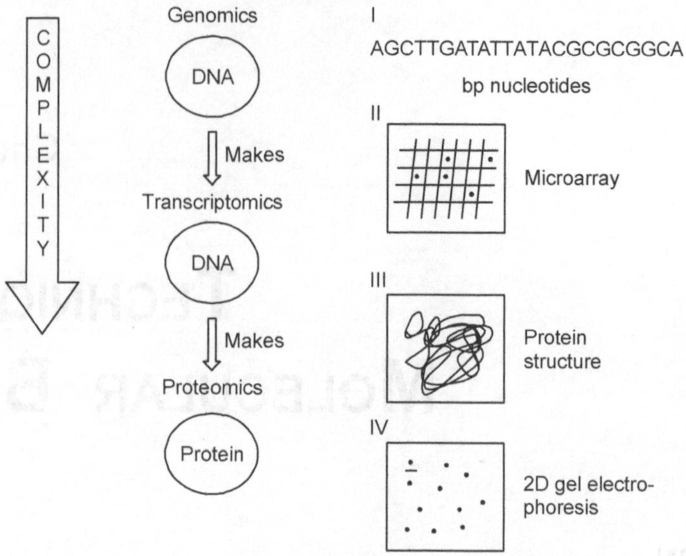

Figure 1.1 Complexity of genomic data processing

Steps

1. Breaking of cells to expose nucleic acid.
2. Separation of nucleic acid from other components.
3. Recovery of nucleic acid.

ISOLATION AND SEPARATION OF NUCLEIC ACID

Isolation of Nucleic Acids

Study of purified nucleic acids have led to many key advances in understanding of DNA and RNA and extraction and isolation of nucleic acid is a key step to subsequent molecular analysis.

Isolation of DNA

Depending on type of specimen, volume required, yield, purity, size of isolated nucleic acid, ease of operation, throughput, cost, use of hazardous reagents, automation of procedure, the most appropriate protocol is selected.

Specimens. Whole blood, plasma, serum tissue biopsies, cultured cells, buccal swabs, paraffin-embedded tissue, CSF, amniotic fluid etc.

(*a*) DNA Extraction

Protocols for DNA extraction can be classified as:

1. Liquid-phase extraction.
2. Solid-phase extraction.

1. *Liquid-phase extraction.* Useful when large quantity of DNA or large sample volumes are involved.

2. *Solid-phase extraction.* They are most commonly used.

Advantage

- Easy to operate.
- Large batches of specimen can be processed.
- High reproducibility.
- Can be automated.

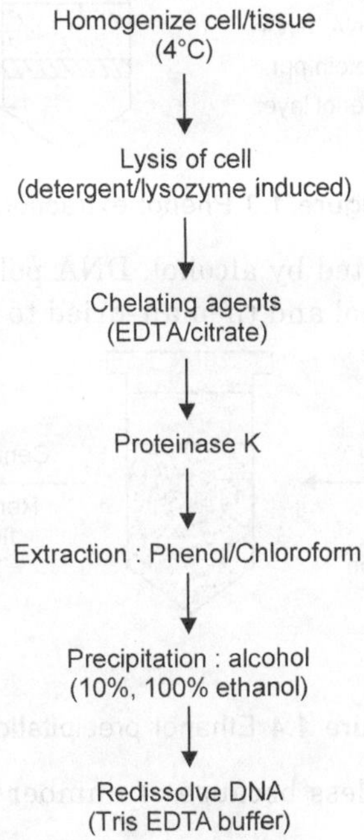

Figure 1.2 Extraction of DNA from cells or tissues

Procedure

Solid-phase extraction

1. *First Step:* Cell lysis—both cell and nuclear membrane envelopes are disrupted.
2. *Next:* Removal of cell proteins—by salt precipitation.

   or Degradation of cell proteins—by enzymes.
3. *Additional Step:* RNase digestion—optional.
4. *Next:* Precipitation of genomic DNA remaining in solution by alcohol.
5. *Next:* Isolation and rehydration of DNA precipitation DNA EXTRACT

   (*i*) Solution is allowed to pass through silica—impregnated filter which binds and purifies DNA from other debris present in the alcohol solution or magnetic particles can be used instead of silica.

(*ii*) Or centrifugation or vacuum manifolds can be used for filtration steps.

The resultant DNA extract can be stored until subsequent analysis.

Liquid-phase extraction

Difference is:

1. In separation of cellular and protein debris from soluble DNA by solvent extraction. *e.g.*, phenol-chloroform protocol.

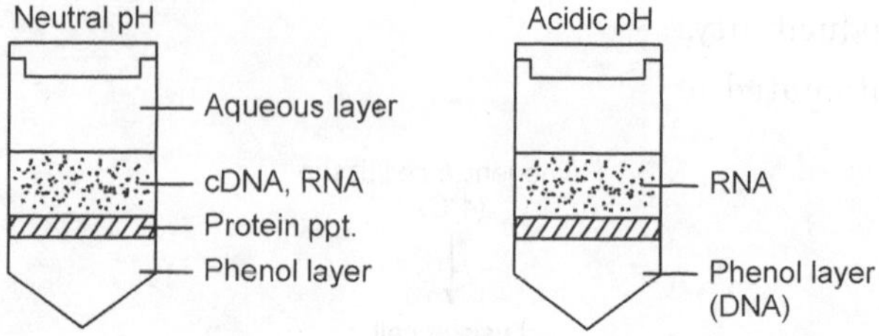

Figure 1.3 Phenol extraction

2. After DNA is precipitated by alcohol, DNA pellet is isolated by careful manual removal of excess alcohol and then air-dried to remove residual drops of alcohol.

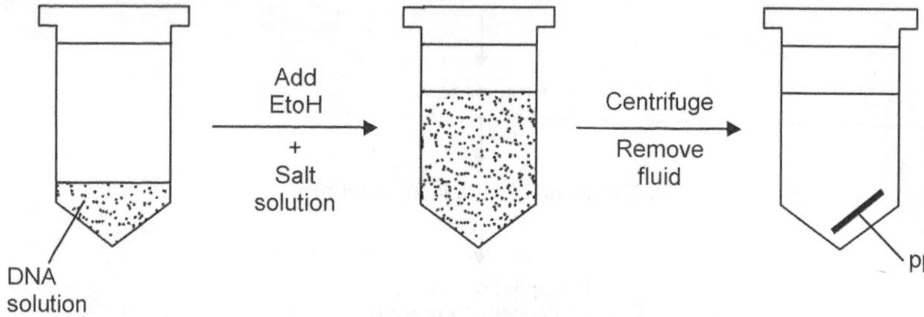

Figure 1.4 Ethanol precipitation

3. Sample throughput is less because of number of manual steps involved in the solution base methods.

(*b*) Elution of DNA

Bound DNA is usually washed and eluted by using nuclease-free water or low ionic strength buffers.

If magnetic particles are used then DNA molecules precoated with magnetic beads are retained placing solution under magnetic field. Magnetic beads are then removed from purified DNA.

Other protocols for DNA extraction

1. Use of isolated columns: 96-well plate formats are available commercially.
2. Automated platforms.

Isolation of RNA

RNA extraction and analysis are required for gene expression studies.

Pecularities of RNA

RNA: Less stable than DNA

- Not protected by double-helical conformation.
- Subject to alkaline hydrolysis via 2′ hydroxyl group of its ribose moiety.
- Degraded by RNA-specific nuclease (RNAases).
- RNAases are ubiquitous, hence difficult to work with native RNA molecules in the lab.
- Thus, special attention is required while working with RNA.

Precautions while handling RNA

1. Due to inherent instability, specimens intended for RNA analysis should be:
   (*a*) processed promptly in fresh state or
   (*b*) preserved immediately by:
      (*i*) addition of preservation agents *e.g.,* RNA later™.
      (*ii*) snap frozen by liquid nitrogen.
2. Number of freeze-thaw cycles should be minimized.
3. Using RNase-free-reagents, plastic ware to avoid RNAase contamination.
4. Clean or decontaminate working surface and equipments with RNase-free detergents or chemicals.
5. Use water treated with DEPC (diethyl pyrocarbonate) for inactivation of RNAase.
6. Care should be taken to avoid DNA contamination. DNAase I treatment in commonly incorporated to digest DNA during RNA purification.

RNA extraction

Procedure

Identical to DNA extraction, RNA extraction is also solution-based and solid-phase extraction protocols.

1. *First.* Cell lysis—Release of RNA tissue specimens need to be ground thoroughly to fine powder form before lysis. This procedure should be performed on either snap-frozen tissue or specimen preserved with RNA stabilizing agents to prevent RNA degradation to release RNA.

   Lysis buffers:

   - include phenol.
   - sodium dodecyl sulfate.
   - guanidinium salts.
   - lyse the cells.
   - inhibit RNAase.
2. *Next.* isolation and purification of RNA from protein and lipids by:

(*i*) phenol-chloroform extraction.

(*ii*) reversible binding to silica.

3. *Next.* precipitation of RNA by alcohol.

Thus, with the above procedure, total RNA comprising of mRNA, rRNA, snRNA and tRNA is isolated.

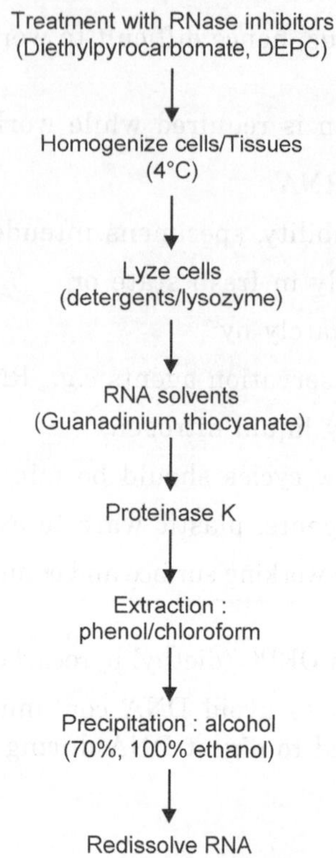

Figure 1.5 Steps involved in extraction of RNA from cells or tissues

Isolation of mRNA

Polyadenylated tails on 3′ ends of mRNA by hybridization to cellulose-bound oligo (dT molecules).

Nucleic Acid Yield and Quality

Principle of Assessment

Nucleic acids absorb UV light maximally at 260 nm owing to its bases. Thus, DNA or RNA yield can be quantified based on this principle.

Methods

1. Spectrophotometric method—gives purity of same.
2. Densitometric method —gives size of isolated DNA or RNA–provides better precision.
3. Automated analyzers—using prefabricated chips and microfluidic channels are available which are both sensitive and precise.

RESTRICTION OF MAPPING OF DNA FRAGMENTS

Restriction mapping involves the size analysis produced by several restriction enzymes individually and in combination.

Enzymes Used in Molecular Biology

Table 1.1 Enzymes used in molecular biology

Molecular Tools Enzymes
1. Restriction Endonuclease.
2. DNA Ligase.
3. Alkaline Phosphatase (ALP).
4. DNA Modifying Enzyme:
(*i*) Nuclease
Endonuclease
Exonuclease
(*a*) DNA-dependent DNA polymerase
(*b*) RNA-dependent DNA polymerase
(*c*) DNA-dependent RNA polymerase
(*ii*) Polymerase
(*iii*) Enzyme modifying ends of DNA
(*a*) ALP
(*b*) Polynucleotide kinase
(*c*) Terminal (deoxy nucleotide) transferase
(*iv*) Others

Restriction Endonuclease

Restriction endonucleases (type II) are one of the most important group of enzymes for manipulation of DNA. They are bacterial enzymes that can cut/split DNA of any source at specific sites. They were first discovered in bacteria *E-coli* restricting the replication of bacteriophages, by cutting the viral DNA. Thus, the enzymes that restrict the viral replication are known as Restriction Enzymes or Restriction Endonucleases.

Types of Endonuclease

Three different types of restriction enzymes are known.

Table 1.2 Types of restriction endonucleases

	Type I	*Type II*	*Type III*
Methylase and endonuclease activity	Single bifunctional enzyme	Separate enzymes	Single bifunctional enzyme

Subunits	Three: R_2 M_2 S_1	Two: One for methylase one for endonuclease (two copies)	Two
Recognition site	Bipartite asymmetric	4–6 bp often palindromic sequence	5–7 bp asymmetric sequence
Cleavage site	Non-specific	Within or close to recognition size	24–26 bp down stream of recognition site
ATP requirement for restriction	Required	None	Required
Practical applications	—	Restriction mapping, recombinant DNA technology	—

Type II Restriction Endonucleases

Type II Restriction Endonucleases recognize certain DNA sequences, usually 4–6 bp in length and cleave them in a defined manner. The sequences recognized are palindromic or of an inverted repeat nature, (they read the same in both directions on each strand). When cleaved they leave a blunt or sticky ended fragments depending on the particular enzyme used.

Table 1.3 Recognition sequences restriction enzymes from various sources

Enzyme (source)	*Recognition sequence*	*Products*	
Hpa II (H. para influenzae)	↓ 5′–CCGG–3′ 3′–GGCC–5′ ↑	5′–C 3′–GGC	CGG–3′ C–5′
Hae III (H-aegyptius)	↓ 5′ GGCC–3′ 3′ CCGG–5′ ↑	5′–GG 3′–CC	CC–3′ GG–5′
Bam HI (Bacillus amyloliquefaciens)	↓ 5′ GGATCC 3′ 3′ CCTAGG 5′ ↑	5′–G 3′–CCTAG	GATCC–3′ G–5′
ECoRI (E. Coli)	↓ 5′–GAATTC–3′ 3′–CTTAAG-G–5′ ↑	5′G 3′–CTTAAG	AATTC–3′ G–5′
Hind III (H. influenzae)	↓ 5′–A-A-GCTT–3′ 3′–TTCGAA 5′ ↑	5′–A 3′–TTCGA	AGCTT–3′ A–5′

Approximately 500 restriction enzymes have been characterized and recognized around 100 different target sequences.

Nomenclature

The nomenclature follows a general pattern:

1. Ist letter: indicates genus name (in capital, italics).
2. Next two letters (in italics) indicate species.
3. Then comes the strain of the organism.

   e.g., Eco*RI* is from Escherichia (E) coli (*co*), strain Ry 13 (R) and first endonuclease (I) to be discovered.
4. This is followed by a Roman numeral indicating order of discovery.

Recognition Sequences

The recognition sequences for type II restriction endonuclease are palindromes with rotational symmetry. They are 4–6 bp, GC rich *e.g.*, *Eco*RI recognition site.

Cleavage Patterns

Most type II restriction endonucleases cleave DNA within their specific recognition sequences and these cuts fragments may have *sticky ends* or *cohesive ends* (Table 1.3). DNA fragments with sticky ends are particularly useful for recombinant DNA experiment.

Fragmentation of DNA with Restriction Enzymes

Type II restriction endonucleases have target sites which are 4–8bp in length. If all the bases are equally frequent in a DNA molecule, then a tetranucleotide is expected to occur on every 4^4 (*i.e.*, 256) nucleotide pairs in a long random DNA sequence.

Table 1.4 Expected number of DNA fragments produced by restriction enzymes from different genomes

Organism	*Genome size (haploid, n)*	*Expected Number of Fragments*		
		4 cutter (4^4 = 256)	*6 cutter (4^6 = 4096)*	*8 cutter (4^8 = 65536)*
E. Coli	4.70×10^6 bp	18,359	1,147	72
Saccharomyces cerevisiae	1.35×10^7 bp	52,734	3,296	206
Drosophilia melangogaster	1.80×10^8 bp	7,03,125	43,945	2,764
Homo Sapiens	2.80×10^9 bp	10,93,750	6,83,593	42,274

DNA Ligase

Sticky (staggered) ends are complementary and will anneal to eachother. These pairing are transient owing to weakness of hydrogen bonding between few bases in the sticky ends, but they can be stabilized by enzyme *DNA Ligase.*

Fragments produced by cleavage with Bam HI.

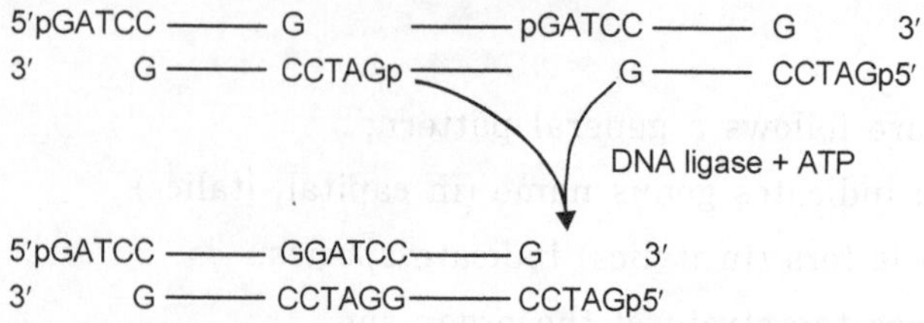

Figure 1.6 Ligation molecules with cohesive (sticky) ends. Complementary ends base-pair to form a temporary link between two DNA fragments which is stabilized by formation of 3′→5′ phosphodiester linkages between these ends catalyzed by DNA ligase.

This covalent joining of ends by DNA ligase enzyme is widely exploited in molecular biology to construct recombinant DNA *i.e.,* joining of DNA fragments from different sources.

Table 1.5 Other Enzyme used in Manipulation of Nucleic Acids

Enzymes	*Use*
1. Alkaline phosphatase	Remove phosphate group to prevent unwanted ligation of DNA. (*i.e.,* prevent recirculation and DNA dimer formation). This allows insection of foreign DNA through DNA ligase.
2. DNA ligase	Join DNA molecule by forming 3′→5′ phosphodiester linkage.
3. DNA polymerase I	Synthesize complementary DNA.
4. Taq DNA polymerase	Used in PCR.
5. Nuclease:	
(*i*) DNAase I	Non-specific endonuclease produce single stranded nicks in DNA.
(*ii*) Exonuclease III	3′→5′ step wise removal of nucleotides.
(*iii*) RNAase A	Cleaves and digests RNA.
(*iv*) SI nuclease	Used in mapping studies single-strand-specific nuclease (degrades single stranded DNA and RNA).
6. Reverse transcriptase (RNA-dependent DNA polymerase)	Synthesize DNA from RNA used in cDNA synthesis.
7. Terminal transferase	Add homopolymertail (nucleotides to 3′ end of DNA).
8. Polynucleotide kinase (PNK)	Transfer terminal phosphate group from ATP to 5′-OH groups of DNA or RNA.
9. Methylase	Methylates specific residuces and protects from cleavage by restriction enzymes.

Restriction Mapping of DNA Fragments

Restriction mapping involves the size analysis of restriction fragments produced by several restriction enzymes individually and in combination (as discussed above).

Restriction Enzyme Digestion

Restriction enzyme recognize specific nucleotide sequence: *recognition sequences* in DNA. Restriction sequences are usually 4, 5 or 6 nucleotides long and restriction enzyme can cut both strands of DNA at specific locations.

There are three ways in which DNA fragments can be cut:

(*i*) *Staggered cut* to leave a 5′ *overhang*: a short single-stranded region of DNA is left that has a 5′ end and overhangs the end of the double-staranded DNA.

(*ii*) *Staggered cut* to leave a 3′ *overhang.*

(*iii*) *Blunt end:* a cut in the same place on both the ends.

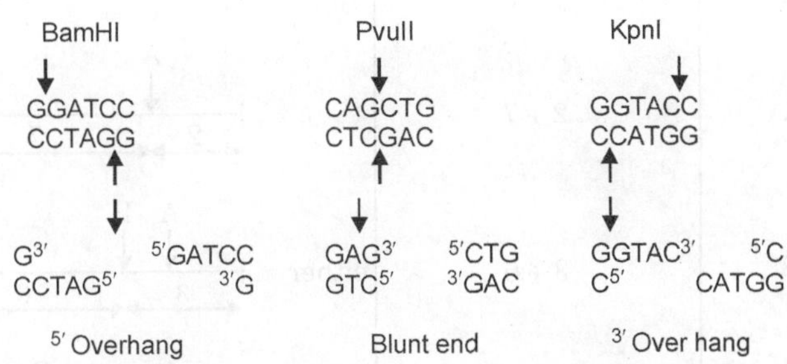

Figure 1.7 Cleavage by restriction enzymes

Restriction Map

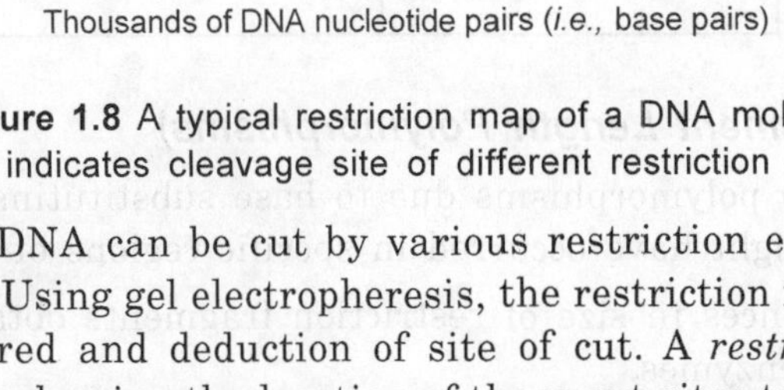

Figure 1.8 A typical restriction map of a DNA molecule (letters indicates cleavage site of different restriction enzymes)

Double stranded DNA can be cut by various restriction enzymes having different recognition sequences. Using gel electropheresis, the restriction fragments are separated, their sizes are measured and deduction of site of cut. A *restriction map* of the DNA molecule can be drawn showing the location of these cut sites termed as RESTRICTION SITES. By using restriction map, different DNA molecules can be compared (*e.g.,* examining evalutionary relationship between two species) without determining their nucleotide sequence.

Also restriction maps are important experimentally in recombinant DNA work, for planning desired cutting of DNA molecule and for monitoring the progress of the experiment.

Taking the following example of mapping of DNA in which restriction sites of two enzymes A and B are mapped.

Cleavage of 9 kb molecule with A gives fragments 2 and 7 kb. So, single A site can be positioned 2 kb from one end. Similarly, enzyme B gives fragments of 3 and 6 kb *i.e.,* B has single site 3 kb from one end. But it is not. However, it is not possible at this state to predict whether it (B) is near to A site or at the opposite end of DNA.

Table 1.6 Restriction Mapping of DNA

Treatment	*Fragment size (kb)*	*Interpretation*
No digestion	9	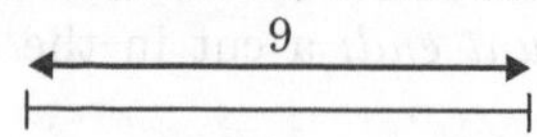
Enzyme A	2 + 7	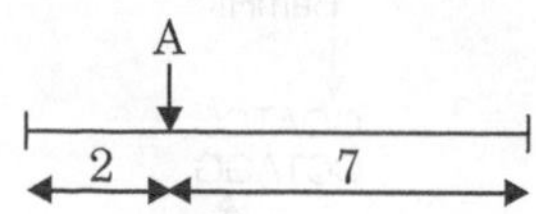
Enzyme B	3 + 6	either 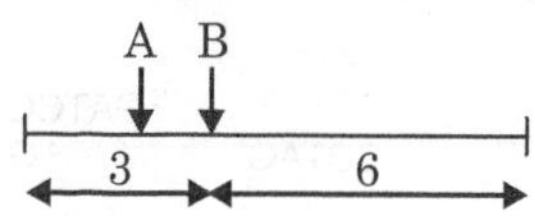
		or 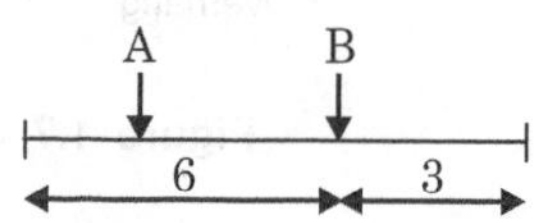
Enzyme A + B	2, 3 + 4	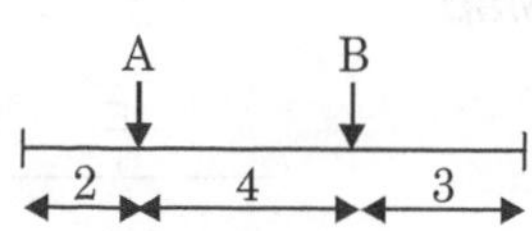
	Alternative result 1, 2 + 6	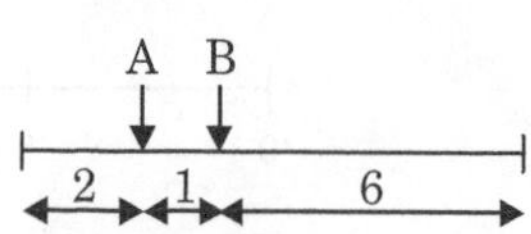

RFLP (Restriction Fragment Length Polymorphisms)

RFLPs are based on polymorphisms due to base substitutins, insertions, deletions and translocation that might have occurred in specific regions of genomic DNA.

This leads to differences in size of restriction fragments obtained due to digestion with specific restriction enzymes.

RFLPs can be detected by DNA probe, southern blotting.

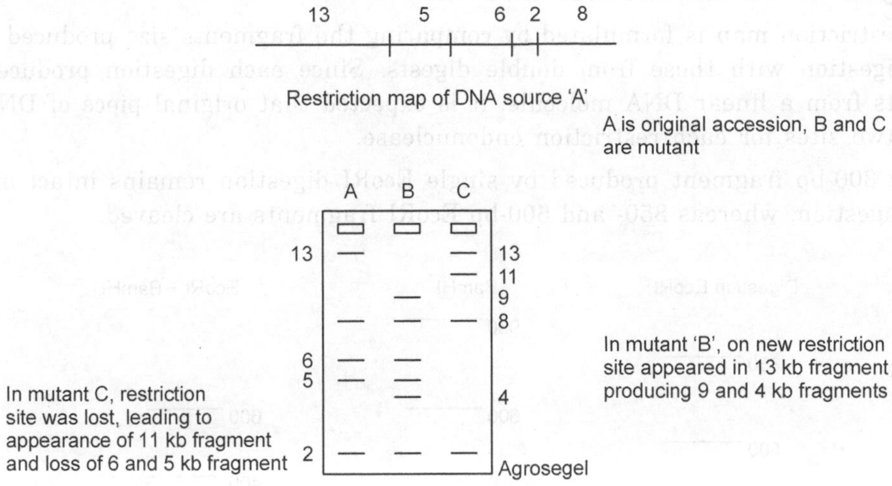

Figure 1.9 Technique involved in detection of RFLPs

The value of RFLPs lies in its ability to be used as markers for human genetic diseases.

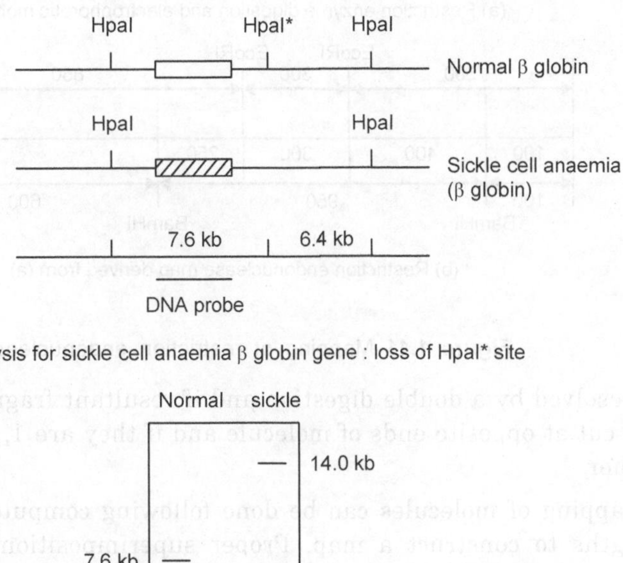

(a) Analysis for sickle cell anaemia β globin gene : loss of HpaI* site

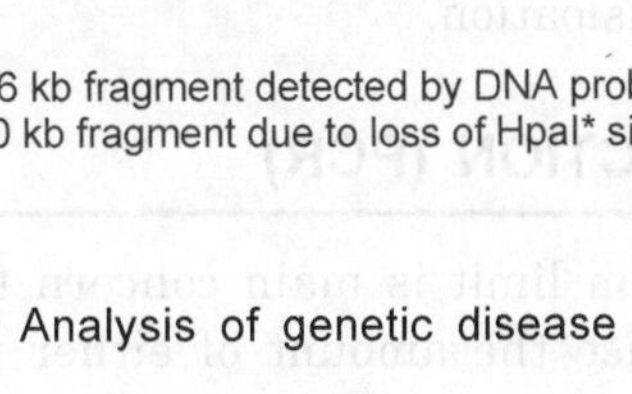

(b) Normal gene yield 7.6 kb fragment detected by DNA probe and sickle DNA yield 14.0 kb fragment due to loss of HpaI* site.

Figure 1.10 Analysis of genetic disease using RFLPs

Mapping of Restriction Endonuclease Site

A restriction map is formulated by comparing the fragments size produced in each single digestion with those from double digests. Since each digestion produces three fragments from a linear DNA molecule, it is expected that original piece of DNA must contain two sites for each restriction endonuclease.

The 300-bp fragment produced by single EcoRI digestion remains intact after the double digestion, whereas 850- and 500-bp EcoRI fragments are cleaved.

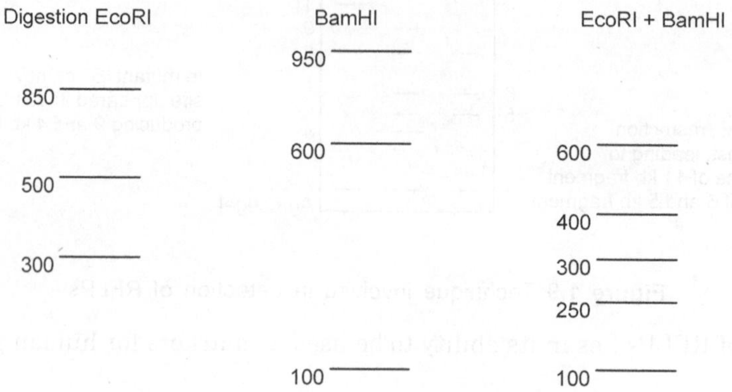

(a) Restriction enzyme digestion and electrophoretic mobility

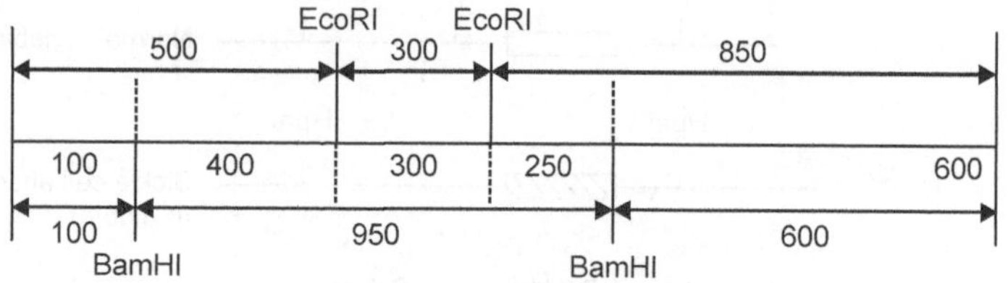

(b) Restriction endonuclease map derived from (a).

Figure 1.11 Mapping of restriction endonucleases

This is resolved by a double digestion and if resultant fragments are 2, 3, and 4 kb, then A and B cut at opposite ends of molecule and if they are 1, 2 and 6 kb, the sites are near each other.

Thus, mapping of molecules can be done following computer analysis of restriction fragment lengths to construct a map. Proper superimposition of restriction map and genetic map of a genomic region or whole genome allows location of genes in absolute physical terms and eventual is isloation.

POLYMERASE CHAIN REACTION (PCR)

Achieving adequate detection limit is main concern for applications of nucleic acid analysis. Techniques that increase the amount of either the target, detection signal or probe are known as methods for amplification of target.

Amplification Methods

Amplification of target includes:

1. PCR.
2. Ligase Chain Reaction (LCR).
3. Transcription-based Amplification (TAS).
4. Transcription-mediated Amplification (TMA).
5. Strand Displacement Amplification (SDA).
6. Lined Displacement Amplification (LDA).
7. Whole Genome Amplification (WGA).
8. Antisense RNA Amplification (RNA).

In target amplification, nucleic acid region around area of interest is copied many times by *invitro* methods. Polymerase Chain Reaction (PCR) is the best known and most widely applied of the target amplification methods.

PCR

It is most widely adopted and routine used method in molecular biology lab.

Requirements

- thermostable DNA polymerase.
- nucleotides of each base (dNTPs).
- target sequence.
- primer (pair of oligonucleotides complementary to opposite strands flanking the sequence to be detected).

Procedure

(*i*) Ist step—target duplex *denatured* into single strands by heat : *denaturation of target.*

(*ii*) *Annealing of primers:* Cooling of mixture and introduction of primers in solution to specifically anneal to complementary sequences on target.

(*iii*) *Polymerization:* Polymerase synthesizes two additional DNA strands containing the primers as 5′ ends and cycle is completed.

(*iv*) *Denaturation:* 2nd cycle also begins with denaturation. Now, there are twice as many strands available for primer annealing and subsequent polymerization.

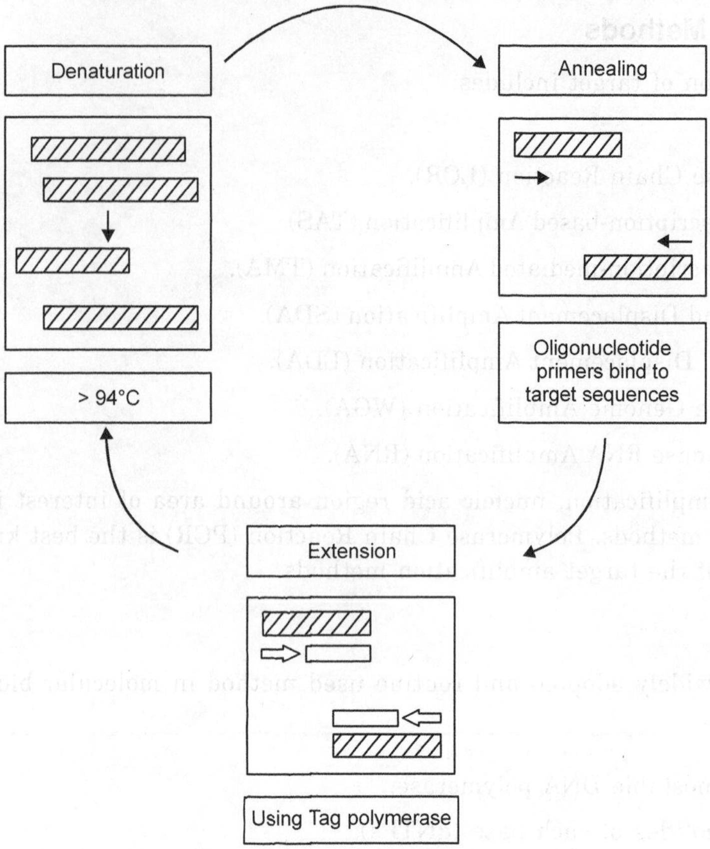

Figure 1.12 Scheme of single PCR cycle

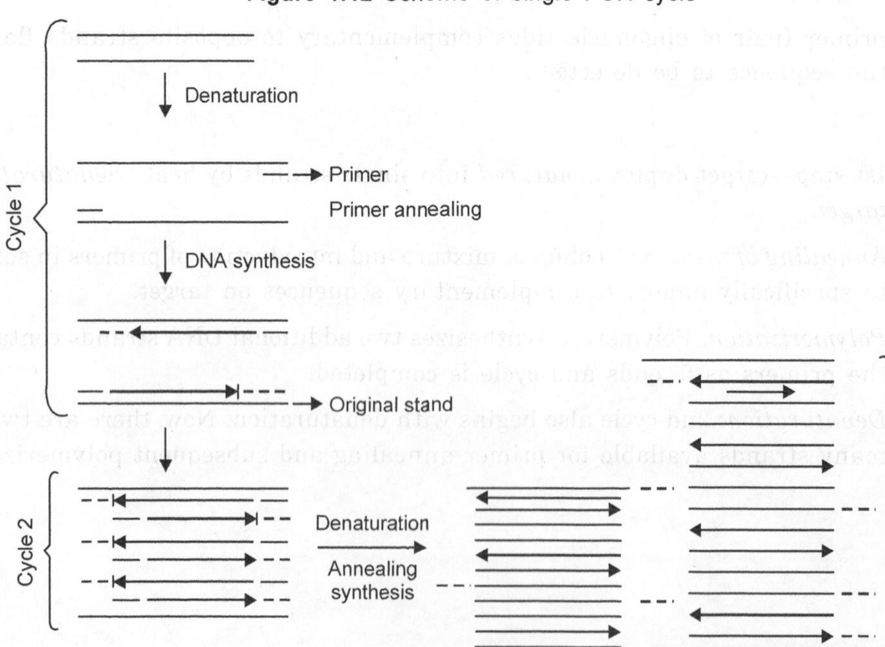

Figure 1.13 PCR

Temperature Cycling

Three temperatures:

1. High temperature—to denature target sequence at (94°C).
2. Low temperature—allows annealing of primers to target (55°C).
3. Optimal temperature—polymerase extension (72°C).

Instrument that takes samples through multiple steps of changing temperature is Thermocycler.

Repetitive thermocycling results in exponential accumulation of product.

$$N_t = N_0 e^r$$

N_t = amount of DNA at time '*t*'

N_0 = initial amount of DNA at time '*t*'

r = 1.386 min^{-1} for PCR

A doubling time of 30 sec in assumed for PCR and starting with only one target copy, takes 23 min (46 cycles) to amplify target to saturation. Thus 0.5 μM of each primer gives 10^{11} copies/μL in a typical PCR reaction.

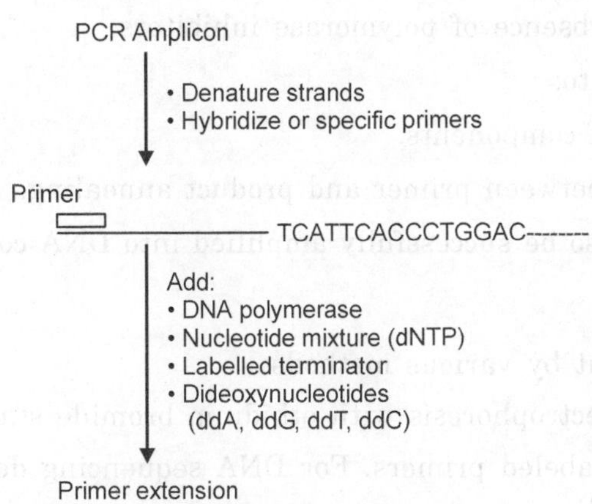

Figure 1.14 Denaturation of PCR amplicon

PCR Efficiency

If efficiency of each cycle is optimal, number of target sequences doubles each cycle (efficiency = 2.0).

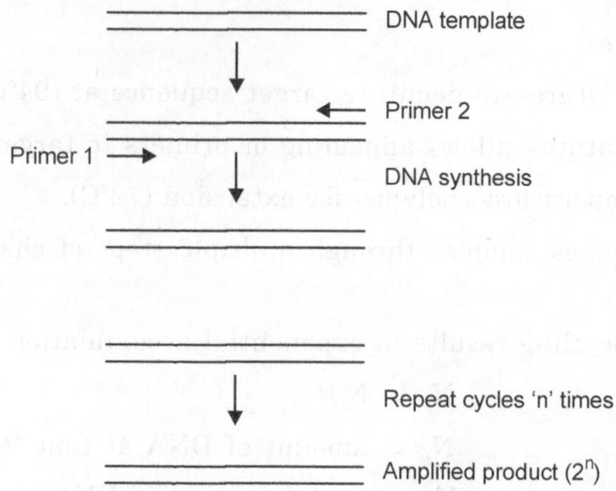

Figure 1.15 PCR provides large quantity of usable specific DNA fragments.

PCR efficience depends on:

- Primer.
- Temperature-cycling conditions.
- Presence or absence of polymerase inhibitors.

Efficiency fails due to:

- Exhaustion of components.
- Competition between primer and product annealing.

RNA targets can also be successfully amplified into DNA copies.

Detection of Products

It can be carried out by various methods:

1. Simple gel electrophoresis with ethidium bromide staining.
2. Florescently labeled primers. For DNA sequencing device (they form part of real-time PCR).
3. Hybridization assays.
4. Automated and closed-tube methods.

Contamination Control for PCR

- Use physically separated areas for preamplification and postamplification steps.
- Use positive displacement pipetles to minimize aerosol contamination.
- Use prealiquoted reagent.
- Do not let the product out of the tube.
- Perform amplification, defection and characterization in a closed tube. Otherwise a minute aerosol droplet contains more than enough target for Robust Amplification.

Different Schemes of PCR

1. Inverse PCR.
2. Anchored PCR.
3. PCR for site directed mutagenesis.
4. Allele-specific PCR.
5. Assymmetric PCR for DNA sequencing.
6. PCR walking.
7. RT (reverse transcribed)—PCR.

Inverse PCR

In inverse PCR, amplification of those DNA sequences takes place which are away from the primers and not those flanked by primer *e.g.,* if border sequences of a DNA segment are not known and those of the vector are known. Then sequence to be amplified may be cloned in the vector and border sequences of vector may be used as primers in such a way that the polymerization proceeds in inverse direction.

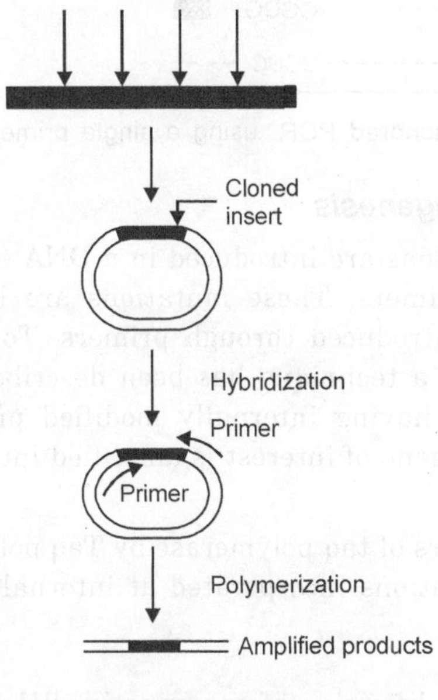

Figure 1.16 Amplification of gene using flanking vector sequences as primers

Anchored PCR

While basic PCR and inverse PCR uses two primers representing the sequences lying at the ends of sequences to be amplified. In anchored PCR, single primer is utilized instead of two. So, only one strand is copied first after which a poly-G tail is attached at the end of newly synthesized strand. Then, this newly synthesized strand with poly G tail becomes template for daughter strand synthesis utilizing an anchor primer with which a poly C sequence is linked to complement poly-G of the template. In next cycle, both original primer and anchored primers are used for gene amplification.

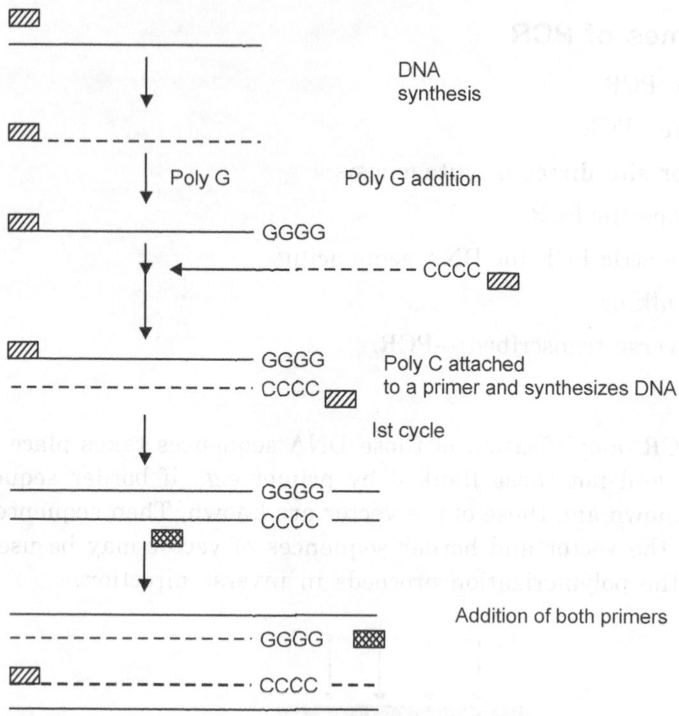

Figure 1.17 Anchored PCR, using a single primer in first cycle

PCR for Site-directed Mutagenesis

In this technique, mutations are introduced in a DNA sequence at desired places by altering the sequences of primers. These mutations are limited to the ends of gene sequence because they are introduced through primers. To introduce mutations at any place of interest in the gene, a technique has been described one having primer at the end of the gene and second having internally modified primer (desired mutation) an *overlap extension*. Where the gene of interest is amplified into two separate segments two separate PCR reactions.

Extension of these primers of taq polymerase by Taq polymerase results in formation of a complete gene with mutations incorporated at internalsites.

Allele-specific PCR

Enables preferential amplification of one genetic-allele over another.

3′ end of one primer are placed at polymorphic site and is extended only if it is completely complementary to the target.

Uses:

- to distinguish a gene for pseudogene.
- for genotypic SNPs.
- determining haplotypes.

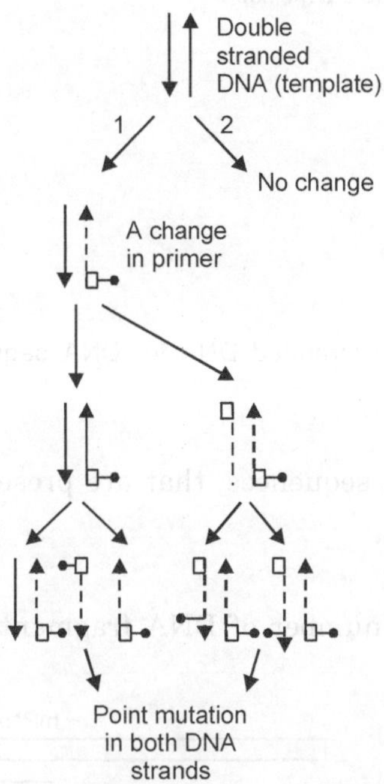

Figure 1.18 Site-directed mutagenesis (Extension of these primers by Taq Polymers results in formation of a complete gene with mutations incorporated at internal sites.

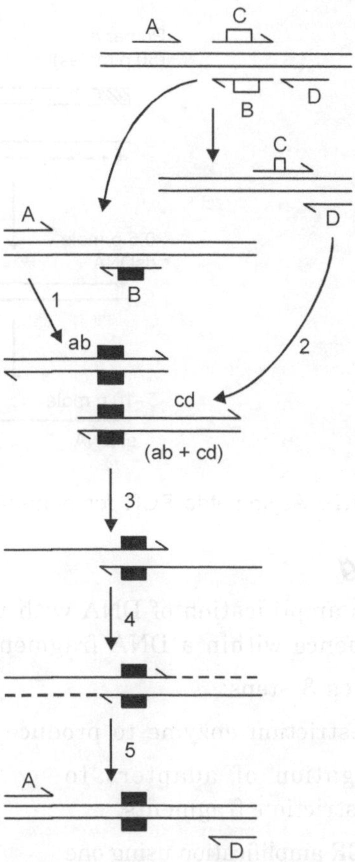

Figure 1.19 Introduction of mutation at an internal site using overlap extension. B, C—internal site overlapping each other A and B, C and D—primers

Asymmetric PCR for DNA sequencing

Using this technique, single stranded DNA can be produced by using two primers in 100:1 ratio, and after 20–35 cycles of amplification. One primer is exhausted and single stranded DNA is produced in next 5–10 cycles.

It uses different concentrations of the two primers of generate more of one strand than of the other.

Uses:

- for sequencing purposes.
- for making single-stranded probes.
- for probe hybridization.

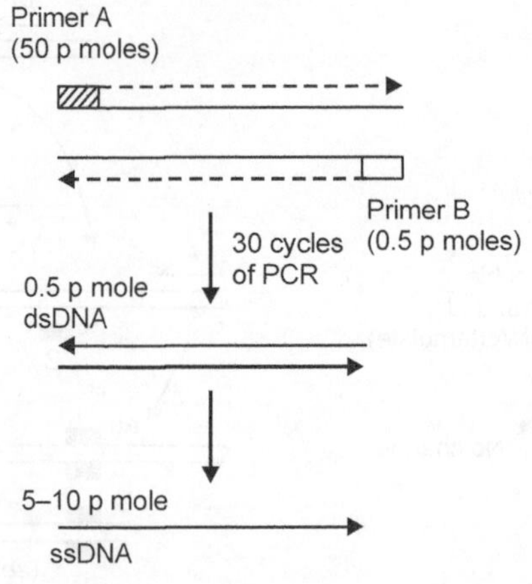

Figure 1.20 Asymmetric PCR for generating single stranded DNA for DNA sequencing

PCR Walking

It allows amplification of DNA with unknown sequences, that are present adjoining a known sequence within a DNA fragment.

It involves 3 steps:

1. Restriction enzyme to produce a large number of DNA fragments.
2. Ligation of adapters to restriction fragments.
3. PCR amplification using one adapter primer and other gene specific primer.

RT-PCR (Reverse transcribed PCR)

RT is used to obtain cDNA for using it as a template for PCR reaction to examine mRNA transcript.

(*i*) Isolation, purification of mRNA.

(*ii*) Reverse transcription of mRNA with reverse transcriptase enzyme to synthesize cDNA.

(*iii*) cDNA is used as a template for PCR using Taq polymerase and specific primers.

Use: Identification of differences in two mRNA samples by using this techniques.

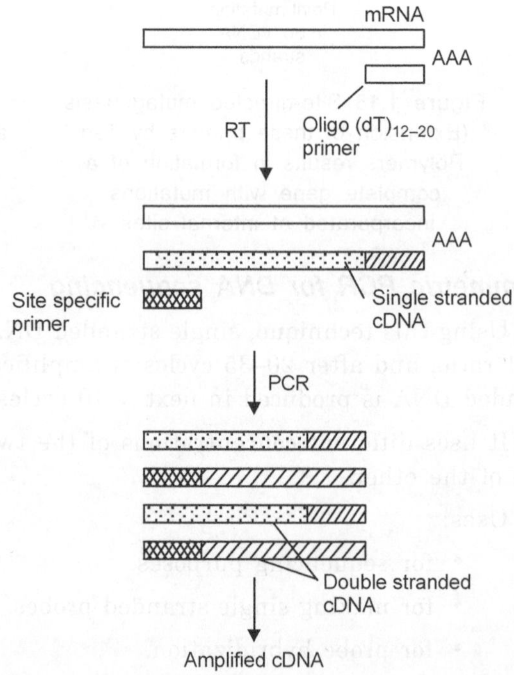

Figure 1.21 RT-PCR

NUCLEIC ACID BLOTTING

They include:

1. Southern Blotting.
2. Northern Blotting.
3. Western Blotting.

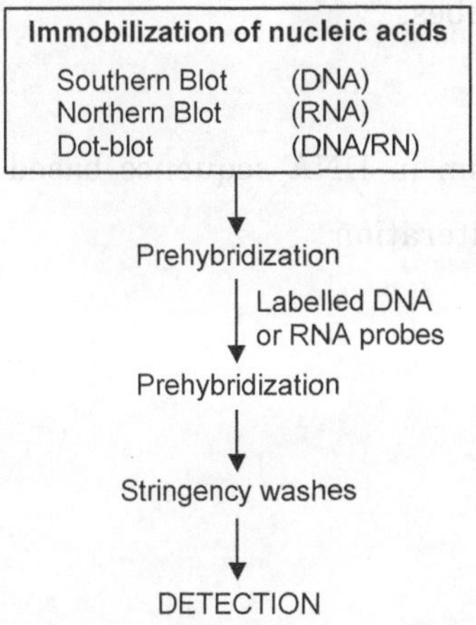

Figure 1.22 Nucleic Acid Blotting Techniques—Outline

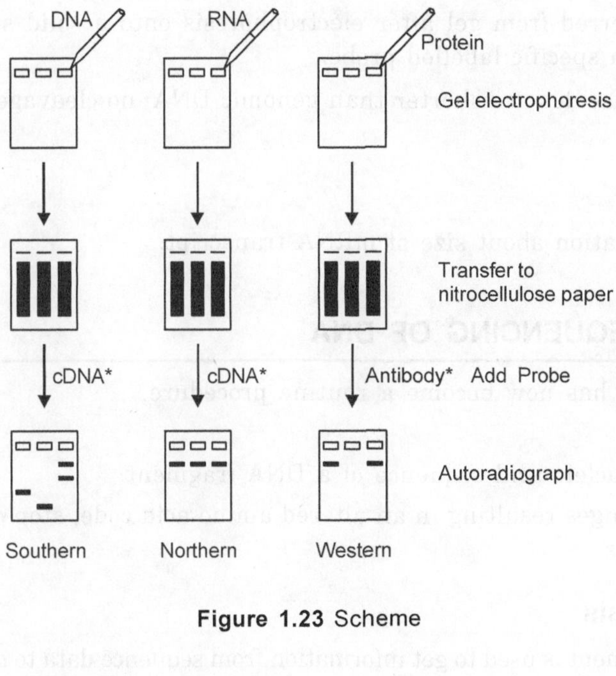

Figure 1.23 Scheme

Southern Blotting

Used to detect DNA.

Procedure

Original sample DNA is digested by a restricted endonuclease, separated by agarose electrophoresis, and transferred by agarose electrophoresis, and transferred to a solid support (nylon or nitrocellulose membrane) followed by selective visualization of fragment using labelled hybridization probes.

Use

- Reveals polymorphism in DNA sequence based on RFLP.
- Detect: structural alteration

  deletion

  duplication

  insertion

  rearrangement

Northern Blotting

Uses RNA rather than DNA as the test nucleic acid.

Procedure

RNA is transferred from gel after electrophoresis onto a solid support followed by hybridization with a specific labelled probe.

Since RNA molecules are shorter than genomic DNA, no cleavage is required before electrophoresis.

Use

Provide information about size of mRNA transcript.

NUCLEOTIDE SEQUENCING OF DNA

DNA sequence has now become a routine procedure.

It determines:

- actual nucleic acid sequence of a DNA fragment.
- base changes resulting in an altered amino acid code, stop codon, deletions, or insertions.

Sequence Analysis

Sequence alignment is used to get information from sequence data to discover information related to functions, structure and evolution.

DNA sequencing
↓
Reconstruction
↓
Physical and genetic map determination
↓
Comparison of sequences to find related proteins
↓
exploring frequently occurring pattern of nucleotide
↓
searching informative elements in protein and DNA sequences
↓
identification of unknown sequence
↓
searching other members of multigene families.

Figure 1.24 Scheme of sequence analysis

DNA Sequencing

It is the process of determination of nucleotide or base sequence of a DNA molecule / fragment. DNA sequencing at present is possible only for 100–800 bp long DNA fragments.

Maxam-Gilbert procedure

In this technique, the DNA fragment to be sequenced is end-labelled by the addition of 32 P-d ATP either at the 5-ends (by the enzyme polynucleotide kinase) or at the 3-ends (by the enzyme deoxy nucleotidyl transfer) of its both the strands.

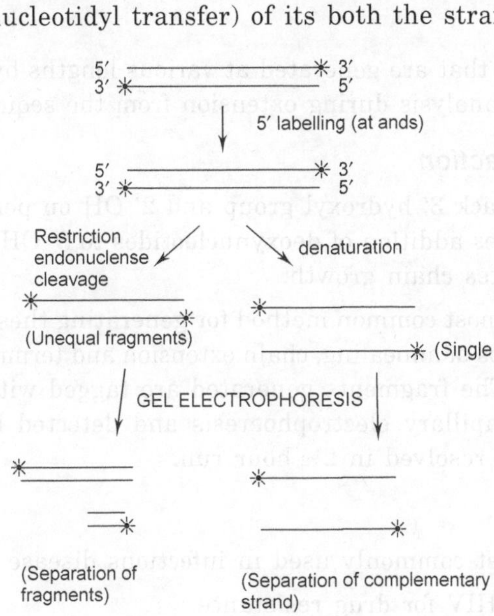

Figure 1.25 Sequencing

This end-labelled fragment is digested with restriction endonuclease to generate two fragments of unequal lengths of which only one end would be labelled. These fragments are separated by gel electrophoresis and sequenced separately. Alternatively, end-labelled fragment is denatured and complementary strands are separated through gel electrophoresis and sequenced separately.

The single end-labelled ds or ss DNA samples are subjected to base-specific chemical cleavage at four sites namely, G, C, G + A/C + T. Then, in four separate reaction mixtures, the DNA samples are partially digested according to base-specific sequences by following steps:

(*i*) modification of concerned bases.

(*ii*) removal of modified base from DNA strand.

(*iii*) Induction of strand break (break in the sugar-phosphate back-bone) in the position from which modified base has been removed.

Such a cleavage generates a mixture of end-labelled DNA fragments of variable lengths. Digests of double-stranded DNA are denatured. Then, they are subjected to electrophoresis separate lanes of the same gel to separate fragments according to their lengths by sequential reading of bands in the four lanes of the gel by auto-radiography, the base sequence is determined.

Sanger Coulson Method

Also termed as enzymatic procedure. The DNA fragment to be sequenced is denatured and the resulting complementary strands are separated by electrophoresis.

Sanger reaction

Generates fragments that are generated at various lengths by incorporation of one of 4 dideoxynucleotide base analysis during extension from the sequencing primer.

Principle of Sanger Reaction

Dideoxynucleotides lack 3′ hydroxyl group and 2′ OH on pentose ring, and because DNA chain growth requires addition of deoxynucleotides to 3′ OH group, incorporation of this base analog terminates chain growth.

Cycle Sequencing is most common method for generating these terminated fragments and involves repeating steps of annealing, chain extension and termination and denaturation by temperature cycling. The fragments generated are tagged with fluorescent dye, then separated by PAGE or capillary electrophoeresis and detected by fluorescent detector. Around 600 bases can be resolved in 2½ hour run.

Use

DNA sequencing most commonly used in infections disease testing:

- genotyping of HIV for drug resistance.
- genotyping of HCV.

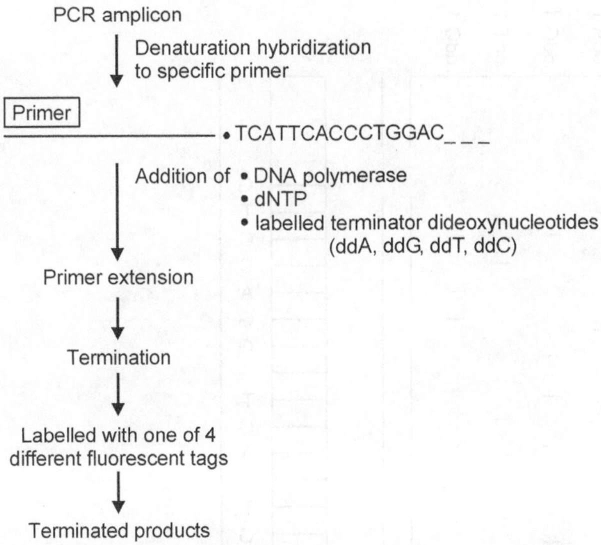

Figure 1.26 Chain termination reaction (Sanger)

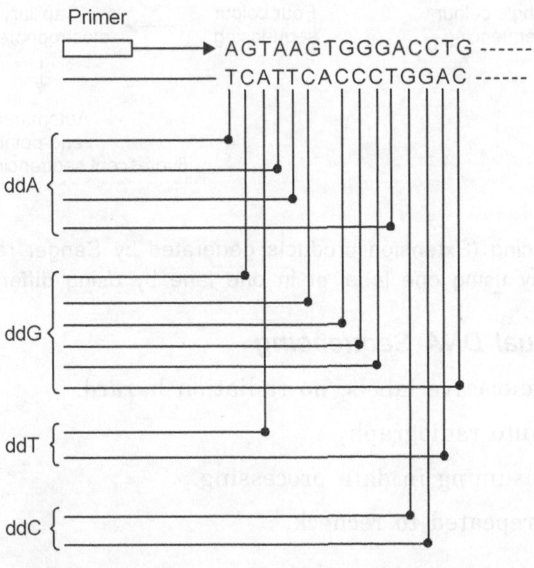

Figure 1.27 Chain termination reaction (Sanger)
(ddA, ddG, ddT, ddC analogues carry different fluorescent tags)

Automated DNA Sequencing

It is also based on sanger-coulson method with two differences:

(*i*) labelling flroescenl labelling is done instead of radioactive labelling used in standard procedure.

(*ii*) track system: single-track system is used instead of four track system.

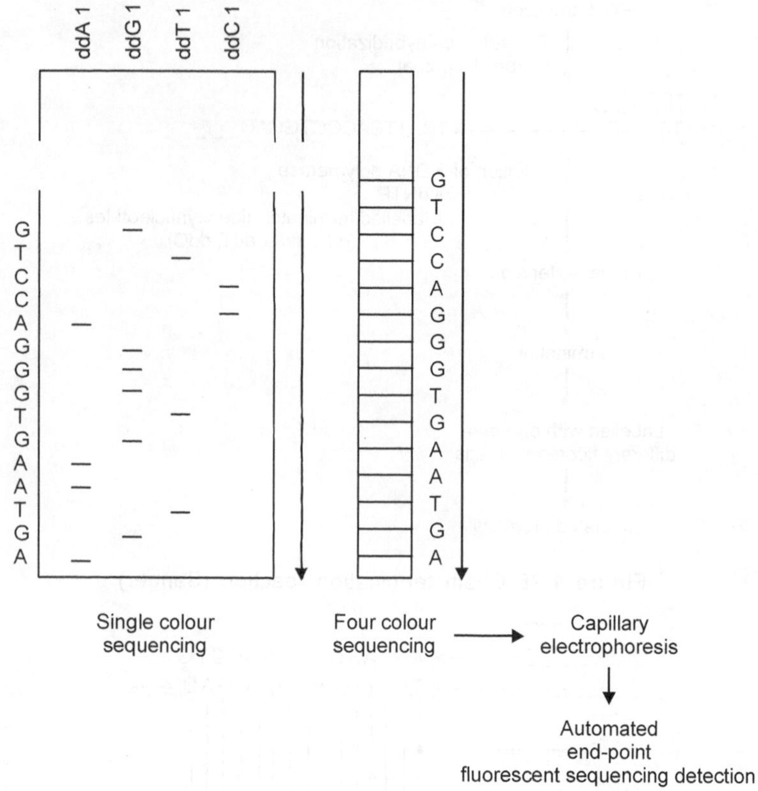

Figure 1.28 DNA sequencing (Extension products generated by Sanger reaction are separated in four lanes by using one lebel or in one lane by using different labels)

Advantage Over Manual DNA Sequencing

(*i*) no use of radioactive labels, no radiation hazard.

(*ii*) no need of auto radiography.

(*iii*) less time-consuming in data processing.

(*iv*) test can be repeated to recheck.

(*v*) fast.

Sequencer

It offers automated specialised tools for working with the output from automated sequences and assists researchers with DNA sequencing automated sequencers alongwith GCG, Mac Vector and Gene Works as sequence entry and multiple sequence alignment editor helps to generate sequence data.

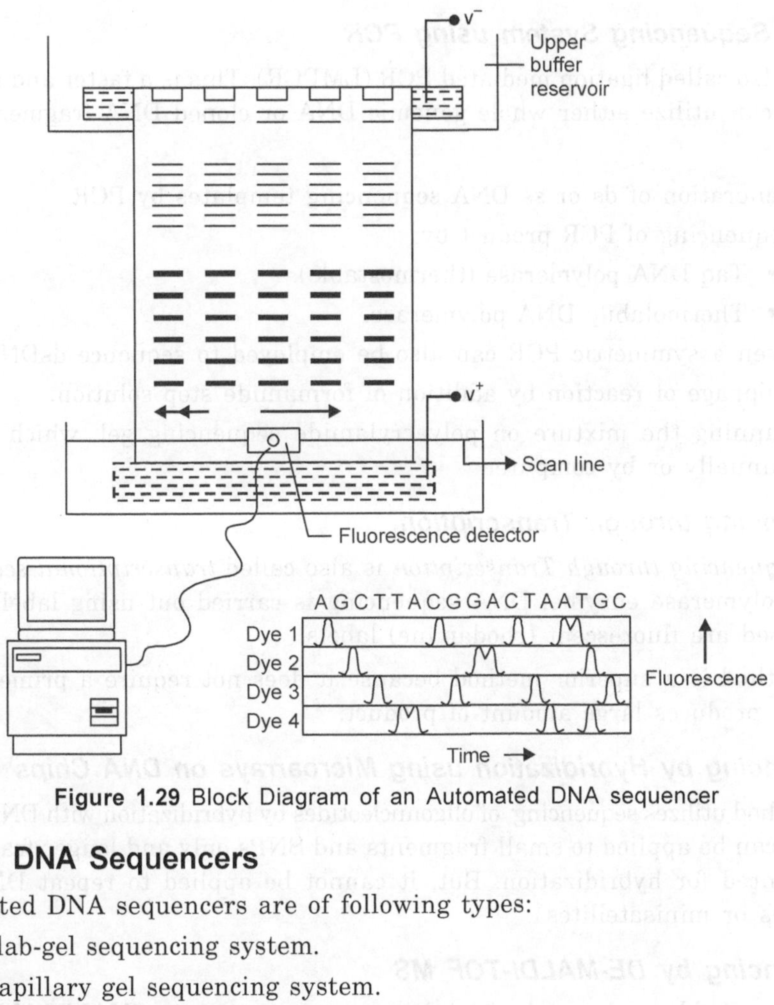

Figure 1.29 Block Diagram of an Automated DNA sequencer

Automated DNA Sequencers

Automated DNA sequencers are of following types:

1. Slab-gel sequencing system.
2. Capillary gel sequencing system.
3. Direct DNA sequencing system using PCR.
4. DNA sequencing through transcription.
5. DNA sequencing by hybrization with microassays on DNA chips.
6. DNA sequencing by DE-MALDI-TOF MS.

Slab-gel Sequencing System

Here, ultrathin (75 μm) slab gels and 96 lanes per gel runs are used. Automated sample loading into each plexiglass block well (filled with PCR dideoxy reaction mixture) with help of capillary action followed by electrophoresis.

Capillary Gel Sequencing System

In this system, automated capillary gel electrophoresis is carried out in a 96 capillary tube filled with a polymerized gel system.

Commercial system available: Mega BASE 4000 (having 384 capillaries).

Direct DNA Sequencing System using PCR

This is also called ligation mediated PCR (LMPCR). This is a faster and more reliable method that can utilize either whole genomic DNA or cloned DNA fragments.

Steps:

(*i*) Generation of ds or ss DNA sequencing templates by PCR.

(*ii*) Sequencing of PCR product by:

- Taq DNA polymerase (thermostable).
- Thermolabile DNA polymerase.

Even assymmetric PCR can also be employed to sequence dsDNA.

(*iii*) Stoppage of reaction by addition of formamide stop solution.

(*iv*) Running the mixture on polyacrylamide sequencing gel, which can be read manually or by computer.

DNA Sequencing through Transcription

DNA Sequencing through Transcription is also called *transcriptional sequencing.* By using RNA polymerase enzyme, DNA sequencing is carried out using labelled 3′ dNTP. The labels used are fluorescent (rhodamine) labels.

This method is a superior method because it does not require a primer (making it faster) and it produces large amount of product.

DNA Sequencing by Hybridization using Microarrays on DNA Chips

This method utilizes sequencing of oligonucleotides by hybridization with DNA microchips. This method can be applied to small fragments and SNPs only and longer fragments need to be fragmented for hybridization. But, it cannot be applied to repeat DNAs such as microsatellites or minisatellites.

DNA Sequencing by DE-MALDI-TOF MS

Matrix assisted laser desorption/ionization mass spectrometry (MALDI-MS) can rapidly acquire DNA sequence information.

It can accurately determine the mass of each fragment arranged by differences of single nucleotides.

This method is applicable to short oligonucleotides and can also be used in combination with Sanger's termination reactions.

Advantage:

It is quick, requires only minutes per sample and no gels, labelling is required.

GENE PROBE, DERIVATION AND ITS DETECTION

Probe

A probe is the nucleic acid whose identity is known and is used to reveal the identity or abundance or a target or sample.

Probes can be unlabelled or labelled with one of a variety of reporter molecules (depending on the technique used).

Types of Probe

Probes can be:

- cloned (recombinant)
- generated by PCR or
- synthesized (oligonucleotide).

They may be DNA, RNA, PNA and single-stranded or double-stranded.

Table 1.7 Nucleic acid probes

Probe	*Type*	*Label*
DNA	• Cell-based DNA-cloning (dsDNA)	Random primer
	• PCR	Nick translation
RNA	• RNA transcription from phage vectors (single stranded)	Run-off transcription
Oligonucleotide	• Chemical synthesis (single stranded nucleotides)	End-labelling

Table 1.8 Methods for Labelling Nucleotide probes

DNA probe	*Label used*
End labelling	^{32}P, ^{35}S
Polymerase-based labelling	^{32}P, ^{35}S
Nick-translation	^{32}P, ^{35}S
Labels Used	*Examples*
Radioactive	^{32}P, ^{35}S
Nonradioactive	Biotin Streptavidin Digoxigenin

Cloned Probes

They consist of a known segment of DNA inserted into a plasmid vector that is propagated by growth in a bacterium.

P^{BR} 322 was one of the first in common use and now many different plasmid vectors are available.

Composition—They may consist of:

- entire plasmid DNA (insert plus vector sequence).
- or purified insert from vector sequences.
- RNA promoter regions adjacent to inserted DNA sequence.

Since only one strand is copied, single-stranded RNA probes are generated that allow production of transcripts in sense or antisense direction.

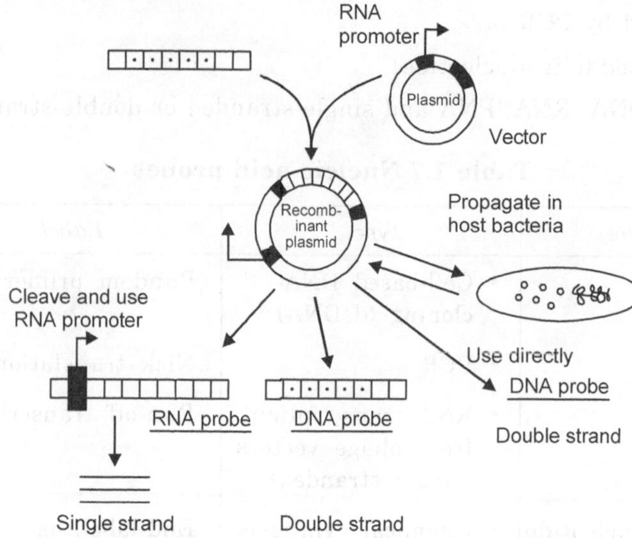

Figure 1.30 Production of Cloned Probes

PCR-generated Probes

They are simple to prepare and are labelled with nucleotides that are radioactive, or fluorescent or have attached affinity labels.

Also, by using biotin-labelled primer, single-stranded probes can be obtained.

Oligonucleotide Probes

Characteristic features of oligonucleotide probe:

- They are easier to obtain than PCR-generated ones.
- Contain 15–45 bases of single-stranded nucleic acids that are chemically synthesized to a specific base sequence.
- DNA oligonucleotide probes are commonly used, but RNA and PNA ones can also be used.
- Oligonucleotide probes are routinely available in public database (*e.g.*, NIH genetic sequence database, public algorithms).
- Oligonucleotide probes are prepared with covalent attachment of a reporter molecule (fluorescent dyes) or affinity labels that facilitate their attachment to solid supports.
- Real-time PCR use fluorescent labelled oligonucleotides.

Labelling of Probes

Nucleic acids are visualized or measured by ultraviolet absorbance and fluorescent dyes. However, they do not discriminate between different nucleic acid sequences *i.e.*, they are not sequence specific. Labelling of these probes solves the problem.

Types of labelling:

- Radioactive label.
- Indirect probe detection.
- Fluorescent label.
- Electrochemical reporters.

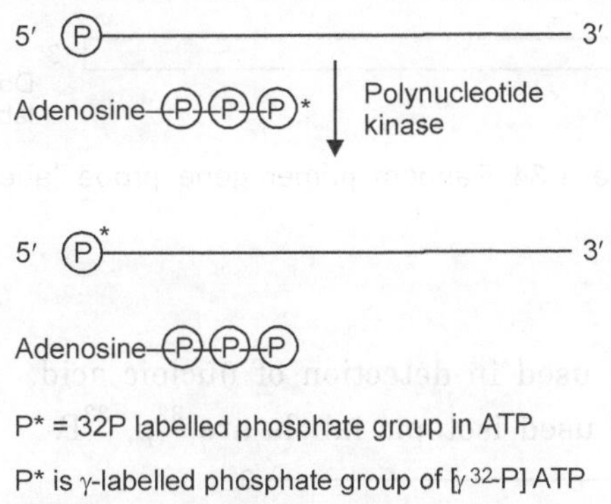

Figure 1.31 End-labelling of DNA probe

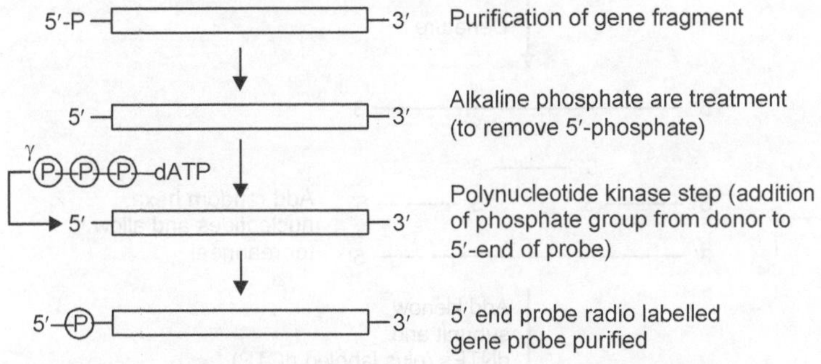

Figure 1.32 End-labelling of a gene probe at 5′ end

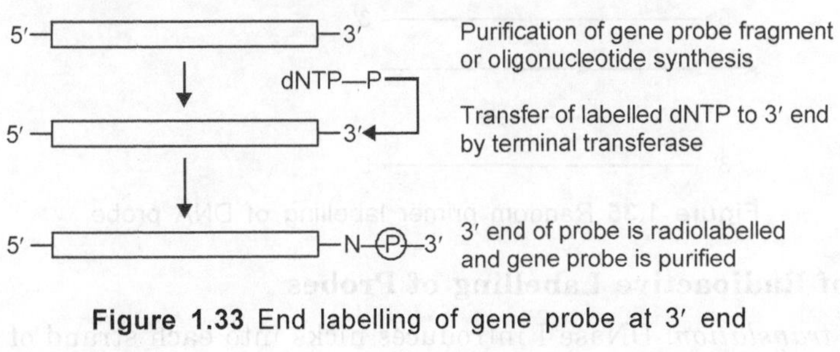

Figure 1.33 End labelling of gene probe at 3′ end

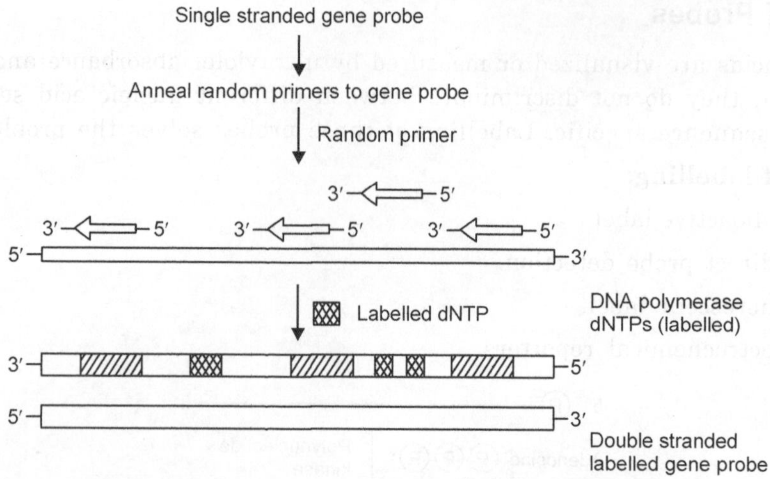

Figure 1.34 Random primer gene probe labelling

Radioactive Probes

These probes are:

- Ist probes to be used in detection of nucleic acid.
- Most frequently used isotopic labels are ^{32}p, ^{33}P.

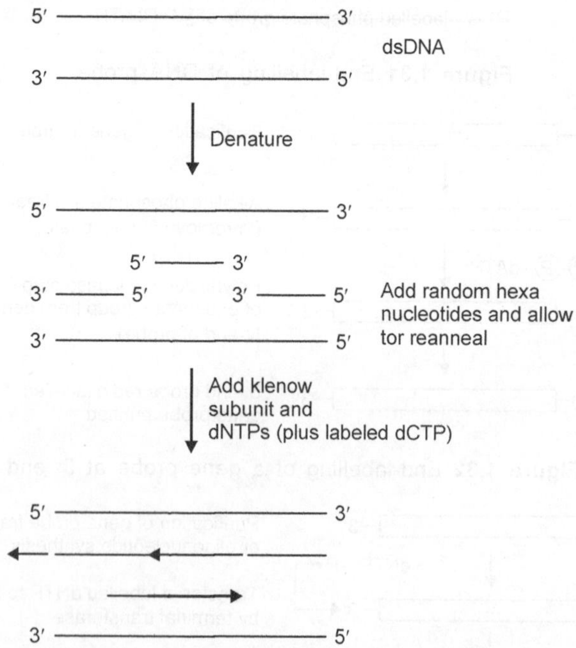

Figure 1.35 Random primer labelling of DNA probe

Methods of Radioactive Labelling of Probes

(*i*) *Nick translation.* DNase I introduces nicks into each strand of DNA randomly and resulting 3′ OH groups form priming sites for DNA polymerase.

(*ii*) *Random priming.* Nucleic acid is denatured and allowed to anneal with short hexamer oligonucleotides of random sequence. The 3′ end of annealed hexanes forms initiation site for DNA polymerase.

(*iii*) *By PCR.* Labelled nucleic acids can also be synthesized by PCR.

Advantage of Radioactively Labelled Probes

- They are sensitive.
- They have high specificity.

Disadvantage

- Short half-life.
- Inherent instability.
- Problem of radio-isotope safety and disposal.

Indirect Probe Detection

It involves nonisotopic probe labelling by using

- biotin-labelled analog of dUTP.
- digoxigenin labelled analog of dUTP.

These affinity labels (biotin, digoxigenin) do not generate detectable signals on their own. They can initiate signal amplification mediated by high-affinity binding with antibodies linked to enzymes (horse-radish peroxidase or alkaline phosphatase) or avidin or streptavidin.

Enzyme activity is monitored according to the enzyme substrate used (chemiluminescent, colorimetric or fluorescent).

(*i*) *Biotinylated Label:* Biotin is an affinity label. Biotinylated probes can be affixed to a streptavidin-coated surface. Following incubation with target nucleic acid, a second probe is added to amplify the signal.

(*ii*) *Chemiluminescence:* Nucleic acid can be linked to organic indicator molecules that emit light when exposed to certain chemicals. *e.g.*, acridinium esters when exposed to H_2O_2 at high pH produce light emission.

(*iii*) *Bioluminescence:* Biomolecules produce light through catalysis of certain substrates. *e.g.*, alkaline phosphatase and peroxidase act on luminescent substrates to emit light. Luciferase is also a bioluminescent molecule used as an indicator of ATP generation in pyrosequencing.

(*iv*) *Electrochemiluminescence:* It is initiated at an electrode surface in the presence of certain chelates of ruthenium.

Fluorescent Labels

Fluorescent labelled probes are preferred reporter for nucleic acid analysis.

Useful in:

DNA sequencing.

Fragment length analysis.

DNA arrays.

Real-time PCR.

Detected by:

Fluorescence polarization.

Fluorescence resonance energy transfer (FRET).

Fluorescence quenching.

Electrochemical Reporters

They detect hybridization-induced changes in electrochemical parameters, such as conductivity or capacitance. Different designs available are:

(*i*) *Attachment of oligonucleotide to electrode surface:* Its binding to complementary target and to an electroactive reporter labelled with ferrocenyl derivative can be detected by voltammetry.

(*ii*) *Use of tethered oligonucleotide:* Reporter probe is attached to a metal nanoparticle that changes conductivity between electrodes.

(*iii*) *Use of unlabelled probes anchored to field-effect sensor:* To detect increase in change following hybridization to target.

Detection of DNA Probe Signal

DNA probes have an advantage of detecting the presence of gene rather than its product. DNA probe signals need to be amplified.

Devices for Amplification of Signals

1. Developing rRNA probes because rRNA genes are present in thousands, thus amplify the target.
2. Use of of PCR technology to generate millions of copies of target DNA sequence to be identified by standard methods.
3. Increasing the signal generating capacity of probe by the following ways:
   (*i*) Concentrating more lable at the site of target molecule (by attaching multiple enzyme molecules to each of its DNA probe)
   (*ii*) Use of multiple probes.
   (*iii*) Attaching multiple enzymes to each of these multiple probes *i.e.,* multiple secondary probes.
   (*iv*) *Amplifore technology:* which uses multiple secondary probes to hybridize secondary probes to hybridize to multiple target specific primary probes.

MICROARRAYS

Micro arrays represent high-density miniaturized arrays of molecular samples. The technology involves a series of probes immobilized on a glass slide as microdots, which are then hybridized with a mixture of test DNA sequences labelled with a fluorochrome.

Preparation

Prepared either by synthesis of oligonucleotide on a DNA chip, or by deposition of available DNA sequences on DNA chip.

Types

1. *DNA microarray*—contain cloned gene sequences, cDNA, ESTs
2. *Antibody microarray*—contain spots of different antibodies.

Table 1.9 Properties of different types of DNA array for expression analysis

Property	*Spotted microarray*		*Affinities*
	Nylon	*Glass*	*Gene chips*
Target size	Typical 100–300 bp		Typical 20–25nt
Target source	Maintained clonesets		• Sequence derived from public and/or private databases • Chemically synthesized
Target composition	dsDNA fragments		Single-stranded oligonucleotides
Probe labelling	Radioactive or enzymatic	Dual fluorescent	Flourescent
Detection	Autoradiography	Confocal Scanning	Confocal scanning
Cost	Low	Moderate	High

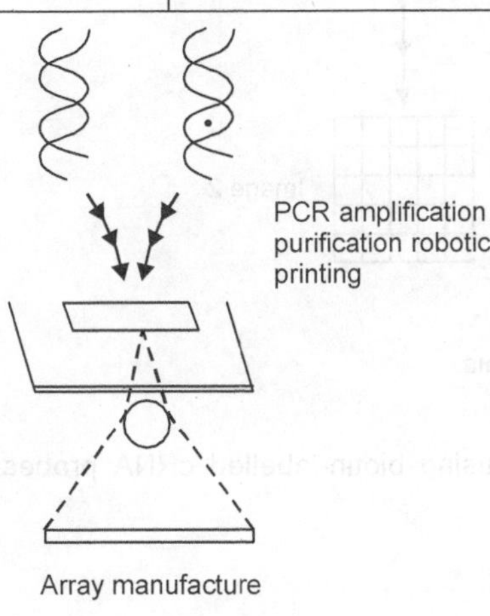

Figure 1.36 Microarray

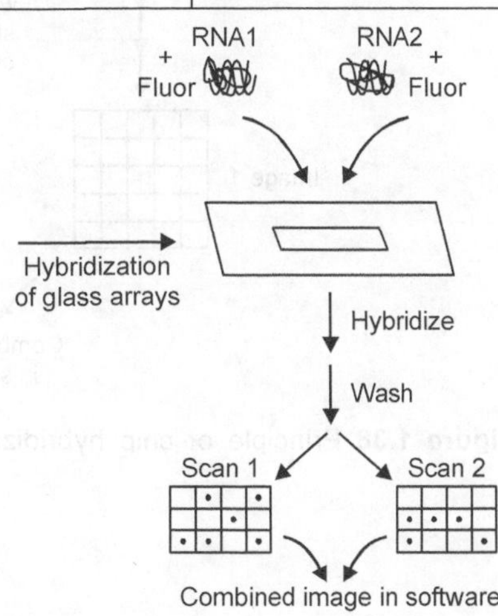

Figure 1.37 Spotted DNA microarray

Table 1.10 Commercial source of clone sets for manufacturing spotted arrays

Company	*Resources*
Research genetics (http://www.resgen.com)	Human Unique collection Mouse Unique collection Rat Unique collection Drosophila cDNA collection
In cyte Genomics (www.incyte.com)	Human Unique collection Mouse Unique collection Candidaalbicans complete ORF collection
Genosys Biotech (www.genosys.com)	E. coli complete ORF collection Bacillus subtilis complete ORF collection

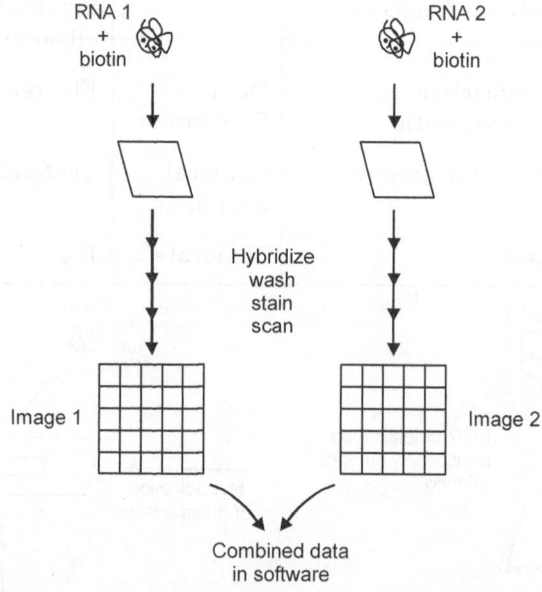

Figure 1.38 Principle of chip hybridization using biotin-labelled cRNA probes

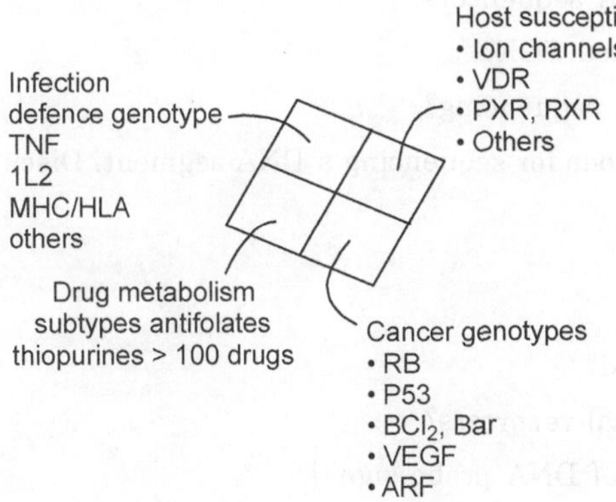

Figure 1.39 Possible design of microarray for diagnostics

SUMMARY

For biotechnology and other applications, it is necessary to know the complete sequence of a cloned gene. The dideoxynucleotide method of Sanger is often used for this process. PCR is a revolutionary procedure with innumerable uses. It allows *invitro* amplification of discrete segments DNA to a million fold. There are four approaches for isolating a human gene : positional cloning, candidate gene cloning, restriction mapping *e.g.,* RFLPs, position candidate gene cloning or cytogenetic mapping.

The DNA fragments can be identified by gene (DNA) probes or microarrays. Microarray or chip technology hold a great promise to biotechnologists in future.

REVIEW QUESTIONS

1. How can you isolate and separate nucleic acids?
2. What are the tools of molecular biology?
3. Short notes:
   (*i*) Restriction enzymes.
   (*ii*) RFLP.
   (*iii*) Cleavage pattern of restriction enzymes.
4. What is temperature cycling in PCR?
5. Enumerate different amplification methods for target amplification.
6. What are different schemes of PCR?
7. Discuss different schemes of PCR.
8. Describe nucleic acid blotting techniques.
9. Describe Sanger reaction.
10. Discuss Maxim glibert procedure of sequencing.
11. Give an account of automated sequencing.

12. Discuss automated DNA sequencers.
13. What is ligated mediated PCR?
14. What is transcriptional sequencing?
15. Describe different methods for sequencing a DNA segment. Discuss its advantages and disadvantages.
16. Discuss microarrays.
17. What is a gene probe?
18. How probes are labelled?
19. What are electrochemical reporters?
20. Describe amplification of DNA probe signal.
21. Draw a scheme for restriction mapping of a DNA fragment.
22. What are cleavage patterns of various restriction enzymes?
23. Give a comparative account of different schemes of PCR.
24. Give a comparative account of different gene probes.
25. Prepare a list of application of microarrays.
26. Calculate a comparative account of probes.
27. Prepare a flow chart for outlining the process of isolation of DNA.
28. Outline the steps of isolation of RNA.
29. Tabulate tools of molecular biology with their functions.
30. Figureout how restriction enzyme recognize sequences.
31. What are RFLPs?
32. Prepare a list of molecular markers used for genetic mapping apart from RFLPs.
33. Give an outline of PCR cycle.
34. How contamination control for PCR is enforced?
35. Outline steps and uses of Southern blot.
36. Outline steps and uses of Northern blot.
37. Give outline of nucleotide sequencing of DNA.
38. What is automated DNA sequencing?

Chapter 2

Techniques in Recombinant DNA Technology

HUMAN GENOMIC PROJECT

Human Genomic Project deciphered 3 billion base pairs that make up the genetic code. In 1988, US National Research Council's special committee formulated a 15-years human genome project, costing some $ 200 million a year. In September 1994, a genetic map with 1 cM resolution was accomplished and a physical map involving 52,000 sequence-tagged sites (STSs) was completed in October 1998.

International Human Genome Sequencing Consortium consisting of investigators from 20 centres located in six countries—UK, US, Japan, France, Germany and China announced completion of a draft sequence in June 2000. The final sequence was accomplished in April 2003, with 99.99% sequence accuracy, with no gaps.

Human Genome

Of the total 3.2 Gb DNA of human genome, 2.9 Gb consists of, weakly staining gene-rich enchromatic proteins, and only 1.1–1.4% sequence encodes proteins.

Estimated number of genes in human genome are between 26,000 and 31,000.

With the decoding of basic sequence, even more difficult task is elucidation of biological functions of these stretches of DNA.

The data generated from the Human Genome Project, new disease-associated genes are being discovered every week. Also, it has given us enability to develop tests for molecular diagnosis and development of new targets for the pharmaceutical industries.

Hap Map Project—International Hap Map Project has been launched to study the patterns of linkage disequilibrium and haplotypes across the human genome and to characterize SNPs (single nucleotide polymorphisms).

ENCODE (Encyclopedia of DNA elements)

This project aims to identify all of the functional elements in the human genome.

Human Epigenome Project

This project aims to elucidate all of the methylation sites in 30,000 human genes.

RECOMBINANT DNA TECHNOLOGY

Definition

Recombinant DNA Molecule: It is a vector into which desired DNA fragment has been inserted to enable its cloning in an appropriate enzyme.

By using restriction enzymes, DNA is cut into suitable fragments and then digated with appropriate fragments to produce a recombinant DNA.

Objective of Producing Recombinant DNA Molecule

1. To obtain a large number of copies of specific DNA.
2. To recover large quantity of protein produced by a gene of concern.
3. To integrate gene of interest into chromosome of target organism.

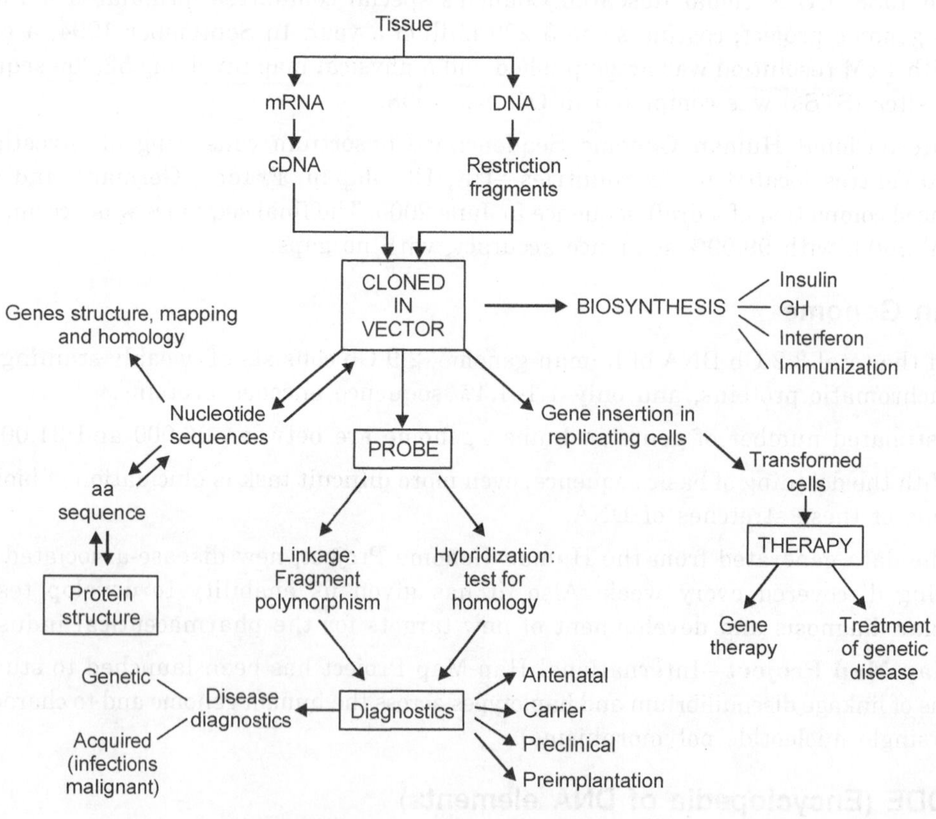

Figure 2.1 Applications of DNA Technology

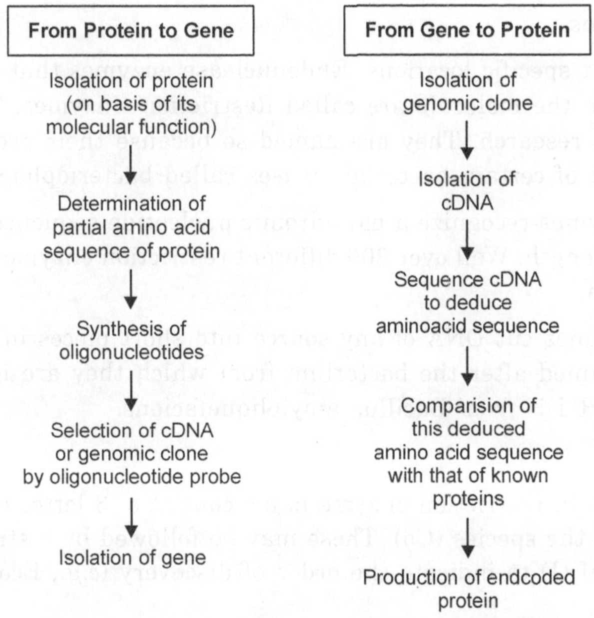

Figure 2.2 Recombinant DNA and genomics.

DNA Technology

Identification of restriction endonucleases, the development of the DNA cloning vectors, introduction of Southern Blot technique and Sanger sequencing and more recent development of Polymerase Chain Reaction (PCR) are important development in the field of molecular biology.

DNA technology has 2 main areas:

- DNA cloning or gene cloning.
- Methods of DNA analysis.

DNA Cloning or Recombinant DNA Technology

It is selective amplification of a specific DNA fragment (or sequence) to produce relatively large amounts of that DNA fragment.

It is of 2 types:

1. in vivo cell-based mechanisms of DNA replication.
2. in vitro polymerase chain reaction.

1. *In vivo cell-based DNA Cloning.* It includes generation of DNA fragments by restriction enzymes and recombination of DNA fragments to form recombinant DNA molecule.

2. *Cell-free DNA cloning or in vitro Polymerase Chain Reaction (PCR)* can be used in produce vast quantities of a target DNA fragment of known sequence.

Basic Tools for DNA Cloning

Restriction Enzymes

They cut DNA at specific locations. Endonuclease enzymes that cut DNA at specific DNA sequence within the molecule are called Restriction Enzymes. They are a key tool in recombinant DNA research. They are named so because their presence in bacterium restricted the growth of certain bacterial viruses called bacteriophages.

Restriction Enzymes recognize a palindromic nucleotide sequence of DNA between 4 and 8 nucleotides in length. Well over 300 different restriction enzymes have been isolated from various bacteria.

Restriction enzymes cut DNA of any source into short pieces in a sequence-specific manner. They are named after the bacterium from which they are isolated *e.g.*, EcoR I is from E. coli, BamH I is from Bacillus amyloliquefaciens.

Nomenclature

The 1st 3 letters in restriction enzyme name consist of 3 letter of the genes (E) and the 1st two letters of the species (Co). These may be followed by a strain designation (R) and a roman numeral (I) to indicate the order of discovery (*e.g.*, EcoR*I*, EcoR*II*).

Recognition

Each enzyme recognizes and cleaves a specific double-stranded DNA sequence that is 4–7 bp long.

These DNA cuts result in:

(*i*) blunt ends *e.g.*, Hpa*I*

(*ii*) sticky (overlapping) ends *e.g.*, BamH*I* : useful in constructing hybrid or chimeric DNA molecules.

Table 2.1 Selected Restriction Endonuclease

Endonuclease	*Sequence specificity*	*Source (bacteria)*
Taq I	↓ TCGA AGCT ↑	Thermus aquaeticus YTI
Pst I	↓ CTGCAG GACGTC ↑	Providencia stuartii 164
	↓	

EcoR I	GAATTC CTTAAG ↑ ↓	E.Coli RY 13
EcoR II	CCTGG GGACC ↑	E.Coli R 245

Recognition Sequence

The recognition sequence for type II endonucleases from palindromers with rotational symmetry (Table 2.1).

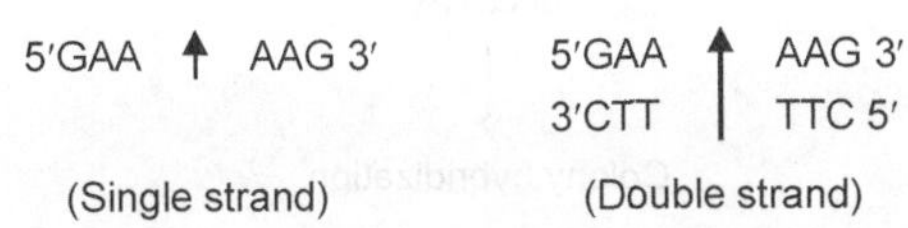

Figure 2.3 Palindromic sequence. (arrow represent axis of symmetry)

Cleavage patterns

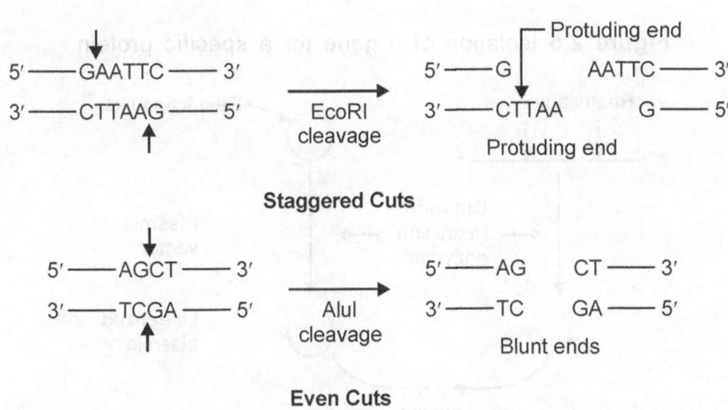

Figure 2.4 Cleavage patterns by restriction endonuclease

Isolation of Desired Gene

The DNA fragments used for cloning are generally obtained in the following ways:

(*i*) genomic DNA fragments from DNA library.

(*ii*) cDNA from cDNA library.

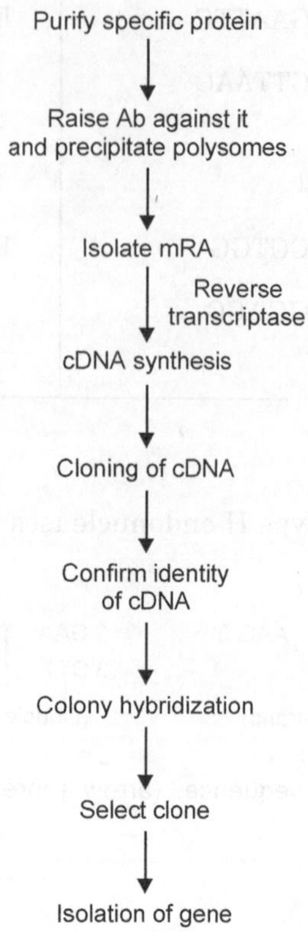

Figure 2.5 Isolation of a gene for a specific protein

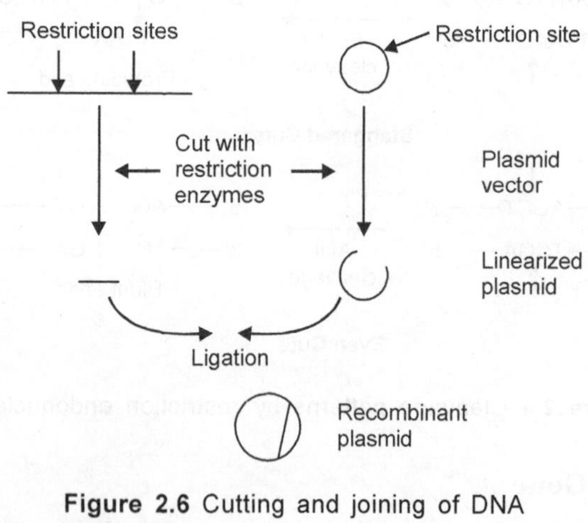

Figure 2.6 Cutting and joining of DNA

Recombination of DNA Fragments

When DNA has been cleaved by a restriction enzyme which produces staggered termini, these are referred to as being 'sticky' or 'cohesive', since they will unite under appropriate conditions with complementary sequences produced by the same restriction enzyme on DNA from any source by enzyme.

DNA Ligase

The union of two DNA fragments from different sources produces Recombinant DNA Molecule.

VECTORS

They are carrier DNA molecule used in cloning process by its own independent replication within a host organism to produce multiple copies itself.

5 main types of commonly used vectors:

plasmid, bacteriophage, cosmid, bacterial (BAC) and Yeast Artificial Chromosomes (YAC).

Plasmid and bacteriophage have limitation of size of DNA that could be inserted.

Cosmid can take up inserts upto 50 kb in size. BACs and YACs allow cloning DNA fragments between 300 kb-1000 kb in size.

Table 2.2 Properties of vector

Properties of Good Vector
• Replicates autonomously
• Size less than 10 kb
• Easy to isolate and purify
• Easy to transform host
• Suitable marker gene for selection
• Ability to integrate into host genome
• Unique target sites for restriction enzyme

Cloning Vector

Vector used for propagation of DNA insert in a suitable host is called Cloning vector.

Expression Vector

Vector designed for expression of DNA insert *e.g.*, for production of protein specified by the insert is termed as *expression vector*. Expression vector are constructed by translational and Transcriptional fusion.

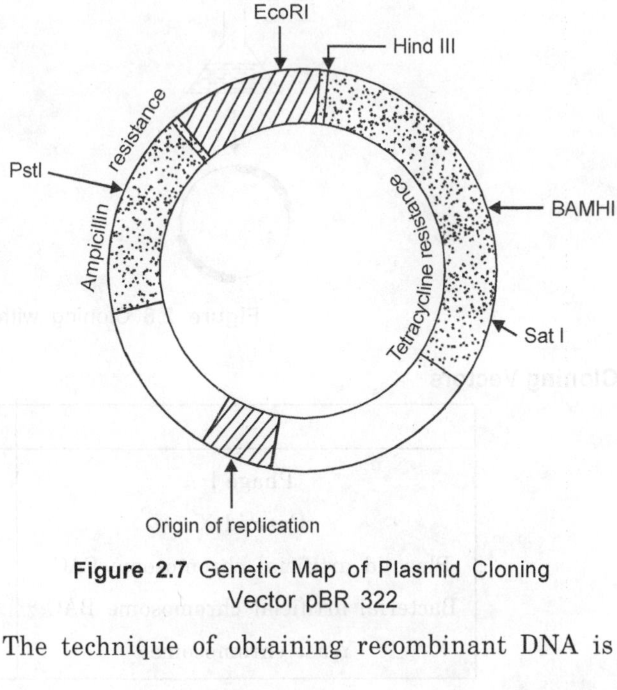

Figure 2.7 Genetic Map of Plasmid Cloning Vector pBR 322

Gene Cloning

Recombinant DNA is product of breakage of a DNA molecule at two desired places to isolate a specific DNA segment and its insertion in another DNA molecule at a desired position. The technique of obtaining recombinant DNA is *Genetic Engineering*.

With the help of this technique, a single copy of gene can be isolated and cloned into an indefinite number of identical copies. This technique is termed as gene cloning and the vectors are called *cloning vectors.*

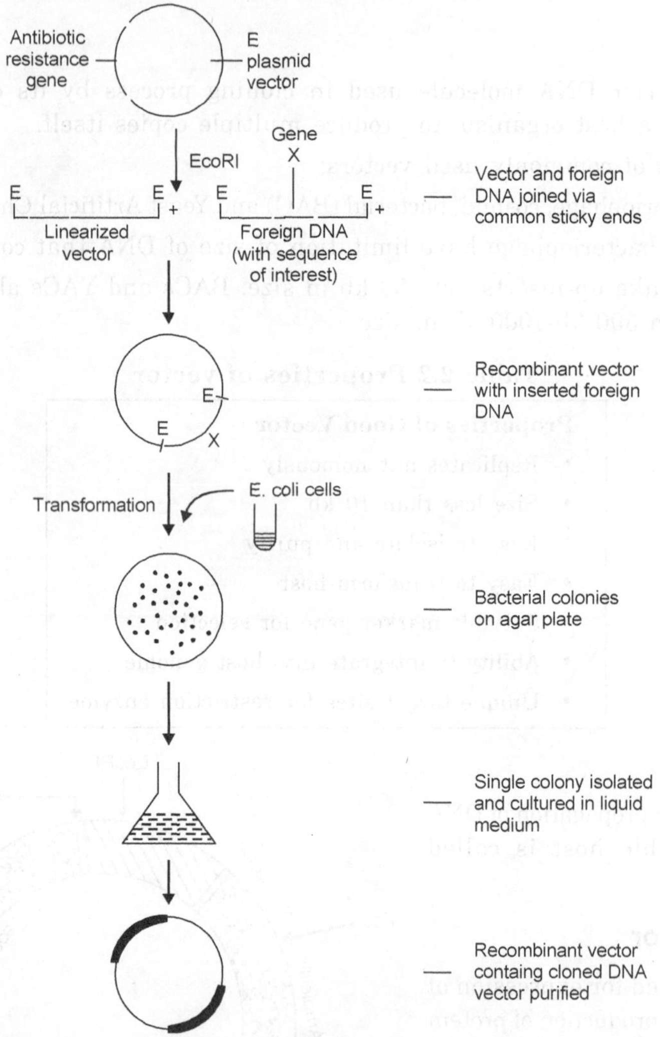

Figure 2.8 Cloning with plasmids

Cloning Vectors

	Foreign Insert Size kb
Phage l	5–25
Cosmid X	35–45
Plasmid artificial chromosome PAC	100–300
Bacterial artificial chromosome BAC	100–300
Yeast chromosome	200–2000

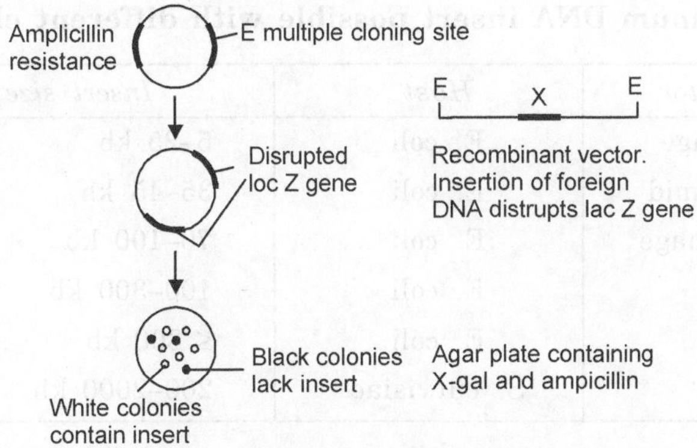

Figure 2.9 Insertion of foreign DNA molecule inactivates lac Z gene and recombinant colonies appear while on agar plate containing X-gal

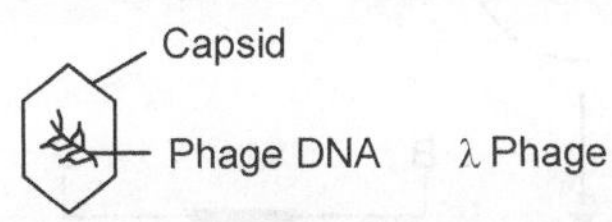

Figure 2.10(a)

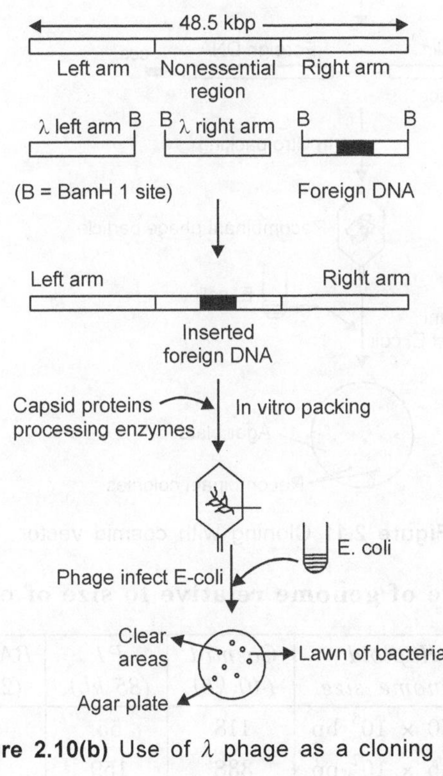

Figure 2.10(b) Use of λ phage as a cloning vector

Choice of Vector

The maximum size of insert that the different vectors will accomodate is shown in the following two tables:

Table 2.3 Maximum DNA insert possible with different cloning vectors

Vector	*Host*	*Insert size*
λ phage	E. coli	5–25 kb
λ cosmid	E. coli	35–45 kb
P1 phage	E. coli	70–100 kb
PACs	E. coli	100–300 kb
BACs	E. coli	≤ 300 kb
YACs	S. curvisiae	200–2000 kb

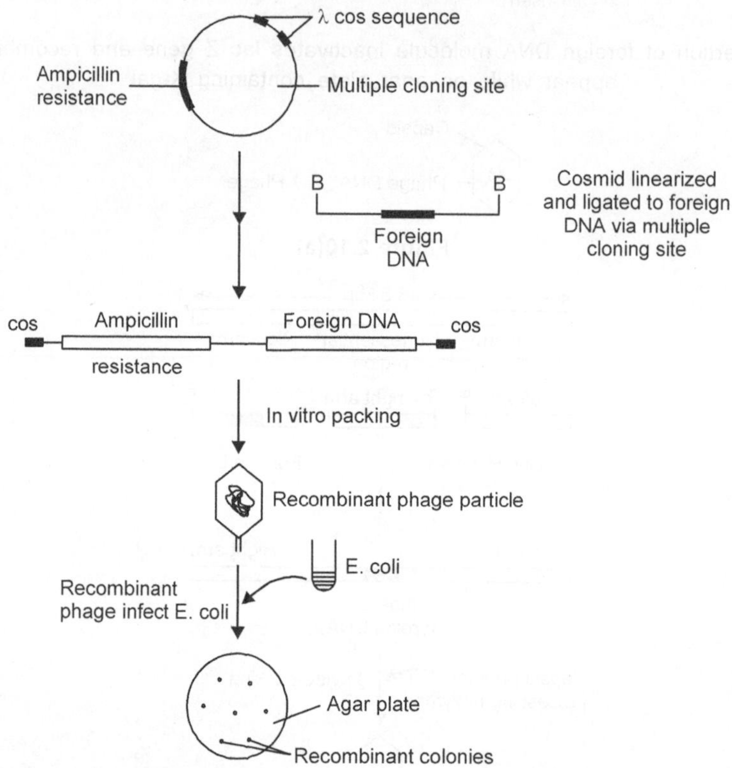

Figure 2.11 Cloning with cosmid vector

Table 2.4 Size of genome relative to size of cloned DNA

Organism	*Haploid genome size*	*Cosmid (40 kb)*	*P1 (85 kb)*	*BAC/PAC (250 kb)*	*YAC (1000 kb)*
E. coli	4.70×10^6 bp	118	55	19	5
S. curvisiae	1.35×10^7 bp	338	159	54	14
D. melanogaster	1.80×10^8 bp	4500	2118	720	180
H. sapiens	2.80×10^9 bp	70000	32941	11200	2800

Transformation of Host Organism

Following introduction of foreign DNA fragment into the vector, the recombinant vector is introduced into modified bacterial or yeast host cells, which multiply and produce large quantities of identical copies of original single target DNA or CLONES.

Recombination Vectors Screening

The recombinant vectors can be screen by various detection systems *e.g.,* loss of antibiotic resistance, immunological or activity assay of protein; products encoded by cloned gene; DNA hybridization with a probe.

Clone Selection

A number of techniques are available for detecting presence of clones within specific DNA sequence inserts and nucleic acid hybridization is most widely used method.

DNA LIBRARIES

A library is a collection of recombinant clones.

Types of Libraries

Genomic Library—prepared from total DNA of a cell line or tissue.

cDNA Library—comprises complementary DNA copies of mRNAs.

Genomic library is prepared by partial digestion of total DNA with help of restriction enzymes to generate large fragments so that most genes remain infect. BAC, YAC, and PI vectors are preferred as they can accept very large fragments of DNA.

cDNA Library: It is a population of bacterial transformants or phage lysates in which mRNA isolated from an organism is represented as its cDNA insertion in a plasmid or a phage vector.

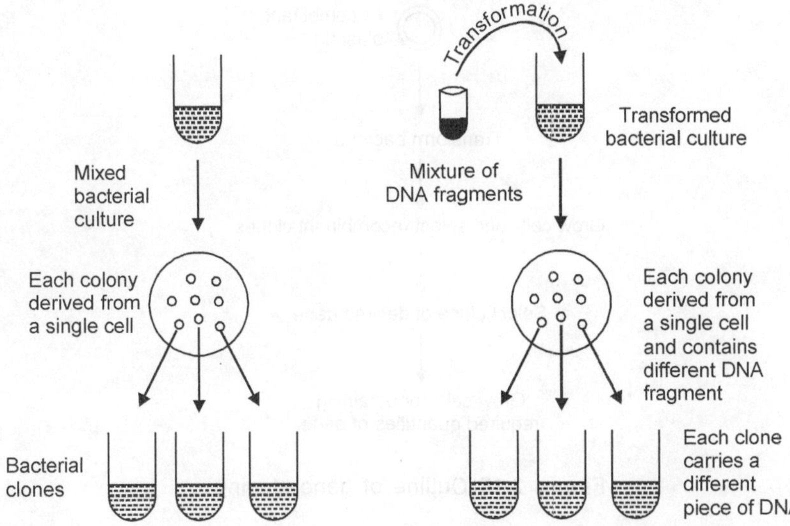

Figure 2.12 Bacterial cloning and Gene cloning

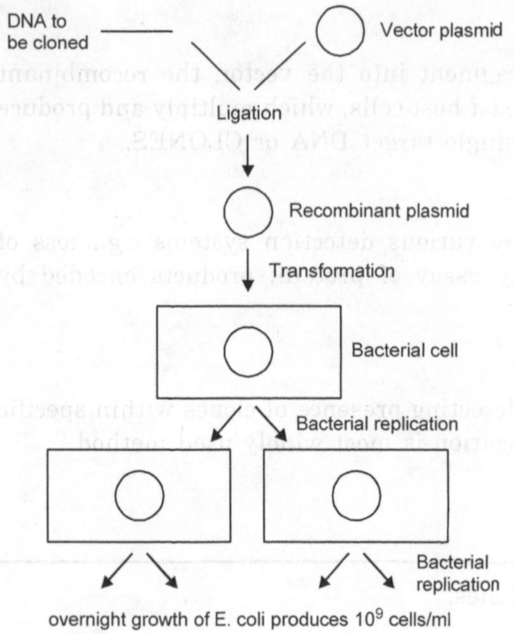

Figure 2.13 Basic outline of gene cloning

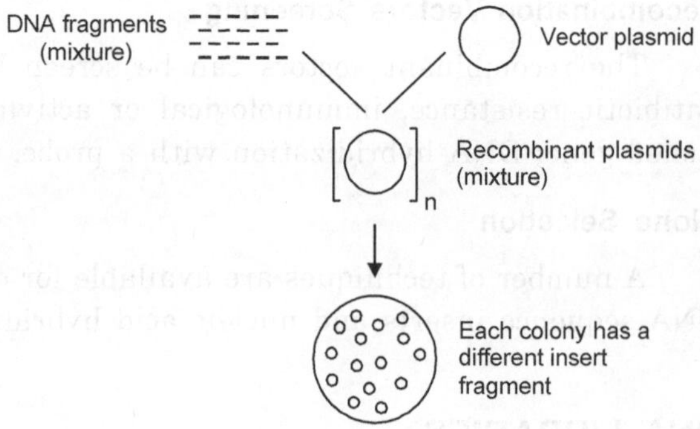

Figure 2.14 Preparation of Genomic Library

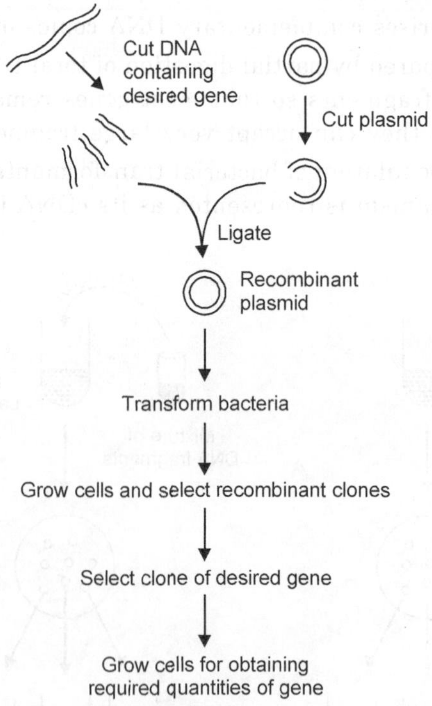

Figure 2.15 Outline of gene cloning

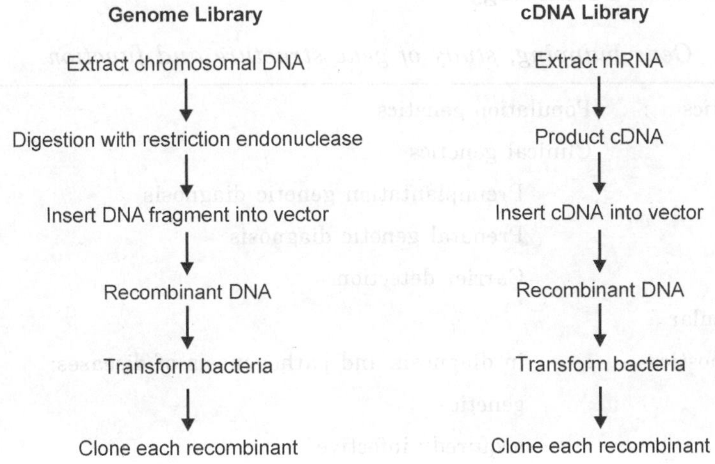

Figure 2.16 Comparison of genomic and complementary DNA (cDNA) libraries construction

Colony Hybridization for Screening of Libraries

Once a genomic library or cDNA library is available, gene sequence can be isolated by **colony hybridization technique.** In this technique, bacteria carrying chimeric vectors are grown into colonies, which are lysed on nitrocellulose filters. Their DNA is denatured *in situ* and fixed on the filter, which is hybridized with a radioactively labelled probe carrying a sequence related to the gene to be isolated, usually cloned cDNA for screening of a genomic library). The colonies carrying these sequences are identified by autoradiograph as dark spots.

If chimeric page particles are taken as vectors, the plaques develop overnight. These plaques can be treated like colonies and the technique is then described as *plaque hybridization.*

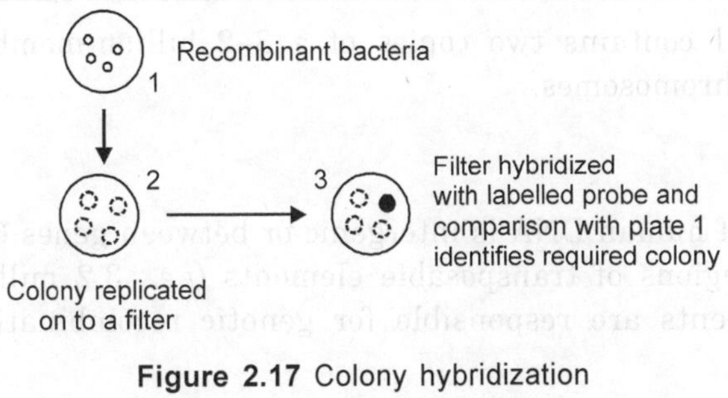

Figure 2.17 Colony hybridization

Searching Specific Genes or cDNA Molecules in Libraries

Probes are used to search for a specific genes or cDNA molecule or to quantitate and define DNA or RNA separated by gel electrophoresis.

The probe must recognize a complementary sequence to be effective.

Applications of DNA Technology

Gene mapping, study of gene structure and function.

Genetics : Population genetics

Clinical genetics

- Preimplantation genetic diagnosis
- Prenatal genetic diagnosis
- Carrier detection

Molecular

Diagnostics : in diagnosis and pathogenesis of diseases:

- genetic
- acquired : infective
  - : malignant

Synthesis of

biologicals : synthesis of hormones, products of immunity:

- insulin
- GH
- interferon
- vaccines

Treatment of genetic disease.

Genetherapy

Cloning.

ANALYSING WHOLE GENOME

Each human cell contains two copies of a 3–2 billion-member sequence code of nucleic acids on 46 chromosomes.

Intergenic DNA

Three quarters of human DNA is intergenic or between genes 60% of which consists of "parasitic" DNA regions of transposable elements (*i.e.*, 3.2 millions in each copy of genome). These elements are responsible for genetic recombination and chromosome structure.

SSRs

Simple Sequence Repeats (SSRs), present in the form of microsatellites or Short Tandem Repeats (STRs) (1–13 base repeat unit) and minisatellites or Variable Number of Tandem Repeats (VNTRs) (14–500 base repeat unit) are present in intergenic DNA. One SSRs on average occurs every 2000 bases.

Uses of SSRs

SSRs serve as markers in

- genetic linkage studies
- forensic medicine
- medical identity testing.

Evolution of SSRs

They are formed by slippage during replication.

e.g., ACACAC, ATAT are most common dinucleotide repeats.

There are 30,000 genes in human genome and each gene covers 27,000 bases of which only 1300 code for aminoacid sequence. These coding regions are EXONS and 9 exons are present per gene (5%). The intervening noncoding regions are INTRONS (95%).

Sequence Variation

Approximately 99.9% of sequence is identical between randomly selected copies of genome (*i.e.*, 1 difference on every 1250 bases).

Most common sequence variations are single base changes termed as SNPs (single nucleotide polymorphisms). Majority of SNPs (97%) occurs in noncoding regions and only 3% are associated with exons.

Of the sequence alterations (mutations) that are known to cause disease, about 70% are SNPs, of which most are missense mutations (49%), fewer are nonsense mutations (11%), 9% are splicing and less than 1% are in regulatory regions.

ANALYSING GENES

The isolation of a specific gene from an entire genome that will discriminate one part in a million and recombinant DNA technology can accomplish this.

Terminology

Genome: Genome represents the total genetic information present in them.

Genome Analysis: It refers to analysis of structural and functional organization of complete genome and it is commonly termed as **Genomics.**

The initial phase of genomics is development of genome maps.

Genome Map: It is a detailed schematic description of the structural and functional organization of the complete genome of an organism.

Aims of Genomics

To obtain DNA sequence of the complete genome which can provide complete nucleotide sequence of genome.

Gene Mapping

Localizing specific genes to distinct chromosomes is termed as gene mapping.

Three Approaches—Physical mapping, Cytogenetic mapping, linkage analysis.

Physical Mapping—determine by physical distances between genes.

Of two types:

(*i*) Low resolution (1-several megabase)

(*ii*) High resolution (hundreds of kb to a single nucleotide).

Low resolution physical mapping techniques include:

- Somatic cell hybridization
- Chromosome specific libraries
- Fluorescence in situ hybridization (FISH)

High resolution physical mapping techniques include:

- pulsed field gel electrophoresis
- high resolution FISH
- DNA sequencing

FISH—Fluorescently labelled DNA probe is hybridized to metaphase chromosomes and examined using fluorescent microscopy. It is a very sensitive technique.

Genetic Map: They depict relative chromosomal locations of DNA markers (genes and other identifiable DNA sequences) by their pattern of inheritance. Three different strategies have been used to construct genetic maps.

Types of Genetic Maps

(*i*) Linkage Maps

(*ii*) Cytogenetic or Cytological maps

(*iii*) Physical maps.

Linkage Map

It depicts order of genetic markers and relative distances between them.

Cytogenetic Map

It depicts location of various genes in a chromosome relative to specific microscopically visible landmarks in the chromosome.

Physical Map

Here, genes are depicted in the same order as they occur in chromosome.

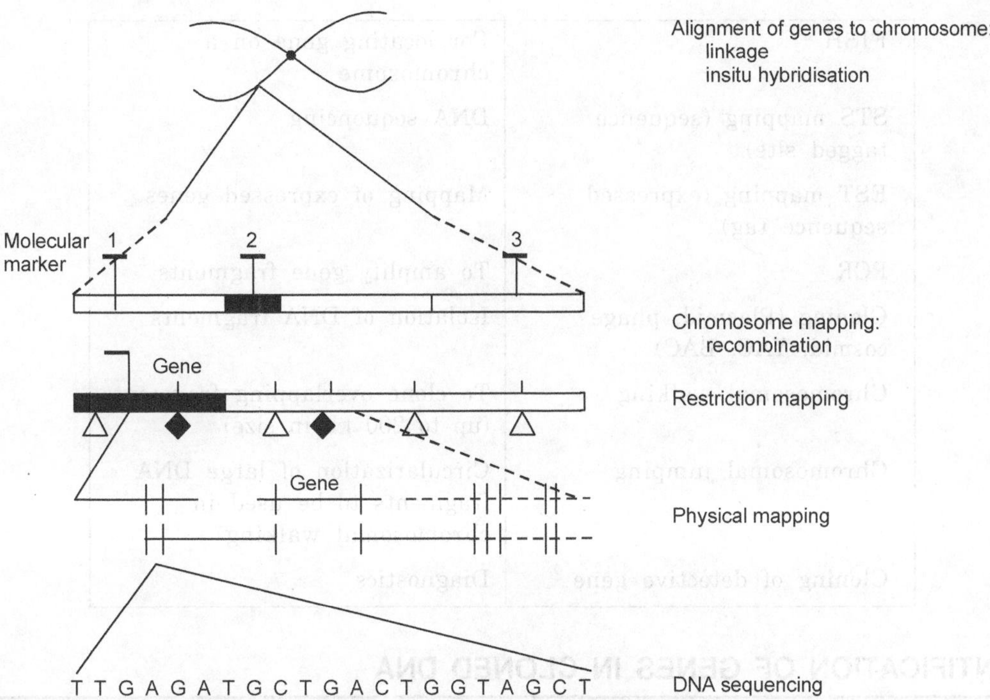

Figure 2.18 Mapping Methods

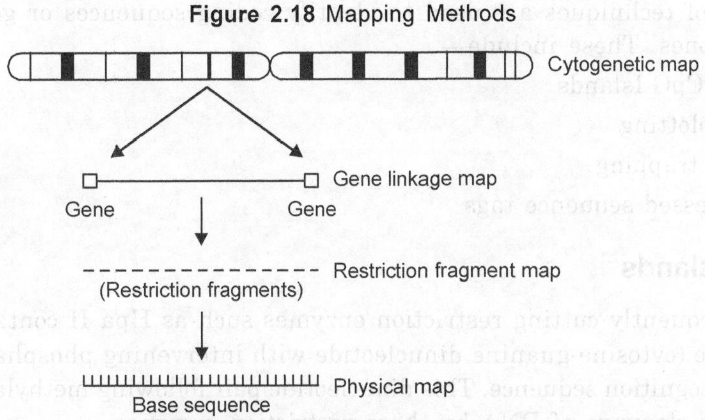

Figure 2.19 Genome maps : different types

Table 2.5 Methods for genome mapping

Method	*Application (use)*
DNA sequencing	Identifies physical map of DNA
Probes	Identify RFLPs, STS, SNPs
Radiation hybrid mapping	To fragment genome into large pieces and locate markers and genes

FISH	For locating gene on a chromosome
STS mapping (sequence tagged site)	DNA sequencing
EST mapping (expressed sequence tag)	Mapping of expressed genes
PCR	To amplify gene fragments
Cloning (Plasmid, phage cosmid, YAC, BAC)	Isolation of DNA fragments
Chromosomal walking	To clone overlapping fragments (up to 200 kb in size)
Chromosomal jumping	Circularization of large DNA fragments to be used in chromosomal walking
Cloning of detective gene	Diagnostics

IDENTIFICATION OF GENES IN CLONED DNA

A number of techniques are used to identify coding sequences or genes with DNA fragments or clones. These include—

1. HTF/CpG Islands
2. Zoo blotting
3. Exon trapping
4. Expressed sequence tags

1. HTF/CpG Islands

Some in frequently cutting restriction enzymes such as Hpa II contain one or more CpG dinucleotide (cytosine-guanine dinucleotide with intervening phosphate molecule) in its nucleotide recognition sequence. This dinucleotide pair following methylation of cytosine residue prevents cleavage of DNA by these restriction enzymes.

CpG dinucleotides occur with one-quarter of the frequency in genome and are non-randomly distributed in genome. Clusters of methylation-free HpaII tiny fragments: *HTF* or CpG islands are found near transcription initiation sites at 5′ end of genes.

About half of genes are associated with HTF/CpG island and 40% of genes show tissue-specific expression of HTF/CpG islands.

2. Zoo Blots

The structure and relative position of many genes have been highly conserved during evolution and in closely related species are termed as HOMOLOGS and usually they are sequences of an important functional gene. Southern blots of DNA from a number of different species is termed a ZOO BLOT.

3. Exon Trapping

By using expression cloning vectors, a suitably modified eukaryotic cell line is transfected to transcribe inserted target DNA into RNA that gets spliced subsequently, Production of abnormal spice product indicates presence of an exon in cloned DNA fragment.

4. Expressed Sequence Tags (ESTs)

Sequence specific primers from cDNA can be designed to identify sequences of expressed genes (ESTs). ESTs can be assigned to a particular chromosomal location by following methods—

- chromosomal hybrids
- radiation hybrids
- FISH
- PCR analysis of gridded arrays.

ESTs provide a rich source of partial sequences of a large number of positional genes responsible for inherited diseases in humans.

ANALYSIS OF HUMAN GENOME DATABASE

Genomic DNA sequence databases for sequence homology to known genes, as well as DNA sequences specific to all genes are available.

About 1500 human disease genes have been identified using **positional cloning** (based on its chromosomal location of a gene).

Positional Cloning

Positional cloning can be done by—*Linkage analysis:*

e.g., Cysfic Fibrosis (CF) has been linked to chromosome 7 and gene was mapped to a region of 500 kb between markers MET and D7S8 at chromosome band 7q31-32.

Also, positional cloning is associated by

(*i*) chromosomal abnormalities *e.g.,*

- Duchenne muscular dystrophy (DMD) X-linked
- Retinitis pigmentosa
- Chronic granulomatous disease.

All these are X-linked.

(*ii*) homology to genes in model organisms.

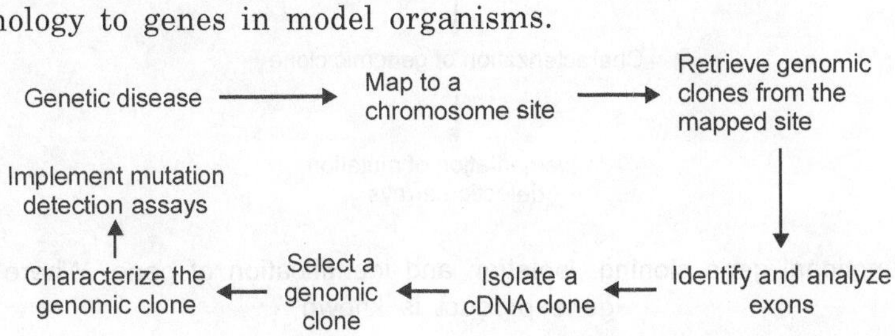

Figure 2.20 Positional gene cloning

Candidate Genes

Those genes which are likely to be involved in the pathogenesis of the inherited disorder are known as *candidate genes.*

Mutations in candidate genes can be screened for by a variety of methods of DNA sequencing.

It has been observed that candidate gene is expressed in the appropriate tissues and at the relevant stages of development.

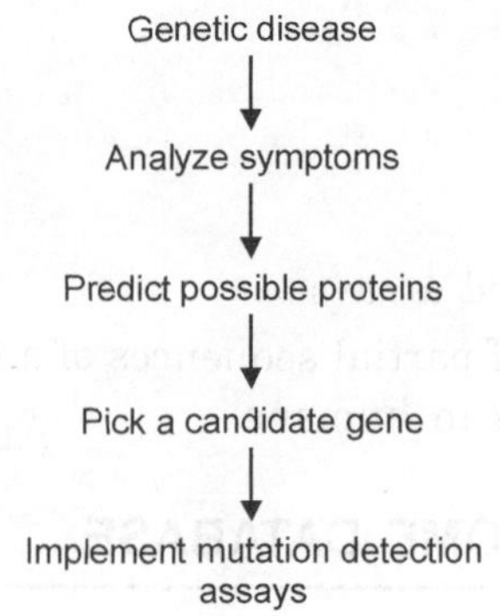

Figure 2.21 Candidate gene cloning

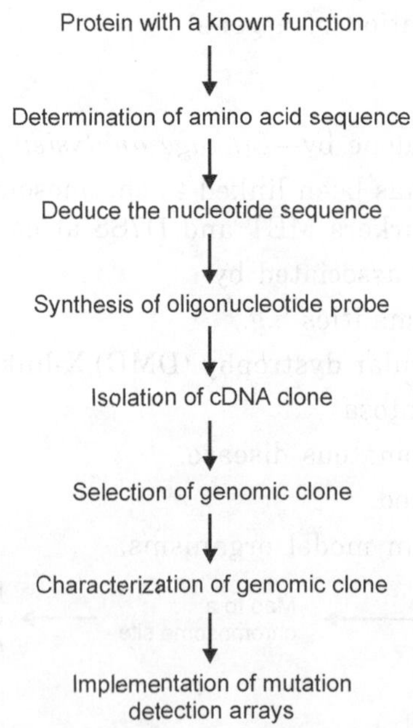

Figure 2.22 Functional gene cloning: isolation and identification of gene. Where sequence of gene product is known

ANALYSING GENE EXPRESSION

Gene Expression

Two main phases of gene expression—

- Transcription.
- Translation.

Terminology

GENOME—is complete set of genetic information.

The complete collection of mRNA transcripts in a cell, tissue or organism at a particular time is referred to as TRANSCRIPTOME and comparative study of mRNA transcripts is TRANSCRIPTOMICS.

PROTEOME—is complete set of translated proteins and global study of translated proteins is PROTEOMICS.

The first methods that were developed allowed investigators to study the expression of a specific RNA or a specific protein. Gradually, methods to compare complex mixtures of gene products have been evolved over time and recent advances have created new terms : transcriptomics, proteomics ....

Analysis gene expression will be discussed in this section under the assumption that polypeptide chain is the end product of gene expression.

Initially study of products of single genes will be discussed followed by study to complex samples.

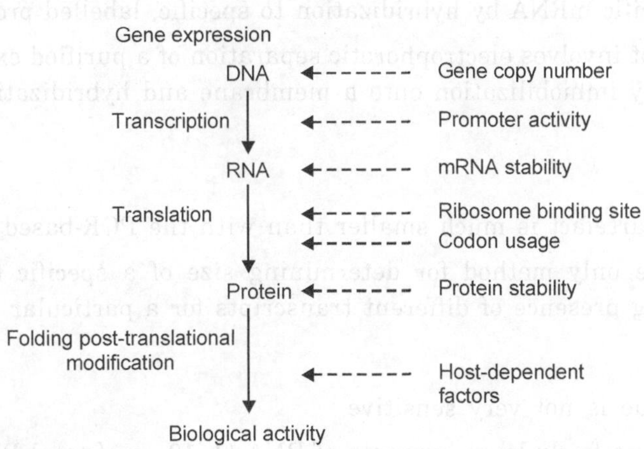

Analysis of Transcription

Techniques for:

(*a*) Analysis of products of single gene

- Northern blot
- RNase protection assay

- reverse transcription PCR
- real-time—RT PCR
- Insitu—hybridization
- Primer extension assay

(*b*) Study of complex samples (Comparing Transcriptomes)

- Differential screening
- Subtractive hybridization
- Differential display
- Array-based methods
- EST arrays
- PCR products arrays

Two Important Points Concerning Measurements of mRNA are:

1. Amount of a specific mRNA in a cell at a point in time is influenced both by level of transcriptional activity and stability of that message.
2. Amount of mRNA present doesn't necessarily correlate with the amount of protein produced.

Techniques for Studying Analysis of Products of a Single Gene

Northern Blots

It detects specific mRNA by hybridization to specific, labelled probes.

A northern blot involves electrophoretic separation of a purified extract of RNA from the cell, followed by immobilization onto a membrane and hybridization with a specific probe.

Advantages

1. Risk of artefact is much smaller than with the PCR-based methods.
2. It is the only method for determining size of a specific transcript and for detecting presence of different transcripts for a particular gene.

Disadvantages

1. Technique is not very sensitive.
2. It requires fairly large amounts of RNA (1–10 μg of total RNA). Sometimes it may not be possible to get sufficient amount of specimen *e.g.,* in case of gene expression of pathogenic bacterium or mRNA level in material obtained by biopsy.

Still this technique is very important tool for detecting products of gene.

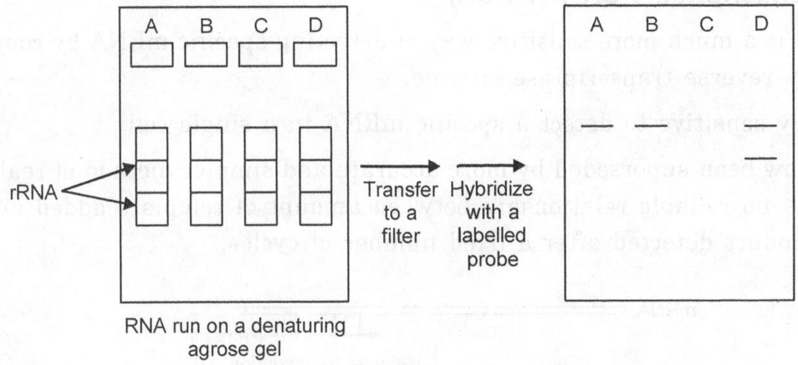

Figure 2.23 Northern Blotting

RNase Protection Assay

When labelled antisense RNA to mRNA preparation, it will anneal to the specific RNA to be measured, forming double-stranded RNA, while non-specific mRNA molecules remain single-stranded.

When RNase (ribonuclease) is added, it will degrade all the single-stranded RNA and double-stranded hybrids formed by annealing the antisense RNA probe to specific mRNA are protected. After RNase digestion, the hybridization mixture is separated by PAGE and radiographed.

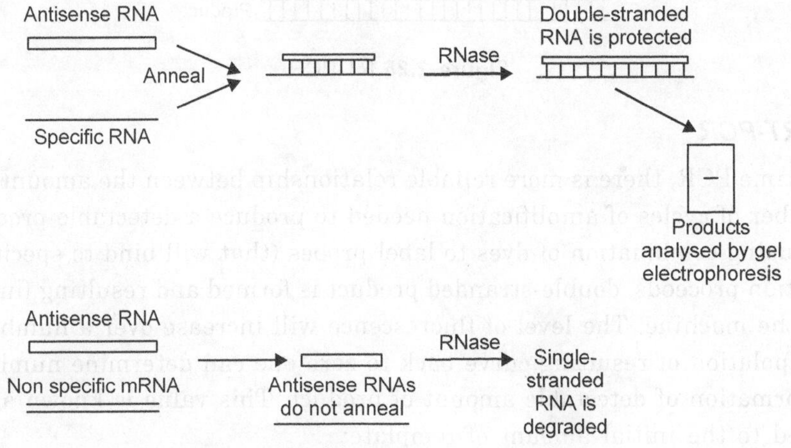

Figure 2.24 RNase protection assay

Advantage

It is more sensitive, quantitative and more tolerant of partial degradation of RNA than Northern blotting.

Disadvantages

1. It doesn't allow determination of size of transcript.
2. It demands more work than Northern blotting.

Reverse Transcription PCR (RT-PCR)

RT-PCR is a much more sensitive way of detecting specific mRNA by copying mRNA into cDNA by reverse transcriptase enzyme.

It is very sensitive to detect a specific mRNA in a single cell.

It has now been superseded by more accurate and simpler method of real-time PCR. Since there is no reliable relationship between amount of template added and ultimate amount of product detected after a fixed number of cycles.

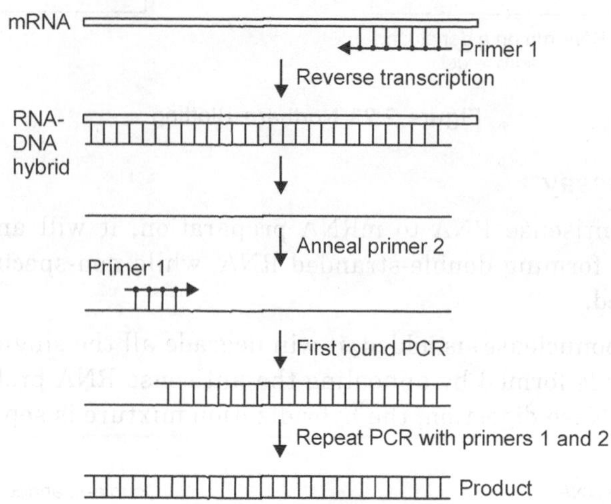

Figure 2.25 RT-PCR

Real-time RT-PCR

In real-time PCR, there is more reliable relationship between the amount of template and the number of cycles of amplification needed to produce a detectable product. This is achieved by using combination of dyes to label probes (that will bind to specific product). As amplification proceeds, double-stranded product is formed and resulting fluorescence is detected by the machine. The level of fluorescence will increase over a number of cycles, and by extrapolation of resulting curve back to zero one can determine number of cycles needed for formation of detectable amount of product. This value is known as **CT value** and is related to the initial amount of template:

higher the value of initial template initially will result in lower CT values.

e.g., If sample A produces a detectable signal after 20 cycles, it has a CT value of 20

Real-time PCR is also an important technique for:

- quantitative detection of specific DNA sequences.
- identification of specific alterations in DNA sequence, and
- medical diagnostic applications.

Block Diagram of an Automated DNA Sequence

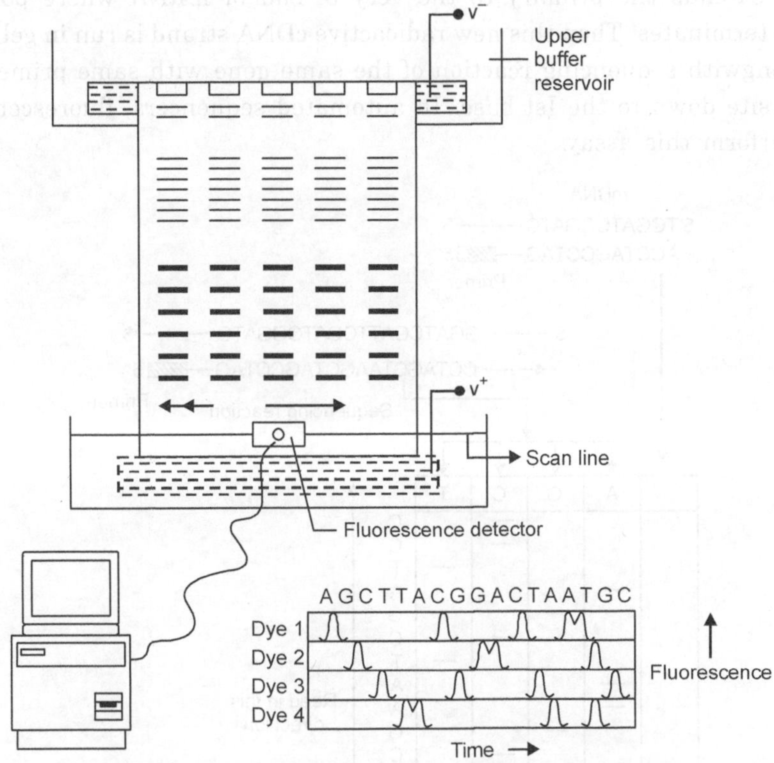

Figure 2.26 Representation of correspondence between fluorescence in a single electrophoresis gene and nucleotide sequence

Insitu Hybridization

In this method, the target is found immobilized within a cell on a microscopic slide and labelled probe is hybridized to cell with metaphase chromosome and following counter staining gene is localized. DNA target is used for gross chromosomal mapping of genes.

Uses

(*i*) Identification/localization of gene

(*ii*) Detection of viruses.

Primer Extension Assay

While studying gene expression, it is important to know how much mRNA is made and where does it start and stop. Studying the 3′ end of a eukaryotic mRNA species is rarely a problem. While constructing cDNA libraries, 5′ end is not always incorporated into cDNA.

The primer extension assay is used for exact mapping of 5′ terminus of mRNA. Firstly Poly-A RNA is purified from a tissue or cell and mixed with radiolabelled oligonucleotide primer complementary to region close to 5′ end of the sequence. Addition of reverse transcriptase extends the primary to the very 5′ end of mRNA where polymerization automatically terminates. Then this new radioactive cDNA strand is run in gel for optimum resolution alongwith sequencing reaction of the same gene with same primer to identify transcription site down to the Ist base. In automated sequencers, fluorescent labels can be used to perform this assay.

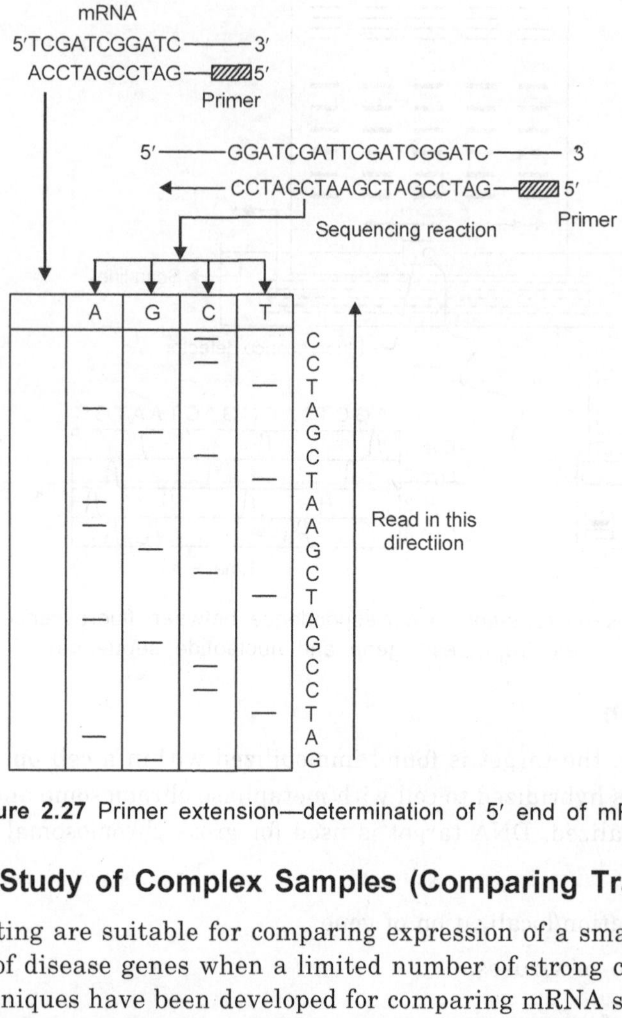

Figure 2.27 Primer extension—determination of 5′ end of mRNA

Techniques for Study of Complex Samples (Comparing Transcriptomes)

Northern blotting are suitable for comparing expression of a small number of genes and identification of disease genes when a limited number of strong candidate genes are known. Newer techniques have been developed for comparing mRNA species expressed in different samples. They include—hybridizations, array based methods etc.

Differential Screening

It is the most primitive method for identifying cloned genes in a gene library.

Two identicate filters containing DNA imprints of gene library are produced.

Two complex mRNA mixtures (A and B) are used to prepare a probe by reverse transcription in the presence radio-labelled nucleotides.

Then, these pools of radioactive cDNA hybridize with duplicate filters separately. Clones that show a positive signal with one probe (say, in B) but not the other, are the candidate clones of expressed genes.

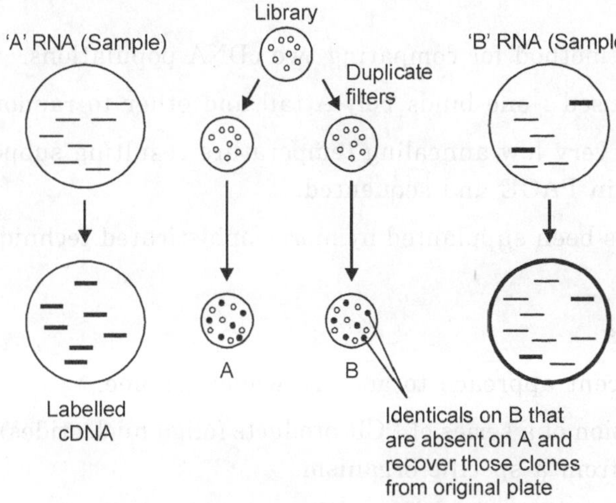

Figure 2.28 Differential screening of a gene library

Subtractive Hybridization

It is an alternative procedure to remove common sequences from the probe and leaving only those which are present in test material.

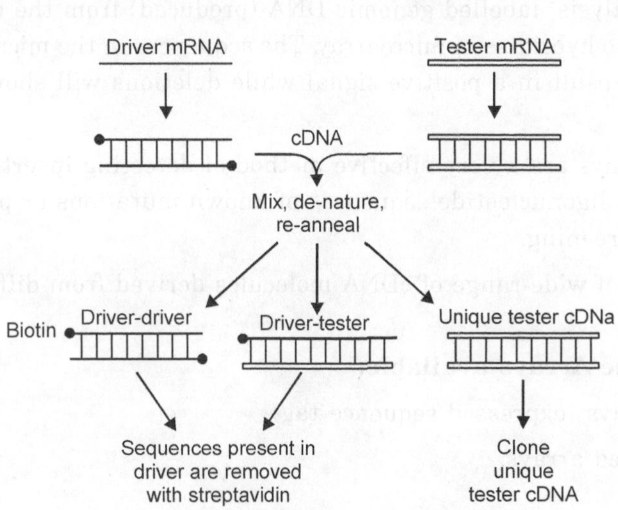

Figure 2.29 Substractive Hybridization

Use: Subtractive tester transcript can be used as a probe for screening a gene library.

Disadvantage

It requires large amounts of mRNA so, PCR combined with principle of above method is preferred (known as representational differential analysis, RDA).

Differential Display

It is a PCR-based method for comparing two cDNA populations.

Two primers are used : one binds poly-A tail and other to random sequence.

Following PCR at very low annealing temperature resulting subpopulation is small enough to be resolved in PAGE and sequenced.

This procedure has been supplanted by more sophisticated techniques such as array technology, RDA.

Array-Based Methods

Array—It is a recent approach to analyze whole genome.

It involves production of a series of PCR products (oligo nucleotides) which correspond to all predicted genes from a specific organism.

To analyze small genome, one can use sequences spaced at regular intervals over the whole genome. A robot is used to produce tiny spots of each fragment in a precisely defined pattern on a treated glass slide. This is the MICROARRAY.

Once the fragments are made, the machine is set up that can produce many identical copies of the same microarray.

In genomic analysis, labelled genomic DNA (produced) from the organism (DNA) to be tested is allowed to hybridize in microarray. The sequences in the microarray represented in target organism result in a positive signal while deletions will show up as absence of a signal.

Thus, microarrays are a very effective method of detecting insertions and deletions. Also, microarray of oligonucleotide sequences of known mutations or polymorphisms in a gene allow quick screening.

Also, presence of wide-range of cDNA molecules derived from different environment can be tested.

Whole Genome Arrays available:

(*i*) EST arrays (expressed sequence tag).

(*ii*) PCR based arrays.

EST Arrays

EST are cDNA cloned where a lab is equipped with a robot to picked every clone from a library.

Also, **transcriptome fingerprint** for cDNA clones from different tissues can be created.

Systematic computer comparison has made it possible to identify which cDNA clones are uniqued. Also, cDNA arrays with non-redundant clones can be produced. By spoting these onto a membrane (macroarrays) or glass slide (microarrays), simultaneous study of majority of genes in humans, mouse and rat genome have been possible.

These microarrays used both 33 P. label and fluorescent labels and data are collected by phosphoimager and microarray readers respectively.

PCR Product Arrays

In EST, at least one clone representing each gene is obtained. However, this objective was not quite achieved in case of human genome.

EST are helpful in identifying genes with open reading frames. Mammalian genome are much larger and complete array of PCR amplified products covering all genes in the entire human genomes is possible.

Translational Analysis

The methods for studying protein expression were developed earlier than DNA cloning methods.

Western Blot

With SDS-PAGE, proteins produced by cell can be analysed and much higher resolution can be obtained by 2D-SDS-PAGE.

To detect a specific protein, and for analysis of its expression, specific antibodies are used in combination with SDS-PAGE. These antibodies can be either labelled themselves or more commonly detected by second labelled antibody.

The analogy with a Southern blot led to this technique being termed Western Blotting. It identifies both presence or absence of a protein that reacts with the antigen as well as its size and an estimate of relative levels of expression.

Immunochemistry and Immunohistochemistry

They help intracellular localization of protein and thus give important clues to its function and incorrect transport of a protein gives important information about a disease phenotype.

2D-Electrophoresis

Involves, isoelectric focussing in one direction and SDS-PAGE in other.

Isoelectric Focussing

All proteins have a characteristic isoelectric point (pI) *i.e.*, the pH value at which they are electrically neutral until they reach a pH equal to their pI at which they are no longer charged. The end result is that each protein will focus at a characteristic point on the pH gradient.

The second dimension separates the proteins according to size.

Thus a pattern of spots is finally obtained that can be compared with other patterns to identify proteins.

pH	*Charge on Protein*	*Movement*
At pH values below pI	protein is positively changed	move towards cathode (–ve)
pH values above pI	protein is negatively changed	move towards anode (+ve electrode)

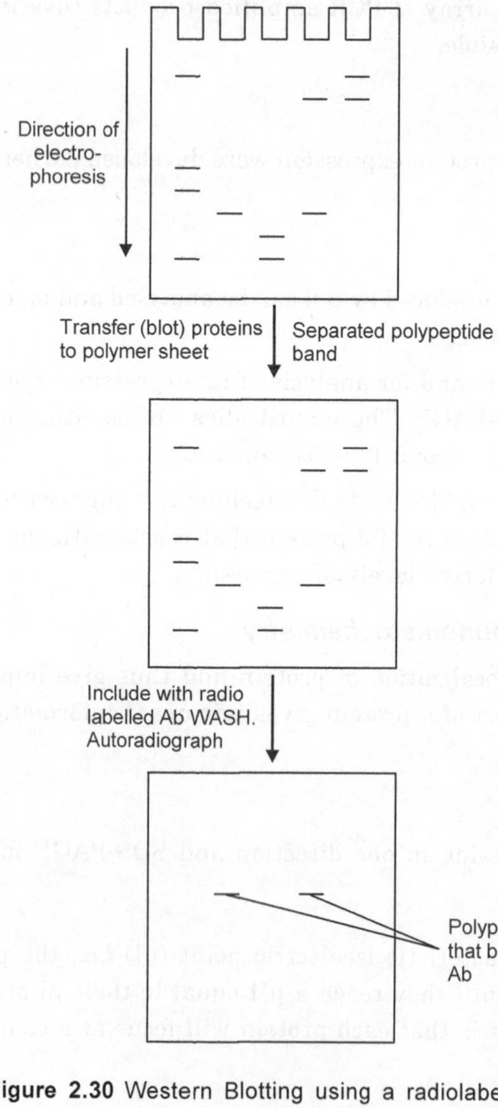

Figure 2.30 Western Blotting using a radiolabelled antibody

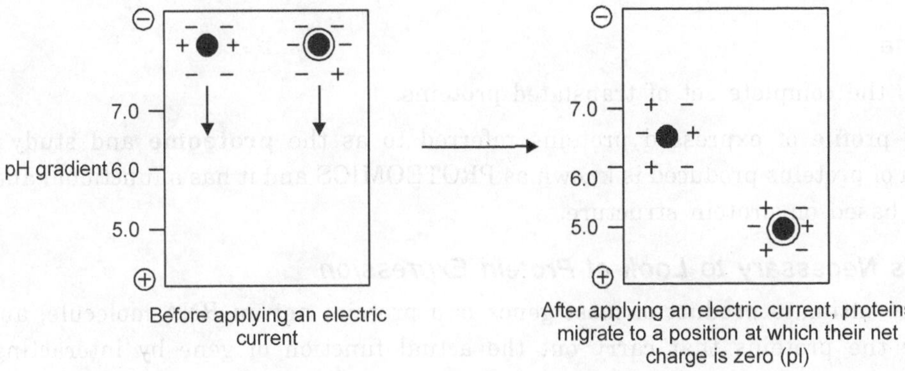

Figure 2.31 Isoelectric focussing (IEF)

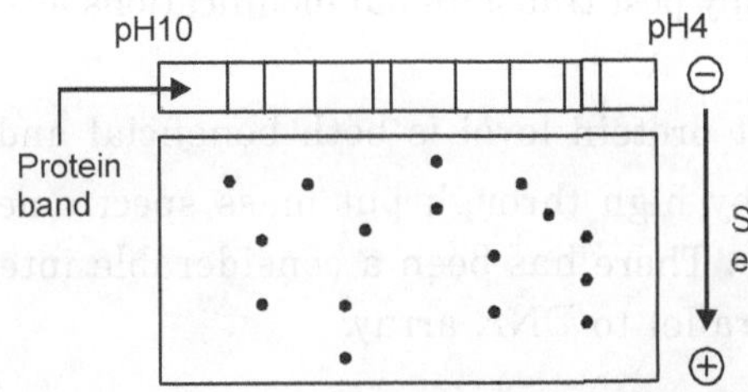

Figure 2.32 2DGE (protein strand is first subjected to ISF in one dimension and then to SDS-PAGE in second dimension)

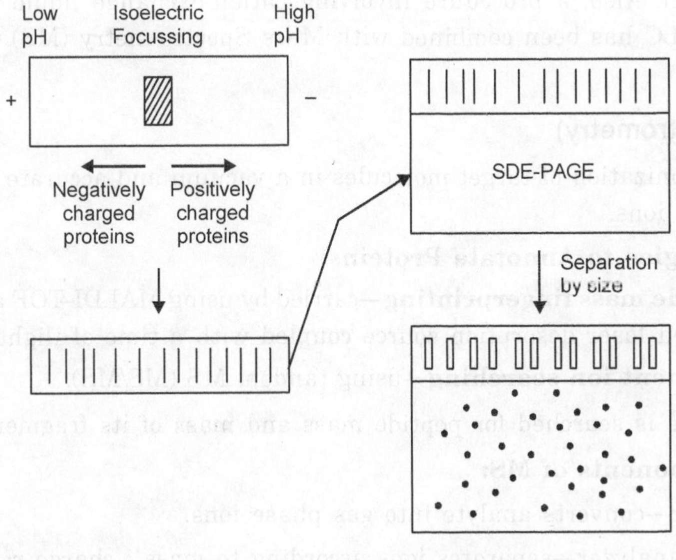

Figure 2.33 2D-protein gel electrophoresis (simplified view)

Proteomics

Proteome

It is the complete set of translated proteins.

The profile of expressed proteins referred to as the **proteome** and study of the spectrum of proteins produced is known as PROTEOMICS and it has a functional anotation of genes based on protein structure.

Why it is Necessary to Look at Protein Expression

Since ultimate product of most genes is a protein, not an RNA molecule, and it is therefore the proteins that carry out the actual function of gene by interacting with cellular and extracellular environment.

Also, many genes are posttranscriptionally regulated, so protein levels may not be related to RNA levels. Further, many post translational modifications are intimately associated with protein function.

Therefore direct analysis at protein level is both beneficial and desirable.

2-D PAGE (2DE) followed by high through put mass spectrometry are widely used technology for proteome analysis. There has been a considerable interest in development of protein arrays as a direct parallel to DNA array.

Alternatives to 2DE

2DE is the workhorse of proteomics and recently this technique has been combined with Reverse Phase Microcapillary Liquid Chromatography (RPMLC) for enhancing the protein separation. Also, a procedure involving cation-exchange liquid chromatography followed by RPMLC has been combined with Mass Spectro-metry (MS) recently *e.g.*, for yeast proteome.

MS (Mass Spectrometry)

It involves ionization of target molecules in a vacuum and accurate measurement of mass of resulting ions.

Two Strategies to Annotate Proteins:

1. **Peptide mass fingerprinting**—carried by using MALDI-TOF analyzer. (Matrix assisted laser desorption source coupled with a time of flight analyzer)
2. **Fragment ion searching**—using tandem MS (MS/MS).

The database is searched for peptide mass and mass of its fragment ions.

Three components of MS:

(*i*) Ionizer—converts analyte into gas phase ions.

(*ii*) Mass analyzer—separates ions according to mass : charge ratio.

(*iii*) Ion detector.

Currents Routes to Protein Annotation in Proteomics

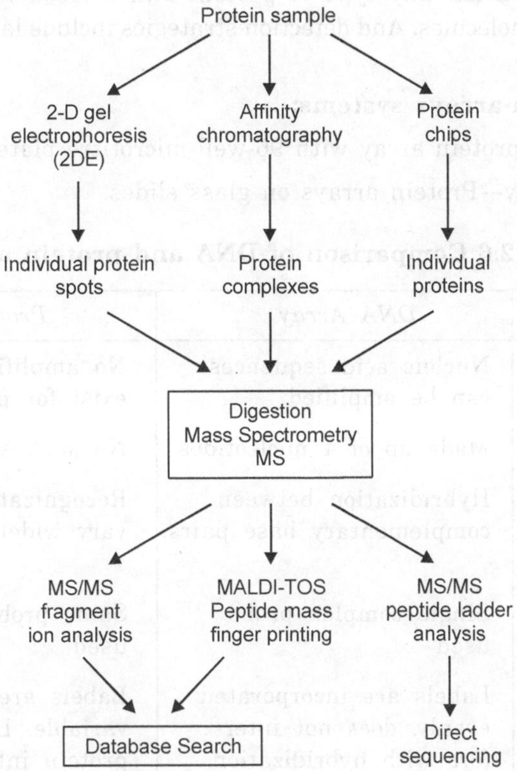

Figure 2.34 Proteomics

PROTEIN ARRAYS AND PROTEIN CHIPS

2DE is an open system for proteome analysis in which all proteins can be detected. For their characterization, it relies on MS.

Protein arrays are emerging as useful closed system for proteome analysis. These are miniature devices in which proteins or molecules that recognize proteins are arrayed on a surface. In concept they are no different to DNA array but they suffer from many practical limitations.

1. No amplication procedure exist for DNA.
2. Recognition parameters vary widely so the same reaction conditions could never be used for all proteins.
3. Labelling of proteins is variable since it could interfere with protein folding, binding.

General Protein Array

Device that can contain any type of protein and is used to assay protein-protein interactions with other molecules. And detection strategies include labelling, surface plasmon resonance.

Different protein-arrays systems:

1. UPA-Universal protein array with 96-well-microtitre plates.
2. Glass microarray—Protein arrays on glass slides.

Table 2.6 Comparison of DNA and protein arrays

	DNA Array	*Protein Array*
Amplification	Nucleic acid sequences can be amplified	No amplification procedure exist for protein
Sequences	Made up of 4 nucleotides	No such sequences
Principle of molecular recognization	Hybridization between complementary base pairs.	Recognization parameters vary widely
Number of probes	Single complex probe used	Same probe cannot be used
Labelling	Labels are incorporated evenly, does not interfere with hybridization	Labels are much more variable. Labelling of protein interfere with protein binding

Type of Protein Microarray Available:

1. Antibody arrays (microimmuno assays)
2. Antigen arrays (reverse immuno assays)
3. General protein arrays
4. Arrays of specific capture agents *e.g.,* aptamers, biochips, SS nucleotides.

Molecular Imprints or Protein Chips

They contain artificial recognition sites for proteins.

Molecularly Imprinted Polymers

(MIPs) depends on ability to emboss a polymeric substrate with recognition molecules. It is yet to be applied to proteome-wide expression analysis on mass-scale.

Broad-Capture Agent Biochips

These devices use broad specificity capture agents. They are commercially available. Protein Chips (Ciphergen Biosystems (nc) bind different classes of proteins and they can be integrated with MS.

Also surface plasmon resonance based protein chip integrated with MS are available.

Solution Arrays

Next generation of miniature protein assay platforms would be based on microfluidics.

SUMMARY

Recombinant DNA technology comprises a battery of experimental procedures to isolate (clone) pieces of DNA containing specific genes. Restriction endonuclease typeII precisely cleavage DNA into fragments of descrete sizes.

Gene cloning can be summarized as: (1) Isolation of DNA from an organism containing target gene that is cut with a restriction enzyme (RE), (2) DNA cloning vector is cut with same RE to digest the source DNA, (3) Two DNA samples are mixed and joined by the action of ligase. (4) This DNA is used to transform host cells and the entire construct is perpetuated.

There are four approaches for isolating a human gene: (1) Functional gene cloning where probes are created to screen cDNA library. (2) Candidate gene cloning to screen mutations responsible for inherited disorder (3) Positional cloning is used when nothing is known about the possible disease or gene product. In involves mapping of chromosome region with RFLP or STRP probes using pedigrees with the genetic disorder. (4) Positional-candidate gene cloning to map a disease gene to a chromosome site, reviewing functional gene and ESTs.

Human Genome Project (HGP) is a massive, multidimensional research project that had the ultimate goal of complete sequencing human genome and was accomplished in April 2003.

Genome analysis is carried out by genome mapping. Genetic map depicts relative chromosomal location of DNA markers by their pattern of inheritance. Genetic maps can be linkage, cytogenetic or physical maps. And genes in cloned area can be identified by a number techniques and EST are commonly used nowadays. Gene expression can be analysed by genomics and proteomics. Genomics includes determination of complete set of proteins encoded by an organism and functioning of genes and metabolic pathways is an organism proteomics is the study of gene products encoded by a genome and function of the encoded proteins. The gene expression is studied by analysing transcription (using Northern blot, RT PCR, *in situ* hybridization and primer extensive assay microarrays) and translation (using Western blot, ISF, immunochemistry). Microarrays are emerging as useful closed system for genomic (DNA microarray) and proteome (protein microarray analysis).

REVIEW QUESTIONS

1. What do you understand by a genetic and physical map?
2. Give an example of map-based DNA cloning using restriction digestion.
3. Describe sequencing.
4. What is DNA library?
5. Discuss advantages of protein array in proteomic research.
6. Discuss various uses of recombinant DNA technology.
7. Describe various blotting techniques.
8. What is gene cloning?
9. What are microarrays?

10. What is mass spectrometry?
11. Compare genomics and proteomics.
12. What is a vector?
13. Compare colony and plaque hybridization.
14. What are SSRs. Give the use of SSRs?
15. Describe sequencing.
16. What is genomics?
17. Give an account of gene mapping.
18. What is EST?
19. Give an account of CpG.
20. What is positional cloning? Enlist its applications.
21. What are candidate genes?
22. What are the two main phases of gene expression? Enlist the techniques for analysis of gene expression.
23. What is a transcriptome? Give techniques for its analysis.
24. Give the use of real time PCR.
25. What are arrays? Give their types.
26. What is translational analysis? Give an account of the techniques of its analysis.
27. What is proteomics?
28. What are the strategies of proteomics?
29. What is mass spectrometry?
30. Compare Maldi with other methods of MS.
31. Enumerate the features of human genome.
32. What is ENCODE?
33. What do you understand by recombinant DNA technology?
34. List the applications of recombinant DNA technology.
35. Enlist the basic tools of DNA cloning.
36. Give a comparison of genomic and cDNA library.

Chapter 3

BIOINFORMATICS AND COMPUTER APPLICATIONS

BIOINFORMATICS : INTRODUCTION

It is the science of using information to understand biology. It is conceptualizing biology in terms of molecules and applying informatics techniques (computer science, applied mathematics and statistics) to organize the information associated with these molecules. Bioinformatics and data mining are two latest areas of research involving computer-assisted management of data generated for biotechnology applications. The information generated in genomics is enormous and its interpretation requires the use of powerful computers and specific softwares.

Computer Network

The internet is a global network of computer networks that link government, academic and business institutions. Computer within the network are referred to as nodes and these communicate with each other by transferring *data packets*. Each computer or network mode has a unique address (IP address) by which it can be identified and can communicate with other nodes.

Genomics

Term genomics has been derived from the word *genome*, which means *haploid* DNA content of an organism.

Term *genomics*, deals with the genome as a whole and had its origin in the *human genome project*, which involved determination of the nucleotide sequence of the whole genome. Today, *genomics* includes sequencing of genomes, determination of the complete set of proteins encoded by an organism and functioning of genes and metabolic pathways in an organism.

Thus, bioinformatics is concerned with development and application of computer software and hardware to acquire, store, analyze and visualize biological information. By providing algorithms, databases, user interfaces and statistical tools, comparison of DNA sequences are possible.

The long term value of bioinformatics and data mining capabilities does not lie so much in developing tools, as it does in converting knowledge or information into products like therapeutics, animal and plant bioreactors in the term of genetically modified organisms, newly discovered genes etc.

Bioinformatics include following important biological data:

1. Gene expression profile.
2. Protein structure.
3. Problem interactions.
4. Microarray (DNA chips).
5. Functional analysis of biomolecules.
6. Drug designing.

Application Areas of Bioinformatics

1. Sequence Analysis.
2. Recognition of genes and regulatory elements.
3. Phylogenetic analysis.
4. Gene expression, expression data analysis.
5. Protein structure prediction.

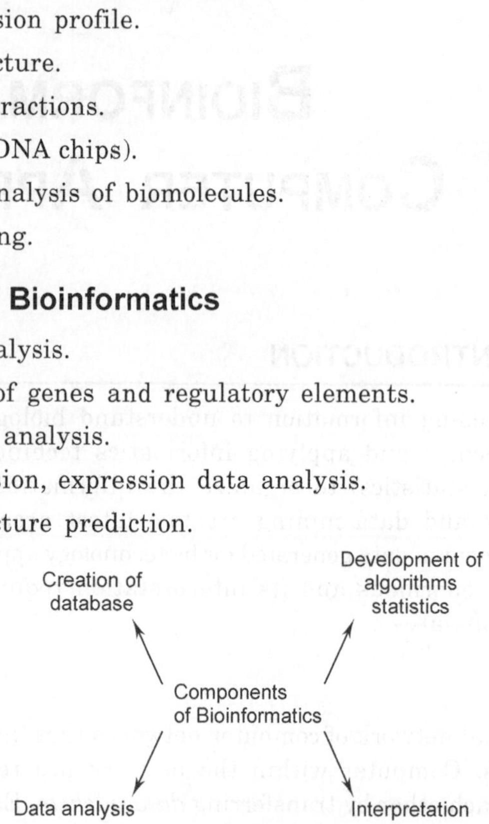

Figure 3.1 Components of Bioinformatics

Aims of Bioinformatics

1. Organization of the data to allow researchers to access existing information submit new entries, and analyze.
2. To develop tools and resources that help in analysis of data. Using these tools.
3. To analyze individual systems in details and make comparisons.

Thus, Bioinformatics has revolutionized the information system in the world. Speed of flow of information, its accuracy & quality has assisted user to plan out their programmer and manage the data to achieve their goals within set time frames.

There is significant industrial interest in Bioinformation currently since the information released by genome sequencing projects would be helpful in medical diagnostics and therapeutics research and development.

Bioinformation promises to lead to advances in understanding basic biological processes and in turn advances in diagnosis, treatment and prevention of various diseases.

Essential to overall success of the Human Genome Project is what is known as Bioinformatics—the establishment of facilities for collecting, storing, organizing, interpreting, analyzing, and communicating the data from project, which can be widely shared by scientific community at large. It is vital for any researcher involved in any aspect of this project to have easy, rapid access to data arising from it. A large no. of electronic databases have been established on world wide web on the internet.

www.nhgri.nih.gov

www.gdb.orgensembl.org.

http://genome.ucsc.edu

www-genome.wi.mit.edu

http-//elegans.swmed.edu/genome.shtml.

www.mgu.har.mrc.ac.uk

www.uwcm.ac.uk/uwcm/mg/hgmdO-html.

These include protein & DNA sequence databases (*e.g.*, Gen Bank, EMBL), databases of human genetic maps (GDB, Geneth on, EPH, CHLC and white head institute sites) and other species (caenorrhabaitis elegenas database), Linkage analysis programs, annoted genome data and the catalog of inheriuted diseases in humans (OMIM : online Mendalian inheritance in man : www3.ncbi.nlm.nih.gov/Omim/).

Thus, developments in Bioinformatics allowing the prospects of identifying coding sequences & their functions.

Bioinformatics & Internet

There are non a large no of genetic database that have sequence information represent a variety of organisms. The largest include. Gen Bank at NIH (USA), EMBL at European Bioinformatics Institute (EBI), Cambridge (UK) and DNA database of Japan (DDBJ) at Mishima in Japan. There are also many data bases within which specialist DNA and protein sequences are stored, all of which may be accessed over the internet.

EMBL	European genetic database ac.a.k	www.ebi.ac.u.ak
Gen Bank	US genetic database	http = // ncbi.nlm.nih.gov
DDBJ	Japanese genetic database	http = // dbj : mig. ac.jp

Internet is a world wide system that links numerous computers local networks, research, commercial and government institutions and establishments, and the world wide web (www).

Bioinformatics Computing

It is the area that involves applications of computational powers of the computer tools and machines on the biological data to help biologists. Lots of biological material is lying in various libraries across geographical locations and is scattered so much that there is no standardization, classification, reusability and applicability of the data. There is lots of data and lots of unanswered questions. Bioinformatics is an area that is capable of solving the queries of evolution and life.

The biologists need to understand about the tools and computational skills being developed for them. While computer scientists are working hard in the direction of mining the expanding data to extract relevant information and patterns, development of tools, algorithms.

Evolutionary Computing

It includes new advance computing strategies paradigms and can be divided into three broad categories:

1. DNA computing.
2. Molecular computing.
3. Quantum computing.

These concepts can be adapted in various computer science applications such as cryptography, artificial intelligence, network communication, computer architecture. This will give rise to system-on-a chip (SOC)-the future of IC technology.

DNA Computing—also known as molecular computing

A DNA computer is basically a collection of selected DNA strands whose combinations will result in solutions to problem. It has the advantage of unique data structure and ability to perform many parallel operations.

Quantum Computing

It involves study of information processing tasks accomplished by using quantum mechanics with advantage of quantum parallelism and superposition of states offering a quadratic speed up.

Another field which is arising is Molecular Computing

Molecular computing is the use of biological molecules for computational devices. It is expected that by 2030, molecular computing will dominate over other computing approaches and it will start generating revenue-producing products by 2050.

The availability of complete genome has opened up a research discipline GENOMICS that deals whole set of genes. With advances in sequencing technology, concept of new high-throughput (experimental) technique come up and the most important being MICROARRAY TECHNOLOGY.

With microarrays, expression of thousands of genes in a cell can be simultaneously measured and probes for all the gene on one microarray chip.

Another important field where high-throughput techniques are used is PROTEOMICS.

Proteomics is the study of proteome-the complete set of proteins in a cell using 2DE and mass spectrometry for identifying proteins by their molecular masses.

These high-throughput experiments produce large amounts of quantitative data posing challenges for bioinformaticians. This new area of biological sciences where computational methods are essential for the progress of the experimental science along with development of algorithm and experimental techniques.

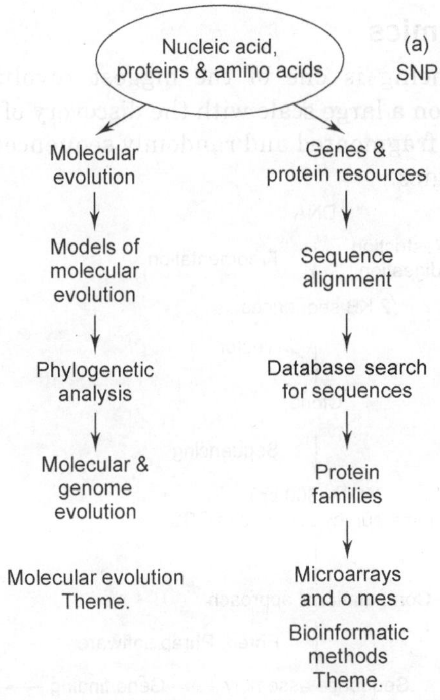

Figure 3.2 Bioinformatics and molecular evolution

The success of genomics and its holistic way of thinking has led to the coining of other 'ome' and 'omic' terms. *e.g.*,

Terminology	*Branch*
Transcriptome:	Complete set of mRNA transcribed in a cell.
Proteome:	Complete set of proteins present in a cell.
Metabolome:	Complete set of chemical reactions involved in metabolic reactions in a cell.

The chief tools of transcriptomics are based on DNA microarrays.

Information Management for 'omes'

After submission of sequences to primary databases one has access them and information that can be shared.

Primary sequence databases analyze the information and high-throughput experiments generate data which can be stored, shared with other researchers and re-analyzed at a later data using newer algorithm. For microarrays, MIAME standard is now being adopted. Databases for complex types of biological experiment, like results of microarray or proteomics experiments need to have well-considered designs to specify relationship between the data they contain and requires a input from both computer scientists and biologists.

Another challenge bioinformatics in the post-genome era is integration of data from many different sources.

Bioinformatics in Genomics

Whole genome sequencing is one of the biggest revolutions in biology. Genome sequencing became possible on a large scale with the discovery of the "short-gun" sequencing strategy, where a genome is fragmented and randomly sequenced, and then pieced together using computational strategies.

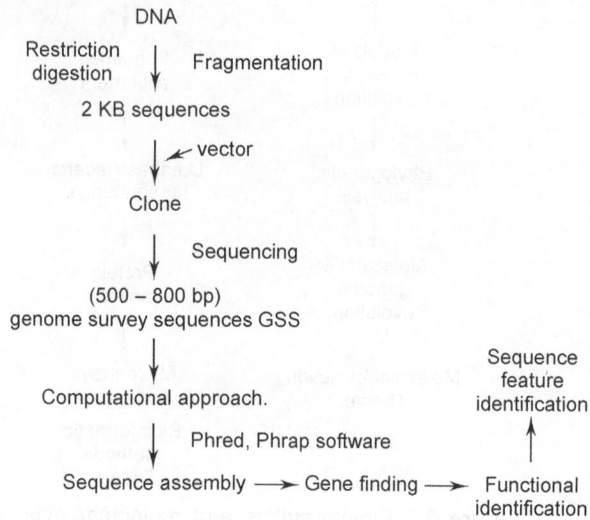

Figure 3.3 Sequence identification

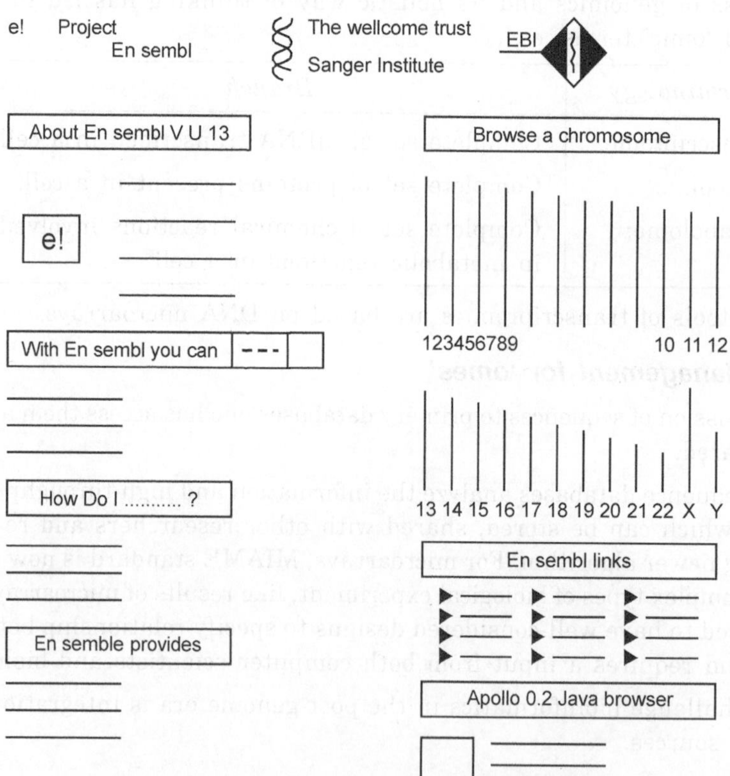

Figure 3.4 Human Genome Server: Web page

History of Bioinformatics

Bioinformatics involves creation, maintenance and use of databases, to which new data on DNA and protein sequences are regularly added. Bioinformation come into existence in 1980s after automated DNA and protein sequencing became possible and computers become central repositories that are accessible world wide. Few years later, bioinformatics established itself as a foundation of future biotechnology. (Table 3.1)

Table 3.1 Chronology of Major events in Genome Sequencing and Bioinformatics

Year	Event
1962	Pauling's theory of molecular evolution
1970	Needleman-Wunsch algorithm
1971	DNA sequencing
1981	Dollitle's concept of sequence molif, Smith-Waterman algorithm
1982	Sequencing of phage lambda genome
1984-1990	Discussion in scientific community for sequencing genome.
1985	Sequence database searching : algorithm
1986	Human genome project proposed
1988	Creation of NCBI (Natural Centre for Biotechnology information) at NIH/NLM.
1988	EMBnet : network for database distribution
Oct. 1, 1990	Human genome project initiated
1990	BLAST
1991	EST (expressed sequence tag) sequencing.
1993	Sanger center (Hinxton, UK)
1994	EBI [European Bioinformatics Institute] Hinxton, UK
1995	Sequencing of H.influenzae genome
1996	Sequencing of yeast genome (Saccharomyces cerevisiae)
1997	Sequencing of E. Coli genome
1998	C. elegans genome sequenced
1999	D. melanogaster genome sequenced
Jun. 26, 2001	Human genome working draft (Homo sapiens) published (90% genome sequenced).

Biological Computing

In early 80s, BIONET (Biology Network was created in Europe to allow use of computers and exchange of software package among its users. This was followed by release of NAPDB (nucleic acid and protein data bank in 1984 which comprised of EMBL'S nucleotide sequence database and protein data bank of 1200 sequences. NAPDB was renamed as COMPEQ and sold to GENOFIT company which released its first PC compatible version with 33 programs. Intelli-Genetics bought the exclusive rights of COMPSEQ with release of PC/GENE packages with many modified releases, the last version being 6.85 version (1995) with 82 programs.

Then come the era of databases and their dictionary. The first to be developed was PROSITE in mid 80s to provide database of protein sequences and structures. This database would be used with SEQANALREF software to analyze and compare sequences. Then 1986, SWISS-PORT protein data bank was developed which is still popular and considered as an important resource for protein sequence and structure.

Following emergence of proteomics in 1990s, databases dealing with 2-D PAGE maps of proteins came into existence namely SWISS-2D PAGE, NIH, USA and EMBL. Europe also developed several databases and softwares.

In mid 1990s, the networking tools and welservers were made available and the field of bioinformatics took off to its full bloom in 21st century.

Thus bioinformatics has emerged as a scientific discipline encompassing the application of computer science and technology to analyse and manage biological data.

Since sequence data is accumulating rapidly and powerful sequence analysis software and newer algorithms are required to transform the sequences into digital symbols.

Only limited alphabet is required to represent nucleotide and amino acid monomers (as digital symbols). The data so generated helps to differentiate genetic data from other types of biological data.

Bioinformatic Tools

The main tools are:

- computer software programs.
- and internet.

A fundamental activity is sequence analysis of DNA and proteins using programs and databases available on the world wide web. Anyone from clinicians to molecular biologists, with an access to net can now freely discover the composition of biological molecules (nucleic acids and proteins) by using bioinformatic tools. The growth of bioinformatics has been a global venture, creating computer networks; and developing software programs for effortless analysis. Multiple international projects are providing gene and protein databases freely to whole scientific community via the internet.

Bioinformatics is an interdisciplinary approach requiring advanced knowledge of computer science, mathematics and statistical methods for understanding of biological phenomenon at molecular level data management, data warehousing, data mining and global communication networking.

The simple tasks used in Bioinformatics concerns with the creations and maintenance of databases of biological information. Majority of such databases are comprised of nucleic acid sequence (and the protein sequences derived from them).

Biological Research on the Web

The internet has changed the mode of searching and exchange of information among scientific community. As soon as data is digitalized, it is distributed from centralized database and most journals are now published online.

In the world of bioinformatics, a simple web search yields tens of thousands of results.

How to Find only useful software data and Scientific Articles?

For finding information on web, one should have the knowledge of search engines and internet.

Web is a means of inter personal and intercomputer contact over networks. Common browsers are Internet Explorer and netscape which present control information, allowing you to trail forward and back or to interrupt a side-trip and allows downloading of information on local computer.

Embedded/highlighted links: They allow jumping around to other pages and sites. They are visible in the material one is viewing and can be distinguished by a high lighted colour, one can return to the calling link (to take up further personal of the page) by following the trail of electronic bread crumbs left behind.

Links: They are of two types

Internal links take the netizen to other portions of text of a current document, image, movie or sounds.

External links allow moving down to more specialized documents up to more general ones, sideways to parallel documents or over to directories that show what other relevant material is available.

Search Engines

A number of search engines namely Atlas, Lycos, Google, HotBot, Northern light, yahoo, Dogpile exist to find way around billions of pages on web.

A researcher should learn how to structure a query to search web and keyword-based database to weed out the majority of the junk data.

The current favourite search engine are Google yahoo. and excellent resource for searching scientific literature in the biological sciences is the free server sponsored by National Centre for Biotechnology (NCBI) at the National Library of Medicine.

This server makes it possible for anyone with a web browser to search the Medline database. Other sources are Lexis-Nexis, Cambridge Scientific abstracts e-Journals *e.g.,* Journal of molecular modeling, Medical Science Monitor have no print counterpart, and displayed on their homepage.

Tutorial programs, reference material are also available on websites government organisations and academic research groups *e.g.*, WCBI (University of Washington Genome Centre) has tutorials on genome sequencing and BLAST sequence alignment program.

Pub Med (www.ncbi.nlm. nih.gov/entrez/query/fcgi) is a valuable source available to biologists. Journals in various fields of namely, molecular biology, biochemistry, genetics, chemical subjects are indexed in Pub Med.

MeSH (Medical subject Heading) is a library of standardised terms and can be used to search via Pub Med.

Role of Text Mining Technologies

To Accelerate Disease-Based Research

Text mining helps scientists of Pharmaceuticals and Biotechnology industries, who are engaged in disease-based research to review the published literature to validate their discovery.

Medline

Medline has thousands of journals and over 15 million abstracts (and over 2,000 abstracted added daily). So, it is physically impossible for any scientist to keep current of the research and explore all of the areas. Thus, to obtain scientific articles pertaining to a topic of interest, special searching softwares are required that scan fastly for terms identical to the query term. Sophisticated software programs have been developed that can understand typical language ambiguities to effectively derive key scientific knowledge from biomedical abstracts.

Almaknowledge Server 2 (AKS2) is a latest text-mining system that examines all abstracts added to medline, applies statistical and rulesbased analyses, that to uncover relationships that exist in scientific literature between diseases, symptoms, drugs, genes, proteins and chemical compounds. It captures formatted data from many sources such as Medline, EntreZGene, UMLS, PubChem. (website is www.activemotif.com). Computational technology of automated text mining available now-a-days can help researchers to be more knowledgable about their disease areas and create more efficient drug discovery processes.

Database

It is an organized collection of data that is stored, formulated accessed and represented in a consistent manner. Databases are the heart of bioinformatics. There are many types of databases depending on nature of information stored and manner of data storage. These databases are accessible to everyone and their web addresses can be found in the references 1st issue of journal Nucleic Acid Research every year (www.nor.oupjournals.org).

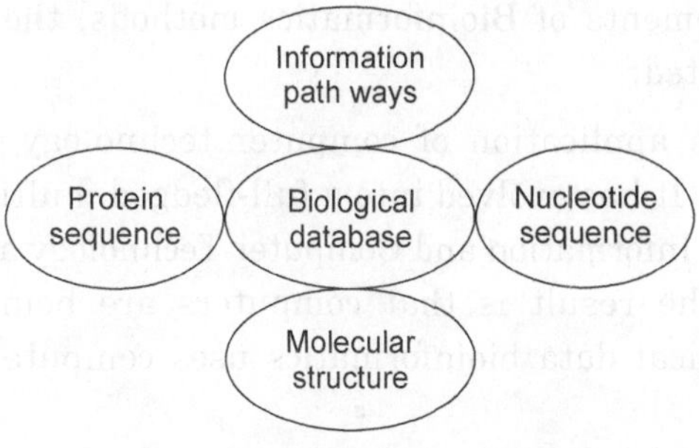

Figure 3.5 Biological Database

Data Ware House

It is a repository (archieve) of information collected from various sources and stored at a single site. This helps user in decision support and analysis on historical data to predict trends.

Bioinformatics and Computer Applications

Bioinformatics is conceptualizing biology in terms of molecules and the applying "informatics" techniques to understand and organize the information associated with these molecules on a large scale. The ultimate goal being to uncover the wealth of biological information hidden in the mass of data.

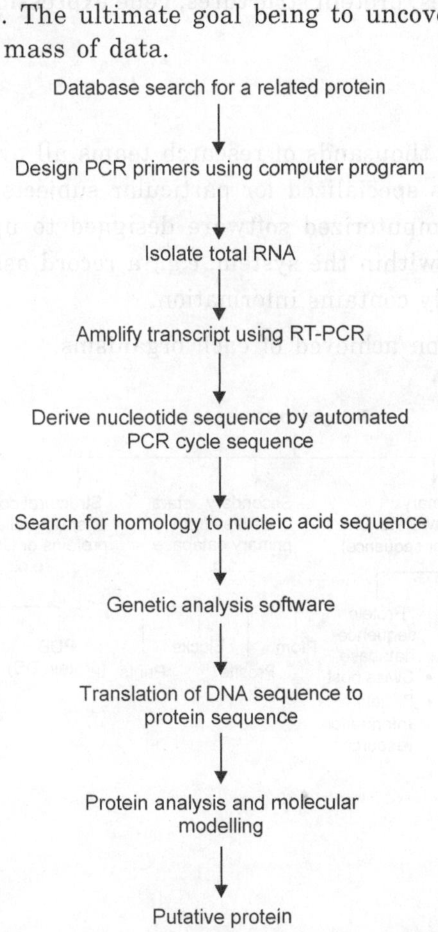

Figure 3.6 Scheme of work using bioinformation to generate protein information

The greatest achievements of Bioinformatics methods, the Human Genome project is currently being completed.

Bioinformatics is the application of computer technology to the management and analysis of biological data. It has evolved into a full-fledged multi-disciplinary subject that integrates developments in Information and Computer Technology as applied to Biotechnology and Biological science. The result is that computers are being used to gather, store, analyze and merge biological data bioinformatics uses computer software tools for data creation.

Three Components of Bioinformatics

1. CREATION OF DATABASES - It involves organization, storage and management of biological data sets. These databases are available on net.
2. DEVELOPMENT OF ALGORITHMS & STATISTICS-This is done to determine relationship among the members of large data sets.
3. ANALYSIS OF DATA & INTERPRETATION-This is done by using first two component to analyze data & interpret results. *e.g.*, analysis of DNA, RNA and protein sequences, protein structures, gene expression profiles and biochemical pathways.

Biological Databases

The data produced by thousands of research teams all over the world are collected and organized in databases specialized for particular subjects. A Biological Database is usually associated with computerized software designed to update, query and retrieve components of data stored within the system. *e.g.*, a record associated with a nucleotide sequence databases typically contains information.

This carries information achieved of each organisms.

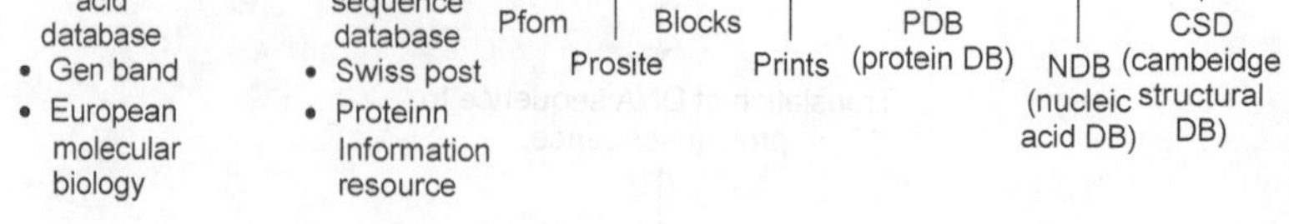

Major Biological Databases

Table 3.2 Major Biologicals Databases

Source	*Subject*
Pub-Med	
Cwwwmcbi.nlm.niogov/ entrez/query-fcgi	Biomedical literature
Path DB (www.ncgr. ar/software/path db/)	Biochemical pathway
KEGG WIT (www. genome adkp/legg)	Biochemical pathway
Protein Data Bank (www.vcsb.org/pdb/)	Protein structure
Gen Bank	
Swiss port (Via Pub med)	protein structure sequence
Entrez Genome	Genome sequence
Gen Bank SRS	Nucleic acid

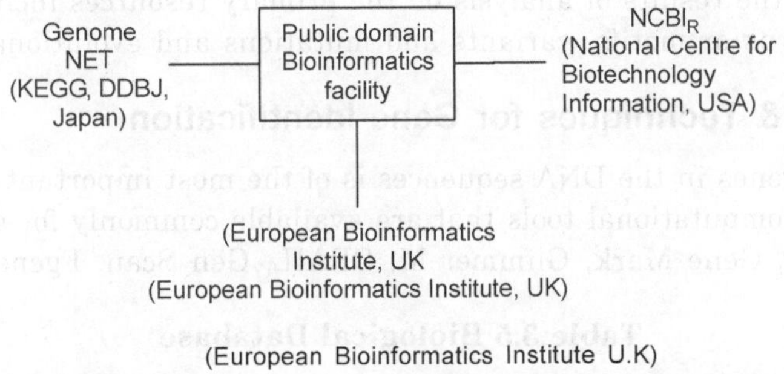

Figure 3.7 Major databases for Bioinformatics

Table 3.3 Algorithms used for searching for genes in DNA sequences

Type of algorithm	*Example*
Neural network	GRAIL
Rule-based system	Gene Finder
Hidden Markovmodel	GENE SCAN
	GENIE
	Gene Mark HMM
	HMM Gene
	FGENEH

Table 3.4

Approaches for data mining
Influence based data mining
Affinity based data mining
Time-delay based data mining
Trends based data mining
Comparative based data mining
Predictive based data mining

such as contact name, input sequence, description of type of molecule, same of source organism, literature citations associated with the sequence.

Primary Databases (Archives)

They represent experimental results but are not a curated review. They contain information and annotation of DNA and protein sequences, structures and expression profiles.

Secondary Databases (Curated)

They contain the results of analysis on the primary resources including information on sequence patterns or motifs, variants and mutations and evolutionary relationships.

Software Tools & Techniques for Gene Identification

Recognizing genes in the DNA sequences is of the most important aspect in genome analysis. Several computational tools that are available commonly for gene prediction in large-scale namely, Gene Mark, Glimmer M, GRAIL, Gen Scan, Fgenes.

Table 3.5 Biological Database

Data base	*Characteristics*
1. **Nucleotide Sequence**	
Database Gen Bank	www.ncbi.nih.gov/GENE BANK/ maintained by National Center for.
EMBL	Biotechnology information (NCBI), USA www.ebi.acuk/embl.
	European Molecular Biology Lab (EMBL) under aeijis of European Bioinformatics institute (EBI), U.K.
Uni Gene	www.ncbi.nih.gov/Uni Gene/

2. **Protein sequence database - PIR**	pir. Georgetown. edu protein information resource (PIR) database provided by National Biomedical Research Foundation (NBRF), USA.
SWISS-PROT	www.expasy.ch/sport
3. **Protein sequence motif database**	
PROSITE	www.expasy.ch/prosite
4. **Macromolecular databases**	
PDB	www.rcsb.org/pdp primary database for 3-D structure of biological macro-molecules.
5. Others KEGG	www.genome.ad.jp/kegg/kyoto Encyclopedia of Genes & Genomes (KEGG) is database with latest computerized information on biomolecules, cell biology and information pathways.

Table 3.6 Utility of various-programs

Program	*Utility/Application*	*Web link*
1. Gene Mark	• To access coding potential of DNA sequences • 1st tool to be employed for prokaryotic genes. • Now exists in separate variants for gene prediction in prokaryotic, eukaryotic and viral DNA sequences.	www.ebi.ac.uk/genemark
2. Glimmer (Gene Locator & interpolate Markov Modeler, John Hopkins & TISR	• To identify coding & regions • Used as primary gene finder tool at TIGR. • modified version designed for plasmodium falciparum : Glimmer M • Glimmer HMM for higher organisms,	www.tigr.org/softlab

3. Grail (Gene reconitions & assembly internet link, Oak Ridge National Lab)	• identifies axons, Poly A sites, promoters, CpG islands, repetitive elements and frameshift errors in DNA sequences by comparing them with data-base of known human & mouse sequence elements	http-//.compbio.ornl.gov.

Biological Information

Bioinformatics is conceptualizing biology in terms of molecules and then applying "informatics" techniques for understanding and organizing the information concerned with these molecules.

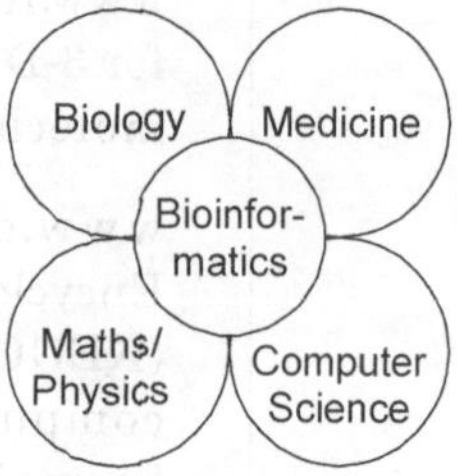

Figure 3.8 Interaction of disciplines that contribute to bioinformatics

The ultimate goal of bioinformatics is to uncover the biological information get a clear insight of fundamental biology of organisms.

The development of bioinformatics not only facilitated the handling and analysis of sequence data but also, the development of sequencing strategies as well.

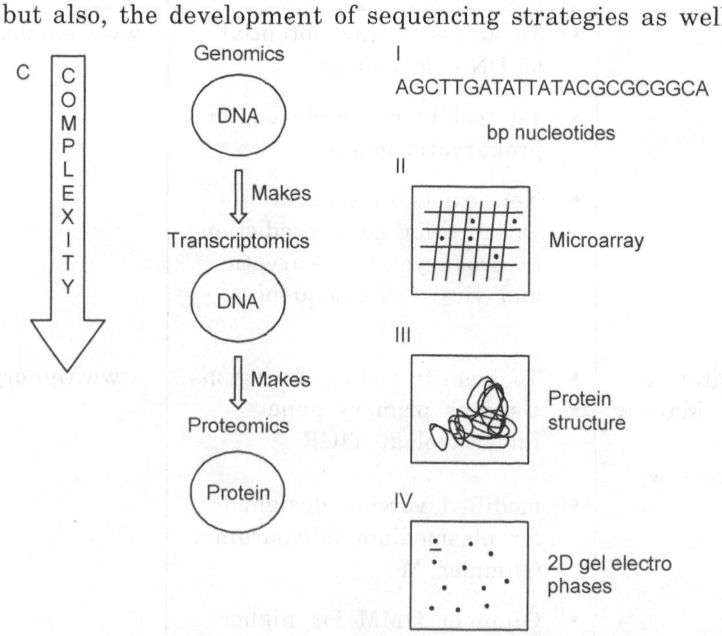

Figure 3.9 Complexity of genomic data processing analysis data interpretation of biological data

Three Components of Bioinformatics

1. Development of new algorithms and statistics to assess relationships among members of data set.
2. Use of these algorithms to analyze and interpret various types of data *e.g.,* nucleotide sequence, amino acid sequences, protein domain structure and protein interactions.
3. Development and implementation of tools *i.e.,* databases that permit access and management of different types of information.

Applications of Bioinformatics

1. Sequencing of macromolecules :

   DNA

   RNA

   Proteins
2. Molecular modelling of biomolecules
3. Tracing evolutionary trees of genes.
4. Sequencing of human genome
5. Prediction of functional gene products Handles vast biological data
6. Drug designing
7. Micro array development

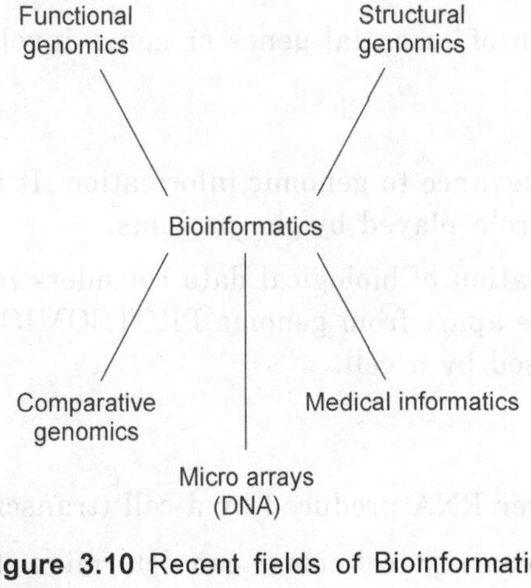

Figure 3.10 Recent fields of Bioinformatics

Three Levels of Bioinformatics

- Analysis of a single gene (protein).
- Analysis of complete genomes.
- Analysis of genes and genomes with respect to functional data.

1. Analysis of Single Cene
   (*i*) Similarity with other known genes.
   (*ii*) Phylogenetic trees, evolutionary relationships
   (*iii*) Identification of well-defined domains in the sequence.
   (*iv*) Sequence features: physical properties, binding sites, modification sites.
   (*v*) Prediction of sub cellular localization.

   Prediction of secondary and tertiary structure of proteins.
2. Analysis of Complete Genome
   (*i*) Location of genes on chromosomes, correlation with function or evolution.
   (*ii*) Expansion duplication of gene families.
   (*iii*) Presence or absence of biochemical pathways.
   (*iv*) Identification of "missing" enzymes.
   (*v*) Large-scale events in the evolution of organisms.
3. Analysis of Genes & Genomes with Respect to Functional Data
   (*i*) Expression analysis, microarray data, on RNA measurement.
   (*ii*) Proteomics.
   (*iii*) Comparison and Analysis of biochemical pathways.
   (*iv*) Detection or mutant genotypes is phenotypes.
   (*v*) Identification of essential genes or genes involved in specific processes.

Functional Genomics

It assigns functions relevance to genomic information. It is the study of genes, their resulting proteins and the role played by the proteins.

Analysis and interpretation of biological data considers information both at level of proteome and transcriptome apart from genome PROTEOMICS is analysis of amount of proteins (proteome) expressed by a cell.

Transcriptome

Is analysis of messenger RNA produced by a cell (transcriptome).

Microarrays. DNA microarray technology can determine expression level of genes. It includes genetyping and DNA sequencing.

GENE expression array allows simultaneous analysis of mRNA expression levels of genes in both benign and malignant tumours.

The promise for Bioinformatics is that public genome data, mixed with proprietary sequence data, clinical data from previous dug efforts and other stores of information could unearthen clues about possible candidates for future drugs.

Datamining

It is a tool that allows the user to access multiple data sources and data types, do transforms and other data preprocessing, utilize a variety of exploratory visualizing tools and application of one or more predictive modeling methods to find an entire solution.

Table 3.7 Datamining Tools

Local sequence alignment tools	BLAST & FASTA	sequence similarity search tool
	Pattern Recognition	sequences & structure
Multiple	Sequence alignment tools :	CLUSTALW, PHYLIP

Applications of Bioinformatics

Apart from analysis of genome sequence data, bioinformatics is now being used for a vast array of other important tasks, include

1. analysis of gene variation and expression.
2. analysis and prediction of gene and protein structure and function.
3. prediction and detection of gene regulation networks.
4. simulation environments for whole cell modeling.
5. complex modeling of gene regulatory dynamics and networks.
6. presentation and analysis of molecular pathways in order to understand gene-disease interactions.
7. designing drugs for medical treatment.

Future Directions

The practice of studying genetic disorders is changing from investigation of single gene in isolation to discovering cellular network of genes, understanding their complex interactions and identifying their role in disease. This will pave way for a new age of individually failured medicine.

Bioinformatics will guide and help molecular biologists and clinical researchers to capitalize on information derived by computational biology. In the coming decades, those research teams will comprise of successful combination of laboratory bench, clinical practice and use of computational tools.

COMPUTATIONAL BIOLOGY

Computational Biology: Introduction

It is the process of involving analysis of sequence information in bioinformatics. This involves finding of genes in DNA sequences, development of methods to predict structure and/or function of proteins, DNA sequences, clustering protein sequences discovered and development of protein models, alignment of similar proteins and generation of phylogenetic trees for examining evolutionary relationships.

Computational biology includes:

(*i*) Finding genes in DNA sequences

(*ii*) Prediction of structure and function of proteins and RNA sequences

(*iii*) Phylogenetic analysis

(*iv*) Evolutionary relationship: biochemical basis of life

The primary objective of computational biology is developing algorithms to enable construction of models to study novel biologic molecules and processes.

Bioinformatics is mainly focussed on collection and evaluation of existing data. On the other hand, computational biology is purely experimental and exploratory, and aims to utilize knowledge of sequence and structure of well-studied proteins for developing computer algorithms capable of predicting primary sequence, 3D structure and function of novel protein.

Also, computer-aided drug designing, and describing of entire range of metabolic activities in a cell with help of computer algorithm are promising. Computational biology promises to greatly accelerate the pace of biomedical research and development of near treatments for human pathologies.

Evolutionary Relationship: Biochemical Basics of Life

One of the most untraced, mysterious and undissected phenomena is LIFE. Scientists in contrast to popular belief of divine origin of life, are bent upon unravelling the mystery of life.

With recent development of biochemical sciences, signal for start of life could be traced down to simple chemical elements (C, H, O, N, P, S, Fe, Cu, *etc.*) that are constituent of all the living organisms.

It is still not possible to reassemble the chemical elements to constitute a living cell once again. But, biochemistry certainly offers an explanation for the basis of life in organisms.

Cell-fundamental Unit of Organism

Cell is fundamental unit of organism through which life is expressed and is a store house of many biomolecules responsible for bioactions in the cell.

Since the cell is a complex organization biomolecules and evidences suggest that a variety of chemical and physical processes occurring on earth or its atmosphere probably led to formation of simple biomolecules and finally complex organization of biomolecules led to origin of life by complex interactions.

A large number of biomolecules are present in living cells such as carbohydrates (mono-, di-, poly-saccharides), proteins, amino acids, enzymes, lipids (fats, oils, fatty acids), nucleotides, (nucleic acids associated histones, acidic proteins), (pigments haemoglobin, chlorophyl) *etc.* Since none of these biomolecules can be expressive of life, it is impossible to pinpoint which biomolecule is living.

The simplest of known living creations are perhaps the viruses which represent organization of protein and RNA/DNA. As viral particle can be stored for very long time in dormant state and they multiply only after being injected into a living cell indicating that reproduction is an important expression of life.

Evolution of Macromolecules

Going by organic chemistry, globe can be traced back to 4 billion years. While decisive phase of biochemistry over past few decades has concentrated on how simple molecules came into being and got organized themselves ultimately to express life processes. The direction of origin of biomolecules has began with non cellular material to prokaryotic cells (with unorganized genetic material) and finally eukaryotic cell (with an organized genetic material).

Origin of Molecules

About 4.5 billion years ago, earth arised from a dust cloud which underwent condensation due to gravitational forces. At that time, lack of any oxygen producing system in atmosphere of earth alongwith highly reducing atmosphere alongwith electric discharge and ultraviolet light from the sun aggregated simple molecules to form complex molecules and probably resulted in formation of ammonia (NH_3) and methane (CH_4) from reduction of nitrogen and carbon. Also, carbon monoxide and carbon dioxide were supposedly present during this prebiotic period. However, origin of water is uncertain, though it seems to be present on earth during this period.

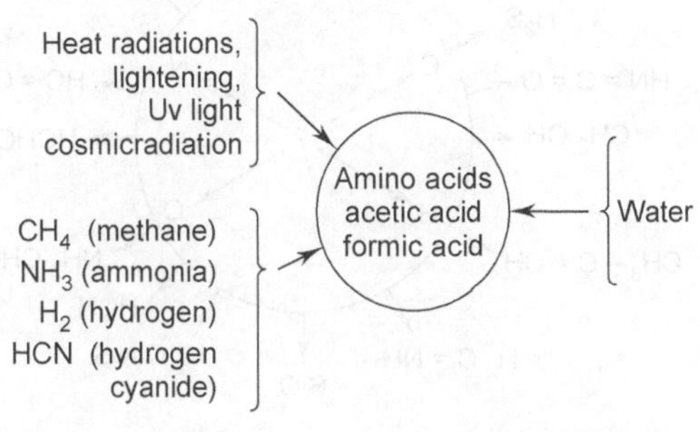

Figure 3.11 Origin of macromolecules of cells

Ammonia, methane, carbon monoxide and carbon dioxide have been discovered in interstellar space and are precursors of macromolecules such as amino acids and proteins. The later have been recovered in samples from terrestrial lava as well as from the moon.

The origin of proteinoid molecule is very well-documented and the next step of interaction of such molecules is to form membrane-like structure and finally leading to better evolved cellular characteristic features operational in cells in due course.

Next major step is flow of energy through development of a catalystic system. No direct evidence regarding biochemical information of forerunners of enzymes or the genetic signal originated are available. In spite of evolution of simple proteinoids or prototypes of nucleic acids, or cell still requires a host of components to be full of life especially a system to extract energy from surroundings and to maintain energy balance.

Origin of nucleic acid seems to have taken place much earlier than the prototype of living cell evolved. Adenine (6-amino purine) is not only the component of information molecules like DNA and RNA, but also a constituent of energy rich compounds such as

NAD and NADP (Nicotinamide Adenine Dinucleotide), FAD (Flavin Adenine Dinucleotide), CAMP (Cyclic Adenosine 3', 5'-Monophosphate), ADP (Adenosine Diphosphate) and ATP (Adenosine Triphosphate). Also, FAD acts as a coenzyme. Adenine can be easily obtained from hydrogen cyanide. Amination of purine ring would have opened avenues for multiple channels in this prototype of a living cell.

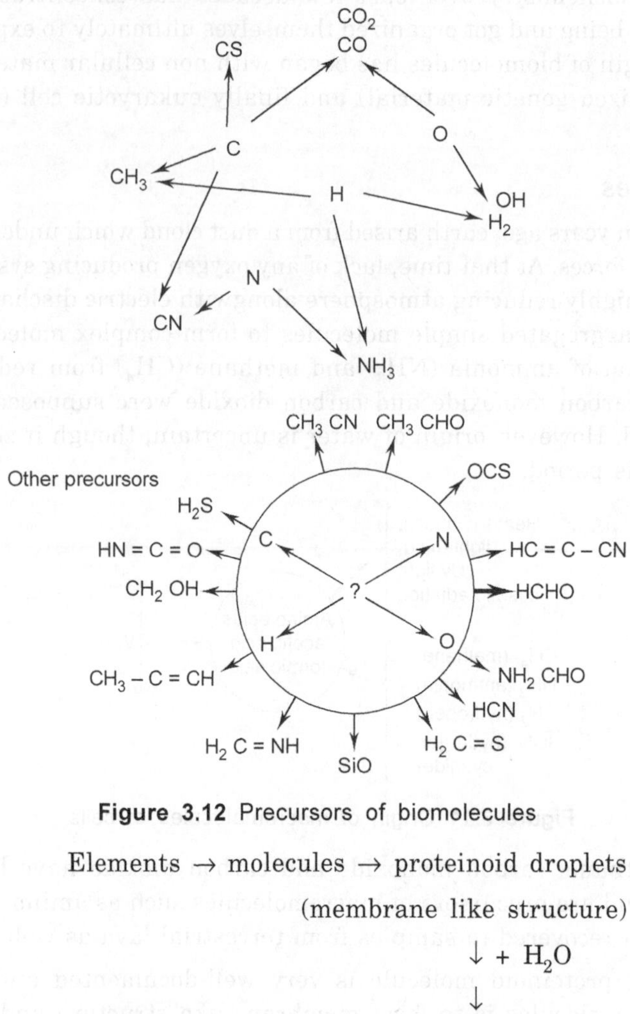

Figure 3.12 Precursors of biomolecules

Elements → molecules → proteinoid droplets

(membrane like structure)

↓ + H_2O

↓

↓

Living cell

Figure 3.13 Molecular assembly of organised cell

Occurrence of errors during duplication of any genetic material resulted in natural selection. These errors usually occur within a single gene and resulting protein may then have one amino acid changed and such changes might be deleterious diminishing or destroying the effectiveness of the proteins produced. Also, several new kinds of protein molecules may be formed which did not exist before. Thus first animate objective cells formed under prebiotic conditions were an aerobic prokaryotic anaerobes. The precursor enzyme operating in these anaerobic prototype living cells under conditions of extremely reducing condition must have been the modern enzyme system including hydrogenase and ferrodoxin (iron and sulphur-containing enzymes). Possibly the ability of cells to utilize vast resource of light energy from the sun originated at a much later stage.

Formation of pigment system with the heme group was perquisite to the formation of an autotrophic cells and photosynthesis emerged 2 billion years ago when the earth's atmosphere was anacrobic and reducing. The four most abundant elements C, H, N and O in human body are needed to make living things were also present in sufficient quantities in earth's crust in atmosphere and in ocean.

After cooling of earth, water and various gases on earth's surface were produced. These gases included substantial amount of CO_2 and traces of O_2 from evolutionary point of view, photosynthetic bacteria are most ancient and were capable of using only reducing compounds. While cyanobacteria had both structural and functional changes in photosynthetic machinergy. It may be added here that photosynthesis occurs in cyanobacteria, chromatophores of purple and green bacteria and in chloroplasts of plants and green algae to evolve oxygen.

Even today, the mechanism of splitting of water molecule to release oxygen evolved subsequently is still not clear, and cyanobacteria have the credit of owning the responsibility of filling up earth's atmosphere with oxygen.

Biological Diversity

Biological diversity is variability among living organisms from all sources of life forms including terrestrial, marine, aquatic ecosystems and ecological complexes.

It includes diversity within species, between species and of ecosystem.

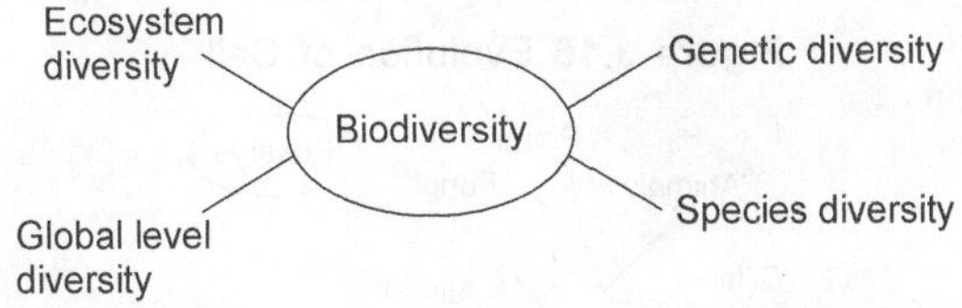

Figure 3.14 Diversity of life forms

Genetic diversity: It is the variation of genes within genes.

Species diversity: It is variation of species within a region.

Ecosystem diversity: It is the variation in a ecosystem where different landform exist to support different and specific variation.

Global level diversity: Of the 5–30 million species of life forms existing at global level only 1.5 million have been identified. They include 3,60,000 species of microorganisms, 3 lac species of green plants and fungi, 8 lac species of insects and 40,000 species of vertebrates. Tropical forests though cover only 7% of total landsurface, are the richest in biodiversity, and more than half of the species on earth live in moist tropical forests. The reason for biodiversity in tropical forest being availability of optimal conditions for evolution and ideal situation for interaction between climate, organisms, soil, time and hereditary in tropics. Thus, tropics have low rate of extinction.

Phylogenetic Analysis

Based on the assumption that organisms with more similar genes evolved from a common progenitor then those with more dissimilar genes. Lineage tree indicates that archea and eukarya are thought to have diverged from each other.

Evolution of complex cell
↑
eukaryotic cell
↑
aerobic prokaryotic cell
↑
Cellular evolution — anaerobic prokaryotic cell – (3 – 9 billion years)
↑
proteinoids
↑
polypeptide and protein formation
↑
macromolecular precursors
nucleosides, nucleotides, amino acids, simple sugars
↑
Chemical and or
Chemical and bioorganic evolution - — light, electric discharge – (4.5 – 5 billion years)
↑
Cosmochemical or evolution — organic molecules (CN, H_2C = O, HCN)
↑
elements(H, C, N, O, P, S, Fe, other metals)
↑
Type of evolution — Evolution of cells Molecular H, C. Years

Figure 3.15 Evolution of Cell

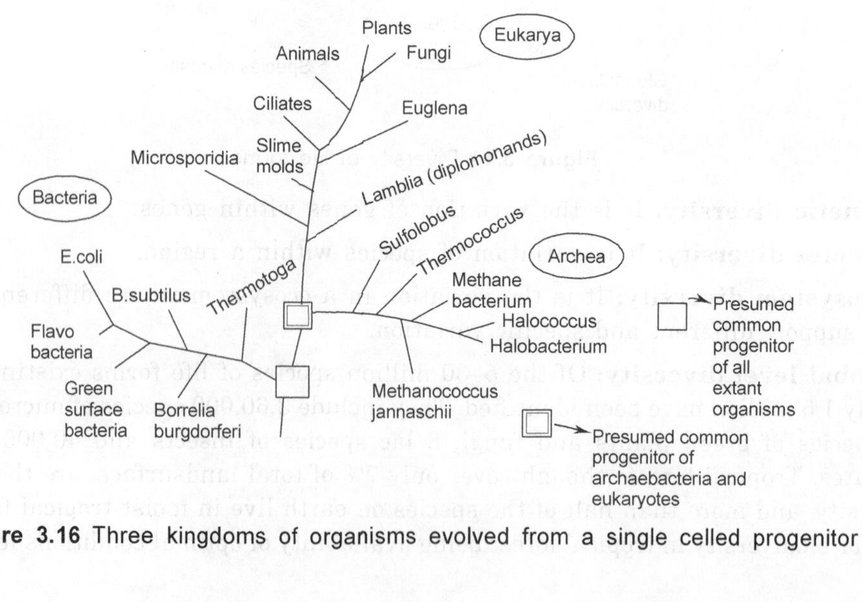

Figure 3.16 Three kingdoms of organisms evolved from a single celled progenitor

Evolution: Evolution is a "change in frequency of genes in a population". Also, it is the heritable changes in a population over many generations. It is error-prone self-replication and variation in success at self-replication. Error-prone means that copies are not always identical to originals and variation in success at self-replication is better explained as the concept of survival of fittest and those with variants are selected by nature to survive (principle of natural selection).

Mutation: Any change that occurs in a DNA sequence that can be passed on to the next generation is mutation. Mutations create new variant sequences in a population and increase genetic diversity.

Genetic diversity is reduced by natural selection and random drift. Balance between mutation, selection, and drift determine the level of genetic diversity in a population. Gene sequences in a population are related to one another via descent from common ancestors. Studies of human mitochondrial DNA indicate presence of a common ancestor who lived in Africa roughly 2 lac years ago. New mutation occurs in a population as single copy and the number of copies of mutation increase or decrease by action of selection and drift. Most new mutations are eliminated from population and occasionally, it may get fixed in the population to the eventually spread through the population.

Molecular Phylogeny

Bioinformatics draws inspiration from a wide variety of quantitative fields including statistics, physics, computer science, engineering to analyze sequence data and protein structure, metabolic modelling data for quantitative analysis of population and ecology. It also provides tools and computational solutions that are critical for understanding biological problems.

Bioinformatic is just not capturing, managing and presenting data derived from DNA and protein sequencing but also, it can be used to investigate the evolution of genes and their protein products and this is termed as *molecular phylogeny.*

To build models of sequence evolution, two approaches are available:

1. *Empirical models.* They are built through comparison of large numbers of observed sequences.
2. *Parametric models.* They are built on the basis of chemical biological properties of DNA and amino acids.

Parametric approach is favoured for DNA evolution studies using parameters such as base frequency base exchangeability and rate heterogeneity.

Base frequency: This parameter describes the frequency of bases (A, G, C and T) averaged over all sequence sites and this is influenced by total GC content.

Base exchangeability: This parameter describes relative tendency for one base to be substituted for another and purine-purine and pyrimidine-pyrimidine base transitions are expected to be more frequent than base transversions (purine-pyrimidine).

Rate heterogeneity: This is the variation in mutation rates in a DNA-stretch due to biochemical constraints, structural features *etc.*

In phylogenetic trees, evolutionary distance is measured in terms of horizontal branch length.

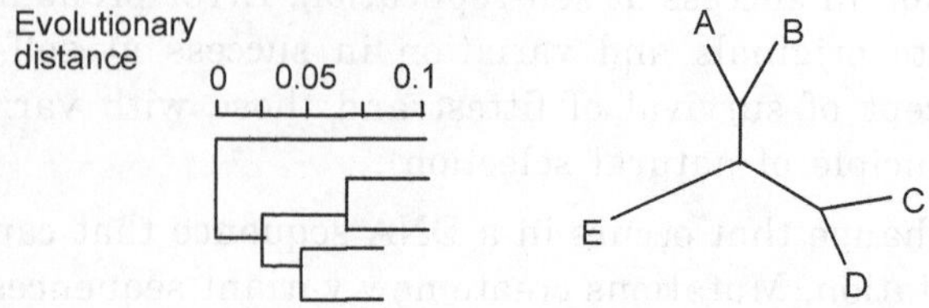

Figure 3.17 Ways of representing phylogenetic relationships

Phylogenetic Analysis

It has been on gross anatomy of species and a phylogenetic tree based on quantitative representation of relationships among species is constructed/drawn. There are certain rules for drawing tree which are based on quantitative nature of sequence relationships. The tree could be hand-drawn trees of life or modern trees which are binary trees using tree-building algorithms. The modern phylogenetic trees have branching pattern and length of branches can be determined by evolutionary distance.

Phylogeny of species has a root which is based on the assumption that all species have a specific common ancestor and phylogenic tree thus derived from sequence data may be rooted a unrooted. However, it is much harder to pinpoint which sequence or pair of sequence in such a tree is the common ancestor.

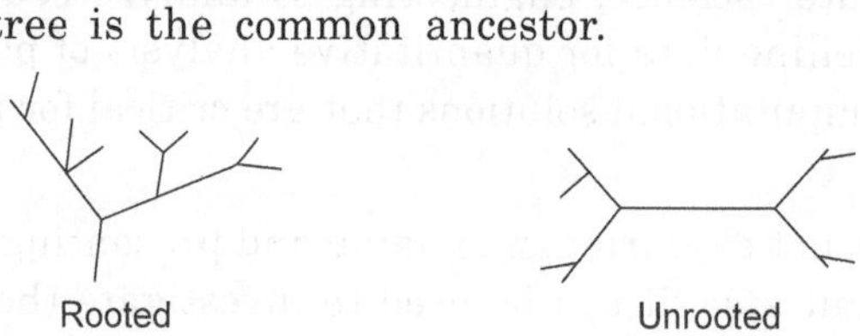

Figure 3.18 Types of phylogenitic trees.

Phylogeny inferred from a protein or nucleotide sequence resembles whole-organism tree of life and provide valuable scientifically valid evidence to support the theories of evolutionary history.

Phylogenetic analysis of a sequence family is most informative about evolution than that of particular gene.

Table 3.8 Properties of trees

- root is common ancestor of all taxa.
- in case of unrooted tree, prediction is done by uprooted tree.
- genes, species are represented by leaves.
- path from root to node represent an evolutionary path.
- paralogues: genes diverged with in same species
- orholoques: genes diverged with species

Steps in Phylogenetic Analysis

1. Alignment strategy
2. Distribution of substitution method
3. Tree building
4. Tree valuation

Phylogeny Methods

Two main categories of phylogeny methods are:

1. Distance method.
2. Character method.

1. Distance method

All possible pairs of sequences are aligned for determination of most similar or closely related pairs. This alignment provides genetic distance between the sequences to predict the evolutionary relationship.

2. Character Method

They are of two types:

(*i*) maximum parsimony method (MP).

(*ii*) maximum likelihood method (ML).

MP method

Here multiple sequence alignment is produced to predict corresponding sequence position.

These sequence position will appear in vertical column.

ML method

In ML method, reliable multiple sequence alignment are obtained and changes in each column in the alignment are examined to find likelihood of a particular tree miscalculated by using expected model of change in sequences.

Methods of Evaluating Phylogenies

To generate a meaningful tree from data using alignment scoring methods should be carefully chosen.

Two ways to test phylogenies are:

1. Jumbling sequence addition order.
2. Boot strap and Jacknife replicantes.

1. *Jumbling sequence addition order:* The simplest way to test a phylogeny is to repeat the analysis several times with different addition orders. All PHYLIP programs and most phylogeny program have JUMBLE option that uses a random number generator to choose which sequence to add at each step.

2. *Bootstrap and Jacknife replicates:* When struck with a single set of data, of finite length, there is no way knowing whether the tree inferred from the data is truely representative of the evolutionary history of the gene family.

Jacknife resampling has largely been replaced by bootstrap resampling. Bootstrap sampling is typically only practical with distance methods where large numbers of sequences must be used.

Applications of Molecular Phylogenetics

1. To study evolution of mammalian orders and construct evolutionary tree of mammals.
2. To study phylogeny of metazoa.
3. To study evolution of eukaryotes.
4. Application of evolution to understanding of developmental biology, evolution of animal body plants, dating of events and application and development of new methods to new sequences.

Genome Evolution

Now that many complete genome sequences are available, comparison of whole sets of genes between species are possible and also evolution of organisms at whole genome level can be studied.

Bacterial genome sequences are now available and its comparison with a large number of species in possible. There is relatively little non-coding DNA between genes in bacteria suggesting selection of the strong efficiency of genome replication to prevent widespread accumulation of repetitive sequences and transposable elements in contrast to eukaryotes.

Parasitic or symbiont bacteria had smallest genomes suggesting that there is a tendency for genes that are no longer necessary for an organism to be deleted from genomes in relatively short period. There is strong evidence that both mitochondria and chloroplasts descended from bacteria that were taken up by ancient eukaryotic cells (Endosymbiosis) and eventually became integral parts of eukaryote. Gene analysis have indicated that mitochondria are related to α-Proteobacteria, present-day Rickettsia and chloroplasts to cyanobacteria with greatly reduced number of genes in these two organellae as compared to the smallest bacterial genome.

Many of the organelle genes have been lost and transferred to nuclear genome and proteins required in organelle are product of nuclear genes. In animal mitochondrial genomes, this process of gene transfer to nucleus appears to have come to an end, leaving few essential genes on the mitochondrial genome that have been stable throughout the evolution of metazoa.

Distance between genes or gene order has given strong information about phylogenetic relationships at specific nodes in a tree. Gene order has the potential to be a strong phylogenetic marker though phylogenetic methods using them are much less developed.

Finding Genes in genome—Genome sequencing

Genome Sequencing: Genome is completely determined DNA sequence of genetic material of an organism.

Genome Sequencing

For knowing the complete genome for an organism, complete mapping of constituents and processes of organism. The technique of locating the gene is GENETIC MAPPING.

A genetic map shows position of genes and is amenable to gene sequencing.

GENETIC SEQUENCING. It deals with deciphering the exact sequence of bases that compose a gene.

Gene mapping involves dividing chromosomes into smaller fragments that can be propagated and characterized followed by mapping them to corresponds to their respective locations on the chromosomes.

Table 3.9 Websites keeping track of status of various genome projects

GOLD	Genomes online database
TIGR	Microbial database
NCBI	Genomic Biology website

GENOMICS is science of mapping, sequencing and analyzing genome and it depends on bioinformatics. The concept of genomics actually began with the conception of Human Genomic Project in mid 80s. This project was started on October 1, 1990 to map and sequence the complete set of human chromosomes and several model organisms. The strategy was to map each human chromosome and then divide them into smaller fragments that could be cloned followed by the mapping and sequencing of each fragment. To achieve this goal, J.Gaig venter and workers (at NIH, USA) devised a new way of finding genes by creating expressed sequence tags (EST). In mRNA (producing proteins) were isolated and copied into DNA molecules and then sequenced a part of DNA molecule to create EST. EST technique generated databases of nucleotide sequences and facilitated construction of a primary transcript map of human genome. EST technique gave feasibility of high throughput gene discovery and is responsible for growth of genomic industry.

After success of EST, whole genome shot gum strategy was devised by venter's team to sequence entire genome. It involved breaking DNA randomly into segments of various size and cloning of fragments into vectors. Since these randomly cleared fragments tend to overlap, or genome assembly program to fit contiguous pieces by matching overlapping ends was used. With the help of their method, sequencing of entire genomes of a few selected microorganisms was carried out successfully namely Uycoplasma genifalium, Haemophilus influenzac Rd, Mycobacterium tuberculosis, Bacillus subtitlis. Celera Genomics was established to sequence human and mouse genomes, which started a commercial era of genomics. With initial EST sequencing giving a estimate of over 100,000 genes in human genomes, genome sequencing actually revealed 30,000 genes (twice that of fruit fly Drosophila melanogaster) with automated sequencing genomes of over 60 organisms have been sequenced and the findings are interesting and unexpected ones. Thus, genomics has undergone expansion and this term in the present context also includes genome function (Further details will be discussed in separate unit on genomics).

Prediction of Structure and Function of Proteins and RNA Sequences

Since bioinformatics involves use of computers to store, retrieve, analyze or predict the composition a structure of biological molecules. Biomolecules include the genetic material, nucleic acids and the product of genes PROTEINS.

For As the nature and priorities of bioinformatics research and applications are changing, it has opened new branches. Proteomics attempts to catalogue and characterize interactions between all gene products and structural genomics attempts to predict structure of all proteins. The details of this section will be discussed in Proteomics and Genomic sub-units.

Information Expression

Cell is the fundamental unit of organization of life and carries multiple informational molecules carrying out bioreactions forming a network of interactions to result in complex grouping and structures.

Each cell is a complex system of human body contains about $6 \cdot 10^{12}$ cells of about 320 different types with variable cell size, for instance, human red blood cell is 0.005 mm in diameter and some neurons are 1 m long.

There are two types of organisms: prokaryotes and eukaryotes.

Prokaryotic cells have simpler structure than eukaryotes and lack any inner cellular membrane.

Eukaryotic cells have a nucleus composed of chromosomes separated from the rest of the cell by a membrane. The chromosomes are the carriers of the genetic material DNA.

Eukaryotes also contain membrane enclosed compartments called organelles like mitochondria, endoplasmic reticulum, golgi complex, lysosomes, centriodes and others which are specialized for particular biological processes.

Four basic molecules of life

They are:

DNA } also called Biological macromolecules
RNA

Proteins

Small molecules

Protein Structure

Proteins are key players among the *biomolecules* in such a way that various cellular activities are involved for the generation of a characteristic shape to a living organism. Scientists have been trying to understand for a long time how protein can carry out diverse functions. Humans are incredible in creativity and adventure and possess higher data processing abilities as compared to supercomputers although computers are extremely efficient at many other tasks. The behaviors of a young child has stimulated us to devise *Artificial Intelligence Networks* that can learn as well as predict but the speed at which human brain can grasp diverse objects and connect them to functional roles is very remarkable. What are the proteins involved which can carry information at such incredible speeds and moreover correlate them intelligently, which is basis of all higher learning special to the human race? The answer again lies in identifying and understanding the structure of protein involved.

Besides this the absence of certain key proteins can produce devastating diseases *e.g.,* Lack of a protein subunit (beta-chain) for the erythrocyte protein heamoglobin can give rise to thalassaemia which affects so many children who can only service on repeated blood transfusions. The presence of mutated beta chain with a substitution of valine for glutamic acid at position 6 results in deformed erythrocytes, called sickle cell anaemia, which is epidemic to certain parts of Africa.

Clearly, we need to understand what is protein and how its involved in our lives.

Network Bioinformatics

Our understanding of biological functions at the molecular levels has been revolutionized by application of "reductionism" by studying preferential express ion of individual proteins. This has given way to a new technique. GRAPH THEORY TO MAP NETWORKS OF BIOLOGICAL INTERACTIONS where mathematics is applied to build individual interactions into pathways.

Since modern high-throughput techniques such as microarrays enable investigator to simultaneously study the status of a cells components at any given time and hybrid-screens and protein chips to identify protein-protein interaction.

Chronology of Network

In eighteenth century Euler developed graph theory and for last forty years Erlos and Renyi initiated the study of mathematical properties of random networks. This was followed by reduction of interacting components to a series of nodes interconnected links or edges to form a NETWORK or GRAPH.

Types of Network

Networks can be directed or undirected, depending upon the nature of interactions.

Directed Network

Interaction between any two nodes has a well-defined direction.

e.g., direction of metabolite flow in a metabolic reaction from a substrate to a product.

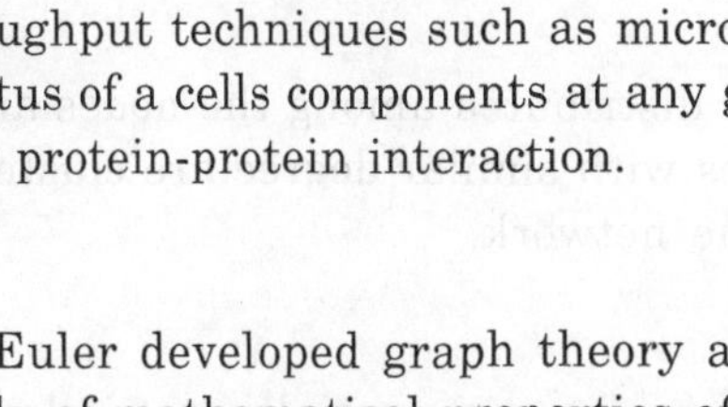

Figure 3.19 Directed network

Undirected Network

Here the links have no assigned direction.

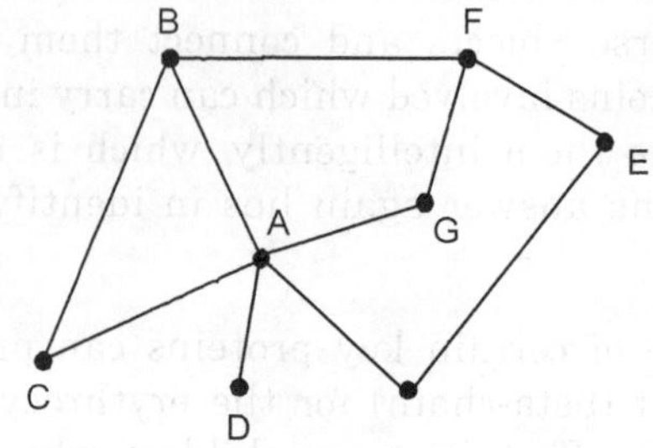

Figure 3.20 Undirected network

e.g., protein interaction networks where link represent a mutual binding relationship.

Protein A can bind protein B and protein B can also bind protein A

Models for Network

They include

- random network models.
- scale-free networks.
- hierarchical networks model.

Random network models

Here, links are randomly distributed among the nodes and they show poisson degree distribution (where most nodes with similar degree are clustered around the mean). Loss of few nodes can fragment the network.

Scale free networks

Here, degree distribution scales exponentially *i.e.*, is logarithmic. This network has an inherent "robustness" and loss of a few nodes do not fragment the network.

Hierarchial network model

This is an extension of scale-free model with coexistence of modularity.

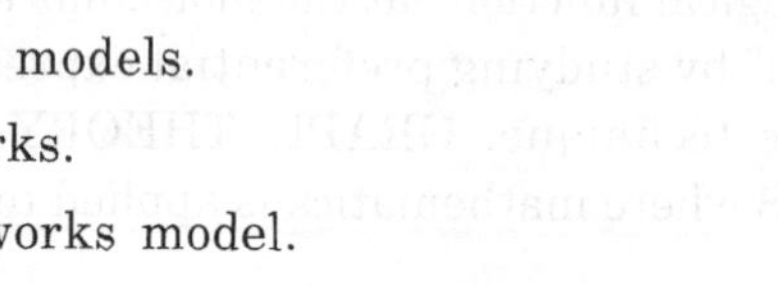

Topological Structure of Biological Networks

Preliminary studies of biological networks have shown that they are hierarchical scale-free networks.

Common features are:

1. Few nodes are more connected and critical to the system
   - Critical hubs in metabolic network are: Coenzyme A

     NAD

     GTP

     ATP
   - Deletion of critical hubs in protein-protein interactions cause death.
2. *Inherent robustness of network:* Modification of node causes a serious breakdown of the system.
3. *Biological networks are modular:* Modularity is thought to have arisen from gene duplication, one of the basic units of evolution.

Practical Significance of Analysis of Networks

1. Network analysis has practical significance in public health programs such as systematic vaccination of entire population for eradication of disease.
2. Mapping of networks of disease transmission: it allows identification of sources of infection and treatment.
3. Mapping of metabolic processes:
   - protein-protein interaction
   - metabolic regulation webs
   - signalling regulation webs
   - transcription regulation webs
4. Designing of theoretical and experimental programs: to study topological and dynamical properties of networks controlling cell-behavior.

Table 3.10 Softwares for Bioinformatics

4 EMBOSS	www.hgmp.mrc.ac.uk
9 RASMOL	www.umass.edu/microbiol/rasmol
10 VMD	www.ks.uiuc.edu/Research/umd
5 GROMACs	www.gromacs.org
7 NAMD	www.ks.uiuc.edu/Research/namd
1 Autodock 3	www.scripps.edu/pub/olson-web/doc/autodoc.
2 Bio Perl	www.bioperl.org
3 Clustal W	www.ebi.ac.uk/clustalw
8 Phylip	http://evolution.genetics.washington.edu/phylip.html
6 Ligbuilder	www.chem.ac-su/chemistry/soft/LIGBUILD.en.html

Neural Networks

Computer scientists have taken inspiration from neuroscience where brain has a complex system of interconnected nerve cells which have capability of processing and storing information. Similarly, computer scientists created *artificial neural networks (ANN)* also termed as *neural networks (NN)* for solving particular problems regarding pattern recognition.

As shown in figure, output from one larger of neurons feed forward as inputs to the next layer.

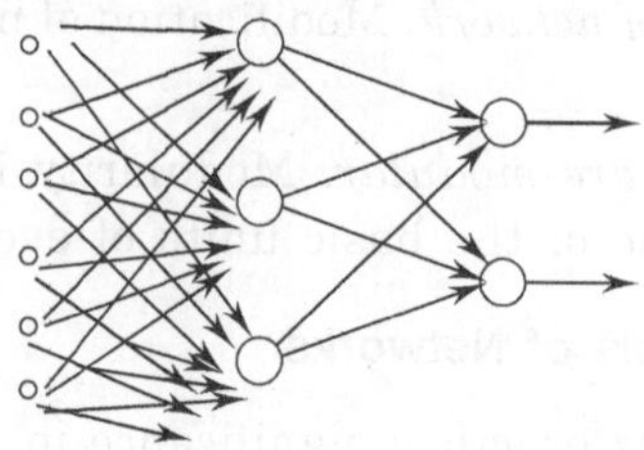

Figure 3.21 Architecture of typical feed forward neural network

In bioinformatics applications, the data are usually short segments of protein or DNA sequences of 10-20 nucleotides. The input to an NN is a sequence and to convert a DNA sequence to input values, for representation one for each base in the sequence (A, C, G, and T). A binary code is used to represent a specific input sequence and inputs from one of each row of four inputs will be set to 1 while the other three are 0.

Thus, a window of six DNA bases with sequence TTCGAA could represented by 24 inputs with values

0001 0001 0 1 0000 1 0 1000 1 000

Also, protein sequences can be coded in this way, using 20 inputs per residue resulting in large networks, with large numbers of parameters to optimize. The number of inputs can be reduced by using quantitative properties of amino acids rather than a binary code. Usually, physiochemical properties of amino acids like hydrophobicity, polarity and surface area are used.

Here also real values are used as inputs and scaled into the range – 1 to 1 or 0 to 1. This makes the network simple and real amino acid properties will have similar inputs. In case of usage of binary code for amino acids, all amino acids appear equally different and network itself learns relevant similarities from the training data.

Neural Networks and Protein Secondary Structure Prediction

Secondary structure of protein is usually represented by three states, α, helix, β helix and loop. Scoring systems that measure propensity of each amino acid for each of the states have been devised and used as the basis of secondary structure prediction methods.

Most straightforward approach for prediction of secondary structure is to represent each input amino acid by 20 binary inputs and to using three output neurons with target part terns (0, 0, 1), (0, 1, 0) and (1, 0, 0) to represent the three structural states possible for the central residue in the window.

Also, weights of each amino acids vary with the position in the window. Some amino acids are stronger predictors of secondary structure than others *e.g.*, for proline, weights corresponding to α-helix output are strongly negative and those for loop output are positive, thus indicating that proline rarely occurs in helices and usually occurs in loops.

Now-a-days, sequences can be automatically submitted to Predict Protein sewer and constricted automatically by PSI-BLAST.

Evolution of Protein Structure

Include of the 15,000 protein structures now known, there are several families in which the molecules maintain the some basic folding pattern over ranges of sequence similarities from new identity down to well below 20% conservation. The general response to mutation is structural change. It is characteristic of biological system that objects we observe to have a certain form that arose by evolution from related objects with similar but not identical form. They must, therefore, be robust to have the freedom to tolerate some variation. We can take advantage of this robustness in our analysis : By identifying and comparing related objects, we can distinguish variable and conserved features and thereby determine what is crucial to structure and function.

Natural variation in families of homologous proteins that retain a common function reveal how structures accommodate changes in amino acid sequence. Mutations that change the volumes of buried residues generally do not change the conformations of individual sheets, but, produce distortions of their spatial assembly. The nature of forces that stabilise protein structures sets general limitations on these conformational changes. Additional constraints derived form function vary from case to case. Families of related proteins tend to retain common folding patterns. However, although the general folding pattern is preserved, there are distortions, which increase as the amino acid sequences progressively change/diverge. With increasing sequence divergence, some regions refold entirely; reducing the size of the core and the distortions of the residues remaining within the care increase in magnitude.

Three-Dimensional Structure of Protein

Proteins perform a variety of roles. The functional properties of proteins depend upon 3-dimensional structures. The linear order or sequence of covalent linked amino acids sequence is defined as primary structure. Depending on the nature and arrangement of amino acids present, different parts of the molecule form secondary structure. The tertiary structure is formed by packing these structural elements into one or several compact globular units called domains. Secondary and Tertiary structure represent the most thermodynamically stable conformation for the molecule in solution and results from non- covalent interactions between the various amino acid chains within the molecule and with the water molecules surrounding it. The important forces which cause linear protein chains to undergo folding in space to characteristic shape that lies to a large extent in chemistry of amino acid residences they contain. Amino acids are broadly divided into three groups

- Hydrophobic.
- Polar, and
- Charged.

and therefore are capable of interacting within the protein in a variety of non-covalent interactions which derive protein to fold in a particular way.

Chemically, proteins consist of a linear polymer main chain with different amino acid side-chains attached at regular intervals

The amino acid sequence of a protein is specified by the nucleotide sequence of a gene. The 3D structure of protein molecules are determined, without further participation of nucleic acid by one dimensional sequences of their amino acids. Proteins fold spontaneously to their native conformations.

Indeed for may proteins, measurements of fractions of molecules in native denatured states as a function of temperature or denaturant contraction imply simple 2 state native-denatured equilibria in which undetectably few molecules are anything but native or denatured. This confirms that any putative intermediates can have no mor than marginally stability. But this makes it difficult to follow the folding transition structurally.

Visualization Techniques for Protein Structure

Consensus networks are methods of visualizing incompatibilies in collection of trees.

A central task in phylogenetic analysis is construction of phylogenetic trees using Markov chain methods and boot strapping. Since large collections of trees are difficult to interpret and drawing of conclusion from them is also problematic. The common practice in this situation is to construct a consensus tree. A newer approach is to visualization of collection of tree which generalizes consensus trees are available and are based on construction of phylogenic networks, the networks which are used regularly by the biologists for visualizing and analysis of complex phylogenetic data sets. Also median networks are used to visualize collection of trees. Median networks were originally designed for the analysis of mitochondrial data. In median network, certain vertices are labelled by elements of X and splits are represented by classes of parallel edges similar to phylogenetic trees :

Two common methods for computing a consensus tree:

1. Strict consensus method
2. Majority rule method

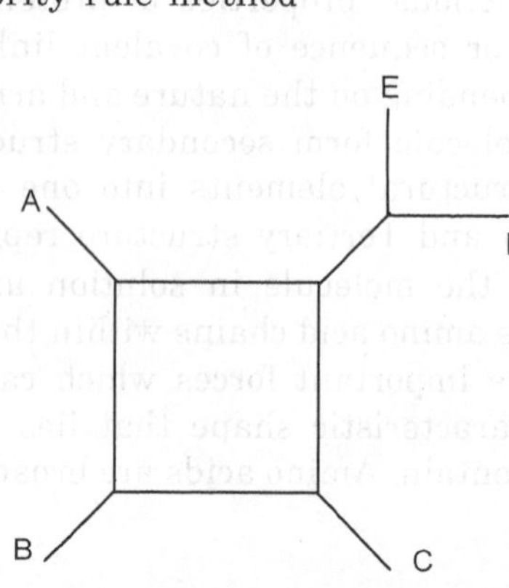

Figure 3.22 Median network associated with the split system

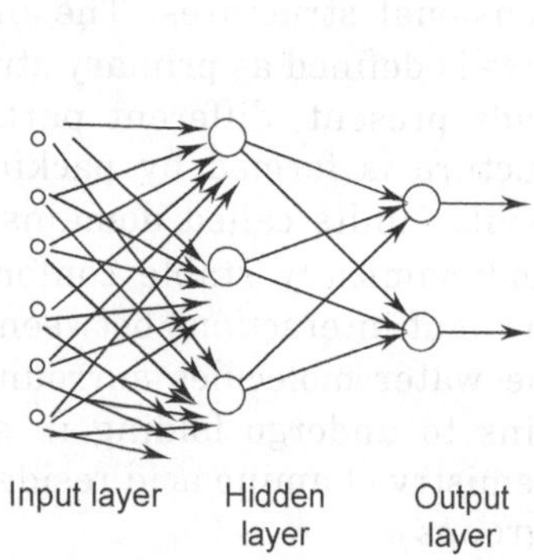

Figure 3.23 Architecture of typical feed forward neural network

Median network associated with split system has been implemented in freely available program spectronet.

Also, number of graphic tools are available for visualizing structure and function of nucleic acids and proteins.

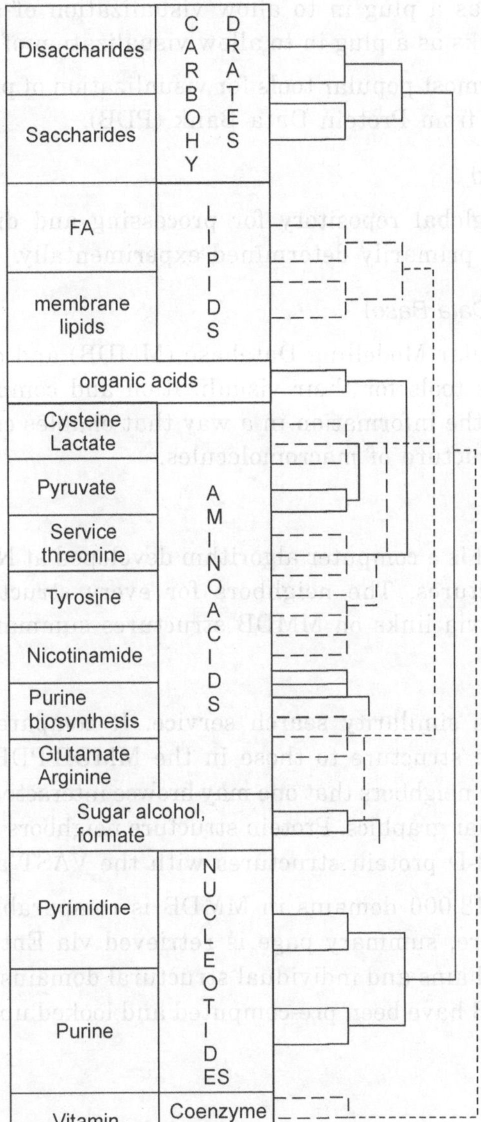

Figure 3.24 Metabolic networks: modularity in networks

1. PROWL

This site provides information on properties of amino acids, bond geometry they allow it also provides other information that is used to make predictions about protein structure based on primary amino acid sequence.

Cn 3D see in 3-D is a sequence alignment viewer for NCBI databases. It allows viewing of 3D structures in if files are downloaded to computer.

2. Chemscape, chine, Rasmol and Protein Explorers

The first two work as a plug in to allow visualization of structures with browser, Protein Explorer also works as a plug in to allow visualization of structures with browser.

Rasmol is one of the most popular tools for visualization of protein structure. It reads molecular structure files from Protein Data Bank (PDB).

3. PDB (Protein Data Bank)

PDB is very large global repository for processing and distribution of 3-D metro molecular structure data primarily determined experimentally.

4. MMDB (NCBI structure Data Base)

Also know as Molecular Modelling Database (MMDB) and contains macromolecular 3-D structures as well as tools for their visualization and comparative analysis MMDB reorganize and validates the information in a way that enables cross-referencing between chemistry and 3andD structure of macromolecules.

5. VAST

Vector alignment tool is a computer algorithm developed at NCBI and used to identify similar protein 3D structures. The neighbors for every structure in MMDB are pre-computed and accessible via links on MMDB structures summary pages.

6. VAST Search

Its NCBI's structure similarity search service. It compares 3-D co-ordinates of a newly determined protein structure to those in the MMDB/PDB database VAST search computes a list of structure neighbors that one may browse interactively viewing superposition and alignments by molecular graphics. Protein structure neighbors in Entrez are determined by direct comparison of 3-D protein structures with the VAST algorithm

Each of more than 18,000 domains in MMDB is comparable with every other one. From the MMDB structure, summary page is retrieved via Entrez, structure neighbors are available for protein chains and individual structural domains. Structure neighbors for proteins already in MMDB have been pre-computed and looked up from MMDB's summary pages.

CDD

Conserved Domain Database is a collection of sequence alignments and profiles, representing protein domains conserved in molecular evolution, is now available in the CD-search service. Protein often contains several modules, each with a distinct evolutionary origin and function. The CD search service may be used to identify the conserved domains present in a protein sequence. To identify conserved domains in a protein sequence, the CD search service employs reverse position-specific BLAST Algorithm.

DART

DART is the **Domain Architecture Retrieval Tool** that can be used to search for proteins with similar domain architectures DART uses pre-computed CD search results to quickly identify proteins with a set of domains similar to that of the query.

Protein Classification

Proteins are classified to reflect both structural and evolutionary relatedness. Many levels exist in the hierarchy, but the principal levels are family, superfamily and fold, as described below. The exact position of boundaries between these levels is to some defers subjective. Evolutionary classification is generally conservative, where any doubt about relatedness exists. New divisions at the family and super family levels can be made as follows:

Family: Clear evolutionary relationship proteins clustered to gather into families are clearly evolutionary related. Generally, this means that pair-wise residue identifies between proteins are 30% and greater.

Superfamily: Proteins that have low sequence identities, but whose structural and functional features suggest that a common evolutionary origin is probable together in superfamilies *e.g.,* action.

Proteins are defined as having a common fold if they have the same major secondary structures in same arrangement and with same topological connections. Different proteins with same fold often have peripheral elements of secondary structure and turn regions that differ in size and conformation. Proteins placed together in same fold category may not have a common evolutionary origin structural similarities arise just from the physics and chemistry of proteins favoring certain packing arrangements.

Overview of Methods of Protein Structure Prediction

Sequence with significant similarity to a protein of known structure

In this case, homology modelling can be used to construct a 3-D model with correct fold, but it does not give accurate loop regions. Homology modeling effectively increases the number of known 3-D structures to a great extent.

Sequence with insignificant sequence Identity

Threading techniques can potentially detect remote homologies. When homologies modelling and threading are inapplicable, in such cases, the prediction problem has to be simplified.

Comparative Modelling exploits the fact that evolutionary related proteins with similar sequences are measured by the percentage of identical residues at each position based on on optimal structural superposition after have similar structures.

Determinants of Protein Structures

The primary structure devotes amino acid sequence and secondary structure denotes regular patterns of the main chain atoms. Tertiary structure is the representation of all atom of whole protein, consisting of multiple chains.

Sequence Determines Structure

A fully unfolded amino acid sequence diluted in the appropriate solvent folds into a unique tertiary structure. This process is usually reversible and is also thought that formation of same secondary structure precedes tertiary organisation. Possible exceptions to this hypothesis constitute molecular chaperons *i.e.,* proteins which assist in protein folding.

Secondary Structure Facilitates Dense Packing

Pauling and corey first introduced the existence of secondary structure elements on theoretical grounds prior to their discovery in protein structures. The main driving force for folding, water soluble globular protein molecules is the needed to pack hydrophobic side chains into interior of molecule.

Function specific motifs of secondary structure

Combinations of few secondary structure segments with a specific geometric arrangement occur frequently in protein structures. Such combinations are termed supersecondary structure/motifs.

Methods of structure prediction for knowfolds

Sequence Alignment

Any sequence analysis starts with database searches for homologous proteins by sequence alignment procedures. When pairwise sequence identity is over 40% alignments procedures are usually straightforward and for others alignments may fail. Multiple alignments improve as data bank grow.

Homology Modeling

Basic assumption of this modelling is that unknown structure (U) and the homologous template protein of known structure (T) have nearly identical backbone structure in the aligned regions. Basic action is to correctly place the side chains of U into backbone of T for sequence identities down to U and T will still have the same fold, but the number of loops inserted grows and divergence between U and T becomes considerable.

Remote Homology Modelling/Threading

It's used for cases with < 25% pairwise sequence identity. Threading has to go through 3 steps:

(*i*) Remote homology between U and T has to be detected.

(*ii*) U and T have to be aligned correctly.

(*iii*) Homology Modeling procedure has to be tailored to the harder problem of extremely low sequence identity.

Prediction of Protein Function

Cascade of inference should flow ideally from

$$\text{sequence} \rightarrow \text{structure} \rightarrow \text{function}$$

However, although one can be confident that similar amino acid sequences will produce similar protein structures, the relation between structure and function is more complex proteins of similar structure and even of similar sequence can be recruited for very different functions.

As protein evolve they may:

1. Retain function and specificity
2. Retain function, but alter specificity
3. Change to a related function or similar function in a different metabolic context
4. Change to a completely unrelated function. An active lactate dehydrogenase and an enolase serve as crystalline in eye lens although they do not encounter the substrates *in situ*.

One problem is that it is not easy to define idea of difference in function quantitatively. In some cases, altered function may conceal similarity of mechanism.

3-D Structure of Proteins

The twenty amino acids are represented as a string of 20 different symbols (*i.e.*, a word over the common alphabet of 20 letters).

Various protein databases have information about the protein sequences and functional roles. They include **SWISS PROT,** the length of a protein molecules vary from a few to many thousand amino acids *e.g.*, insulin consists of 51 amino acids, while action has 28,000 amino acids. The primary structure of protein being linear, carries information regarding its folding. The secondary structures are often seen as folded in form of α-helix or β-sheets joined by loops which further fold with the help of non-covalent forces: hydrogen, bonding, vander Waals force, disulfide linkages to adopt a stable 3D structure called tertiary structure making the protein more compact.

The quarternary structure is formed by association of more than one chain of amino acids *e.g.*, hemoglobin has four chains attached to an iron molecule.

The techniques to visualize protein structure are optical microscopy, X-ray crystallography NMR spectrometry and advanced electromicroscopy.

Since amino acids vary greatly in charge, size, hydrophobicity and other physical properties.

Principal component analysis (PCA) is a way of visualizing the important features of multidimensional data etc., such as tables of amino acids. PCA chooses coordinates that linear combinations of the original variables in such a way that the maximum variability between the data points is explained by the first few coordinates.

Clustering analysis is another way of looking for patterns in complex data sets.

Databases for Protein Structure

For protein sequence analysis, primary, composite and secondary databases are available which stake different information in totally different formats.

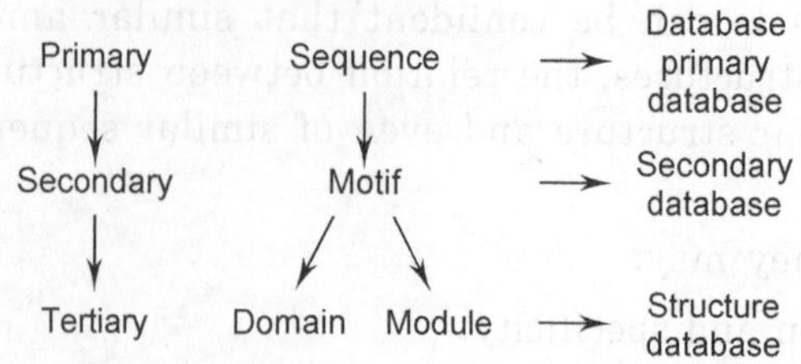

Figure 3.25 Level of protein sequence and structural organisation

Table 3.11 Primary nucleic acid and protein Sequence database

Nucleic acid	*Protein*
EMBL Gen Bank DDBJ	PIR MIPS SWISS-PROT TrEMBL NRL-3D
Protein sequence database PIR MIPS SWISS PROT	(PIR1-PIR4)

PIR-Developed by National Biomedical Research Foundation (NBRF) in early 60s. PIR1-PIR4. It has 4 sections that differ in terms of the quality of data and level of annotation.

SWISS PROT is a protein sequence database to provide high-level annotations including descriptions of the function of the protein, and of the structure of its domains, its post-translational modifications, variants and so on. The structure of SWISS-PROT make computational access to different informative fields both straightforward and efficient. This has become most widely used protein sequence database in the world.

Composite Protein Sequence

DATABASES with details of their primary data source.

NRDB	*OWL*	*MIPSX*	*SP + Tr EMPL*
PDB SWISS-PROT PIR Gen Pept	SWISS-PROT PIR Gene Bank NRL-3D	PIR-4 MIPS SWISS PROT NRL-3D EMTrans MIPSH	SWISS-PROT Tr EMBL

Composite databases render sequence searching more efficient because they obviate the need to interrogate multiple resources.

Secondary Databases

Secondary Database	*Primary source*	*Stored information*
BLOCKS	PROSITE/PRINTS	Aligned motifs (blocks)
IDENTITY	BLOCKS/PRINTS	Fuzzy regular expressions (Patterns)
PROSITE	SWISS-PROT	Regular expressions (patterns)
PRINTS	OWL	Aligned motifs (finger prints). Secondary Databases

Type of information stored is different and based on single, multiple motifs and full domain alignments.

Secondary databases contain pattern data, *i.e.*, diagnostic signatures for protein families. These signatures encode the most highly conserved features of multiple aligned sequences that are often crucial to the structure and function of the protein.

Protein structure related resources may provide a useful adjunct to the databases available for sequence analysis, and will become increasingly important as more 3D structures are solved.

Advances in computer technology will play a major role in simplying the table of sequence analysis in the future. Developments such as **CORBA** (facilitates distributed programming) *internet object-oriented programming language Jawa* are poised to create a new generation of interactive tools that allow seamless investigation of remove information systems at the desktop.

In addition 1D, 2D, and 3D visualization tools will offer new ways of interacting dry compute outputs to transform sequence, motif and structure information into biological knowledge.

There are approximately 20,000 protein structures deposited in public databases.

Nucleic Acid

Nucleic acids are carriers of biochemical information. DNA can be single or double stranded and has 4 different nitrogen bases, namely purines: adenine (A) and guanine (G) and pyrimidine: Cytosine (C) and thyronine (T). The different nucleotides can be linked together in order to form a polynucleotide.

—A—G—T—C—C—A—A

The ends of polynucleotides are marked 5′ and 3′ and by convention DNA is usually written with 5′ left and 3′ right, with the coding strand at the top.

Specific pairs of nucleotides can form weak bonds between them and A binds to T, C binds to G. Such interactions are individually weak and when two longer complementary polynucleotide chains meet they tend to stick together.

```
5′—C—G—A—T—G—C—A—A—C—G  3′
   |  |  |  |  |  |  |  |  |  |
  —G—C—T—A—C—G—T—T—G—C  5′
```

Vertical lines between two strands represent the forces between them and A-T and G-C pairs are called base-pairs (bp). The length of a DNA molecule is usually measured in base-pairs or nucleotides (nt).

Central Dogma of Molecular Biology

Gene Expression

The scheme of DNA → RNA → Protein indicates that DNA codes for proteins indirectly through process of transcription and translation.

DNA $\xrightarrow{\text{transcription}}$ RNA $\xrightarrow{\text{transcription}}$ Protein

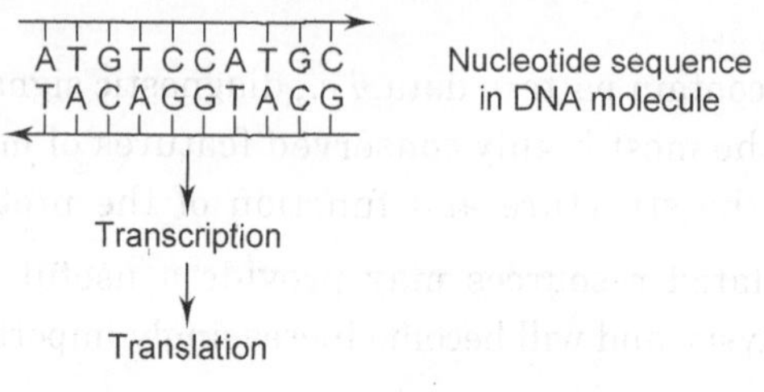

aa chain Met—Ser—The—Alu—Val—Leu—Glu

DNA triplets encoding each aa ATG—TCC—ACT—CGC—GTC—CTG—GAA

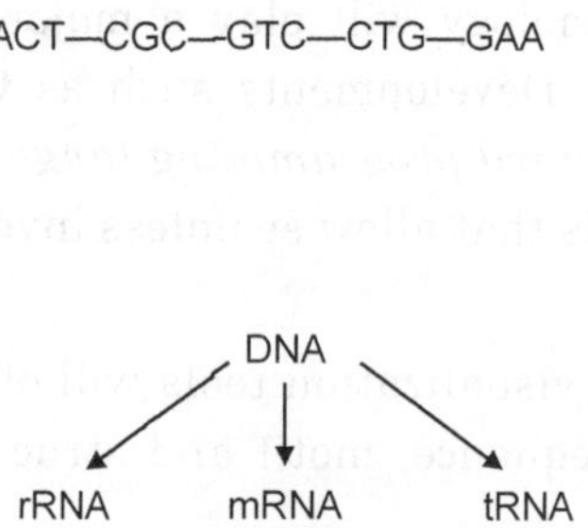

Figure 3.26 Central dogma of molecular biology

The central dogma is the fundamental principle of molecular genetics and summarizes how the genetic information in DNA becomes expressed in the amino acid of sequence in a polypeptide chain.

It is believed that in the earliest forms of life, RNA serves both for genetic information and catalysis and with higher forms the information role was transferred to DNA and catalytic role to protein. However, RNA became locked in central location of process of information flow.

GENE

Genome of an organisms in the totality of DNA present in a single cell. Human genome is composed to 3 billion base pairs of DNA divided among 46 chromosomes that are present in every human cell. Each chromosome contains many genes.

Genes are basically physical and functional unit of heredity. Genes carry instruction regarding making of proteins. There are 30,000-40,000 genes in human genome less than 2% of human genome contains genes (coding regions) and rest of the genome is believed to be involved in providing chromosomal structural support and in regulating the amount of proteins produced in the different cells of the body and at different times.

The genes that make proteins are needed for basic functions are active in most cell types. Genes coded for proteins that have more specific functions are only activated in cell types where that protein is needed. It is by expressing different genes and hence producing different combinations of proteins that the different cell types can fulfill their roles.

Proteins in fact perform all of life's essential functions and any change in DNA sequence can have disastrous consequences. They can be in the form of production of faulty, misformed protein, over-or under production of a protein resulting in the complete disruption of certain cellular processes and hence causing disease.

Mutation

It is a change in DNA sequence and can lead to genetic disorders disease.

Bioinformatics-Genomic Revolution

The bioinformatics has developed out of the need to understand the code of life, DNA. Massive DNA sequencing projects have been evolved further adding to the Science of Bioinformatics. The ultimate goal of bioinformatics is to cover the wealth of biological information hidden in sequence data for obtaining a clear insight into the fundamental biology of organisms in order to use it for enhancing the standard and quality of life of mankind. Also, in future, area of molecular medicine will help to produce customized medicines; in environment it will identify water-cleaning bacteria and in agriculture, production of high yield low maintenance crops.

This interdisciplinary research area of bioinformatics is an interface between biological and computational sciences and would have profound effects on human health, agriculture, environment energy, industry, pharmacology and biotechnology.

GENOMICS

Genomics is a science of mapping sequences and analyzing genome.

Types of Genomics

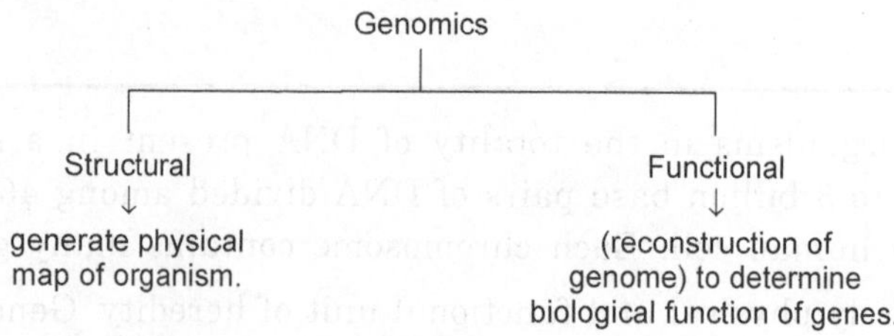

Figure 3.27

Structural genomics

It involves high through put DNA sequencing, and its assembly, organization and management. It is the initial phase of genome analysis and generates genetic, physical or transcript maps of organisms. Now, structural genomics encompass determination of 3-D structure of all proteins.

Functional genomics

It deals with reconstruction of genome for determination of biological function of genes and their interactions. Here, biological investigation for studying a single gene or proteins is used to design experiments using for identifying functions statistics and computational analysis.

Genome Sequencing

Sequencing the genome provides a basis for discovering all the genes, studying their relationship and future experimentation.

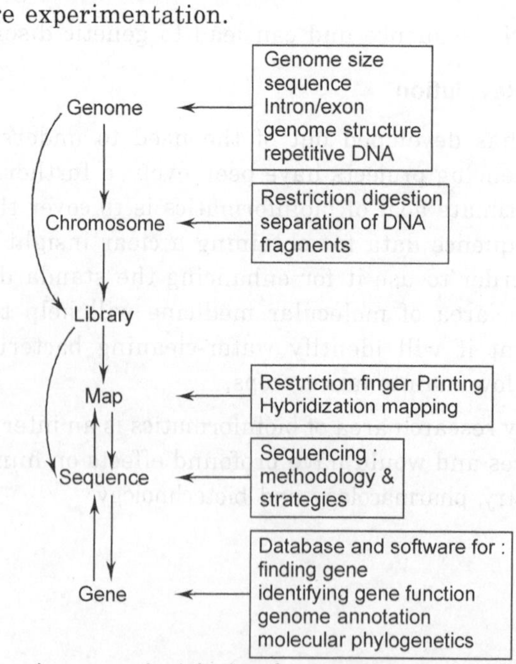

Figure 3.28 Roadmap: methodologies for mapping and sequencing genomes

Techniques of Genome Sequencing:

- Random shotgun sequencing
- Gene prediction
- Mapping
- Sequencer.

Random Shotgun Sequencing

Random shotgun libraries of genomic DNA containing small (2 kb), medium (10 kb) and large BAC library (80-100 kb) insert plasmid vectors are constructed. This is followed by DNA sequencing at both ends of inserts of clones plasmid libraries. The overlapping sequences are identified by a computer based program, which joins them into one continuous stretch to generate sequence information.

Gene Prediction

Using computer programs/algorithms (computational biology), gene prediction can be carried out. Contig map can be created by using restriction maps to generate clones with their subsequent sequencing.

Pattern of inheritance helps to identify the type of genetic defect responsible for a condition and if gene association/inheritance is not known, then **positional cloning** (going from phenotype back to gene) can be of help.

Mapping

A gene linkage map can be calibrated to chromosomal banding patterns in case of deletion or translocation of parts of chromosomes. Approaches for coordinating these patterns are :

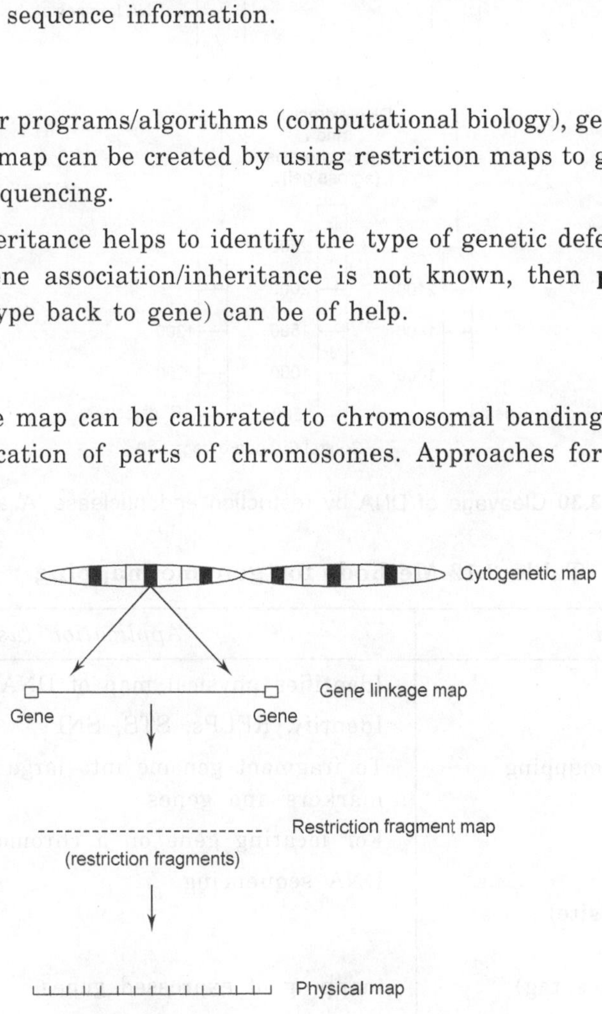

Figure 3.29 Genome maps: different types

(*i*) FISH (fluorescent insitu hybridization) — here, a fluorescent labelled prove sequence is hybridized with chromosome to produce a resolution up to 1 kbp on photography. It is used to detect linkage, chromosomal abnormalities.

(*ii*) *Radiation hybrids.* Used for somatic cells with irradiated chromosomal fragments called radiation hybrids. Hybridization of fluorescent probe with panel of somatic cell hybrids helps to identify chromosome that contains probe. Now obsolete.

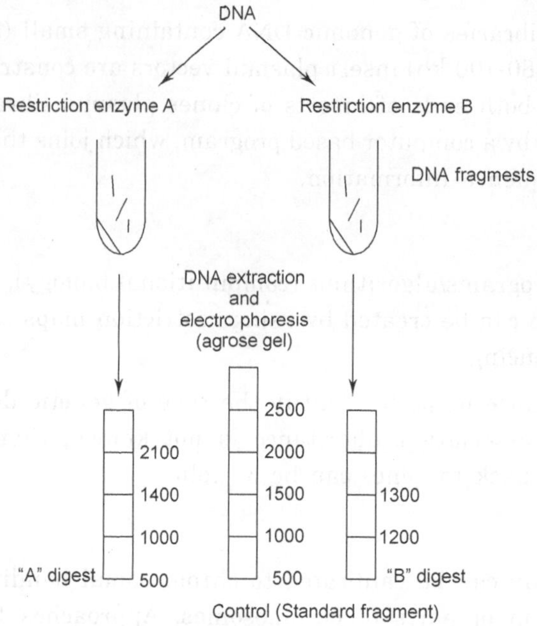

Figure 3.30 Cleavage of DNA by restriction endonuclease 'A' and 'B'

Table 3.12 Methods for genome mapping

Method	*Application (use)*
DNA sequencing	Identifies physical map of DNA
Probes	Identify, RFLPs, STS, SNPs
Radiation hybrid mapping	To fragment genome into large pieces and locate markers and genes
FISH	For locating gene on a chromosome.
STS mapping (sequence tagged site)	DNA sequencing
EST mapping (expressed sequence tag)	mapping of expressed genes
PCR	To amplify gene fragments

Cloning (plasmid, phage, cosmid, YAC, BAC)	Isolation of DNA fragments
Chromosomal walking	to clone overlapping fragments (upto 200 kb in size)
Chromosomal jumping	circularization of large DNA fragments to be used in chromosomal walking.
Cloning of detective gene	Diagnostics

Construction of a restriction map:

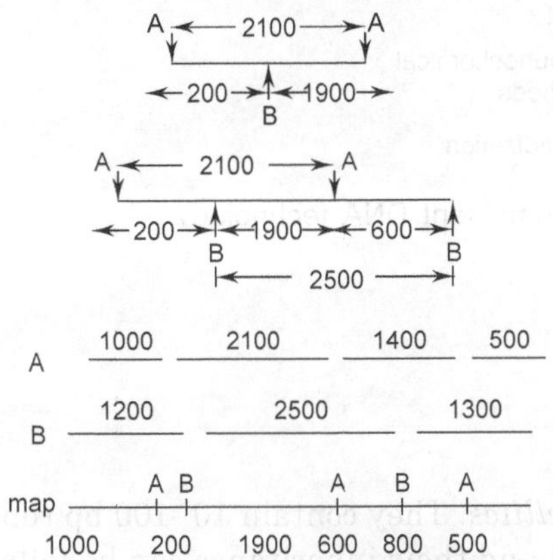

cleavage site of enzyme of A and B in 2100 bp long fragment

cleavage site of enzyme in 2500 bp long fragment

A restriction map (for enzyme A and B)

Figure 3.31 Construction of a restriction map

Isolation of a gene for a specific protein

purify specific protein

↓

raise Ab against it and precipitate polysomes

↓

isolate mRNA reverse transcriptase

↓

cDNA synthesis

↓

cloning of cDNA

↓

Confirm identity of cDNA

↓

colony hybridization

↓

select clone

↓

isolation of gene

Figure 3.32 Overview of strategies in Recombinant DNA technology

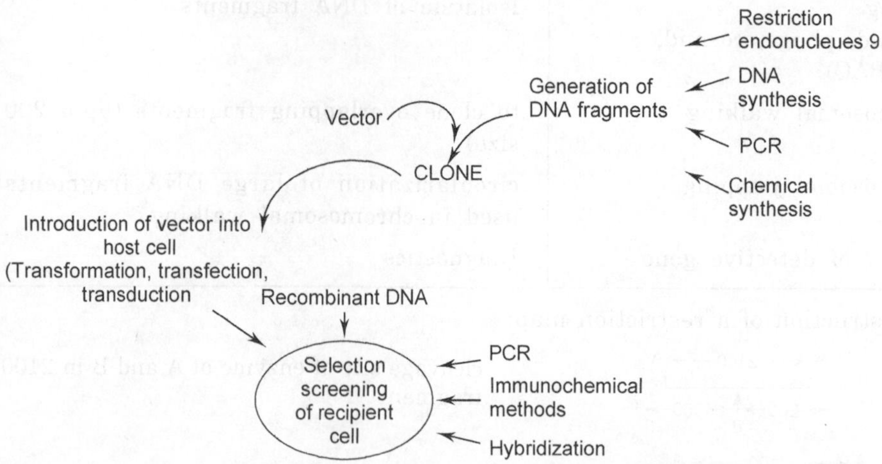

Figure 3.33 Overview of strategies of recombinant DNA technology

Maps of Genome

They include:

VNTRs

(Variable Number Tandem Repeats) or *mini-satellites*. They contain 10 -100 bp repeats which appear once or several times in any individual and their inheritance can be followed in a family. VNTRs can be mapped into a disease phenotype, used as genetic fingerprints in paternity and criminal cases.

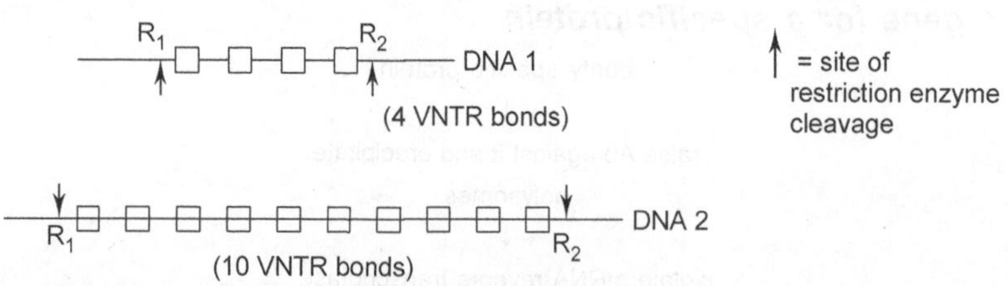

Figure 3.34 VNTRs : two different DNA molecules with different number of copies (bands) of VNTR

Uses of VNTR

- Mapping of genome
- DNA finger printing
- Detection of genetic diseases *e.g.,* Huntington's choria (V NTR) exceed 40 repeat units).

STRs

(Short Tandem Repeat Polymorphism) or micro-satellites. They contain 2-5 bp repeated 10-30 times and have more even distribution over human genome. They are helpful in identification of disease genes.

CONTIG MAP

It is a series of overlapping DNA clones of known order along a chromosome from an organism of interest *e.g.*, YACs or BACs contain human DNA integrated into yeast all or E.coli respectively.

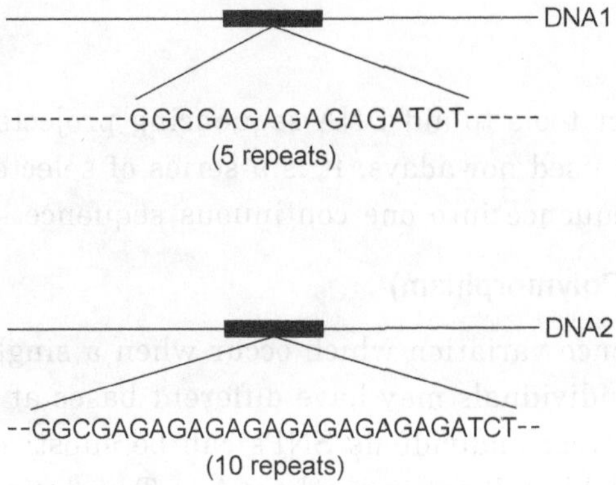

Figure 3.35 STRs (simple tandem repeats): Two variants of DNA molecules with repeating units of a dimmer nucleotide.

STS

(Sequence tagged site). It is a 200 - 600 bp long sequence region of DNA that appears in a unique location of genome and can be mapped by PCR.

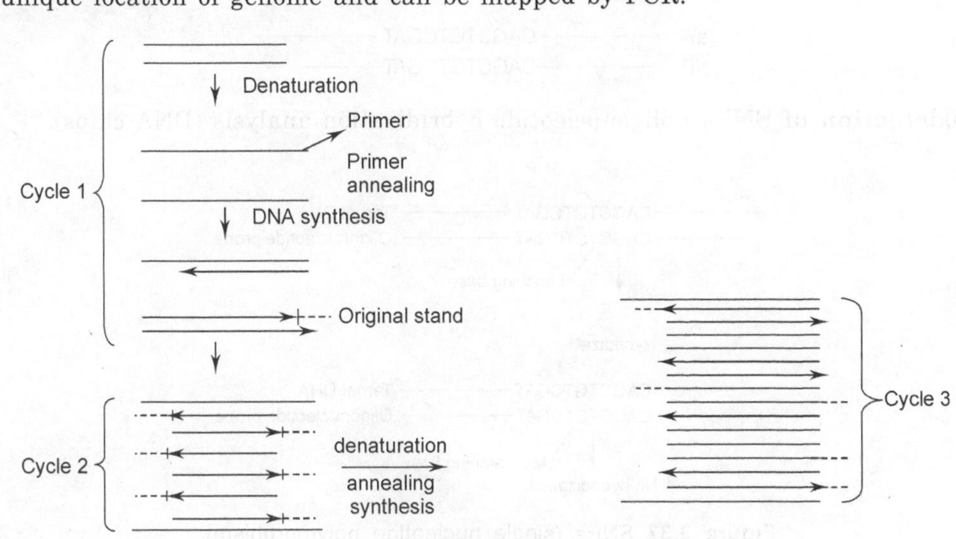

Figure 3.36 PCR

Human gene mapping

The aim of genome projects was to develop a high resolution genetic map (2-5 CM). Before that consensus maps of 7-10 CM were available and recombinant DNA technology has increased the genetic mapping resolution.

Genetic mapping is followed by construction of a physical map of region sequenced. Physical map can be chromosomal (or cytogenic) map, cDNA map, cosmidcontig map, macrorestruction map and high resolution physical map. It is achieved by using the regular techniques namely, DNA cloning, hybridization, PCR, restriction enzymes, and gel electrophoresis.

Computer tools

A variety of computer tools to aid DNA sequencing projects are available and GCG fragment assembly tool is used nowadays. It is a series of selected programs to assemble overlapping nucleotide sequence into one continuous sequence.

SNPs (Single Nucleotide Polymorphism)

They are DNA sequence variation which occur when a single base (A, C, G, or T) is altered so that different individuals may have different bases at their positions resulting in a genetic variation between individuals SNPs can be substituted, inserted or deleted and classical example is sickle cell anaemic where A $\rightarrow$ T mutation in globin gene changes Glu $\rightarrow$ val, creating a sticky surface on hemoglobin molecule (leading to polymerization of deoxy form).

Not all SNPs are linked to disease and they may not be within function regions, SNPs occurring within exons are mutations to synonymous condos causing substitutions that do not significantly affect protein function.

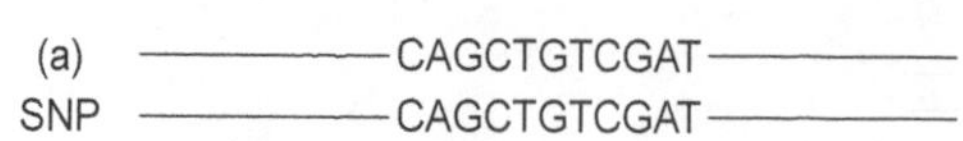

(*b*)**detection of SNPs :** oligonucleotide hybridization analysis (DNA chips).

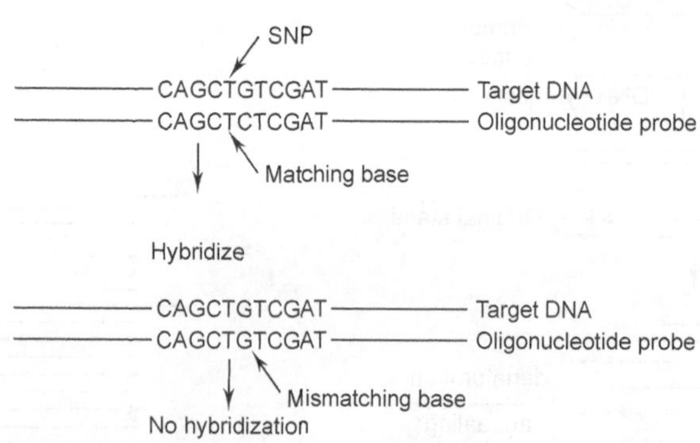

Figure 3.37 SNPs (single nucleotide polymorphism)

Sequence Analysis

Sequence alignment is used to get information from sequence data to discover information related to functions, structure and evolution.

DNA sequencing
↓
Reconstruction
↓
Physical and genetic map determination
↓
Comparison of sequences to find related proteins
↓
exploring frequently occurring pattern of nucleotide
↓
searching informative elements in protein and DNA sequences
↓
identification of unknown sequence
↓
searching other members of multigene families.

Figure 3.38 Scheme of sequence analysis

Sequencing

It offers automated specialized tools for working with the output from automated sequences and assists researches with DNA sequencing into mated sequences along with GCG, Mac Vector and Gene Works as sequence entry and multiple sequence alignment editor helps to gene sate sequence data.

DNA Sequencing

It is the process of determination of nucleotide or base sequence of a DNA molecule/ fragment. DNA sequencing at present is possible only for 100 - 800 bp long DNA fragments.

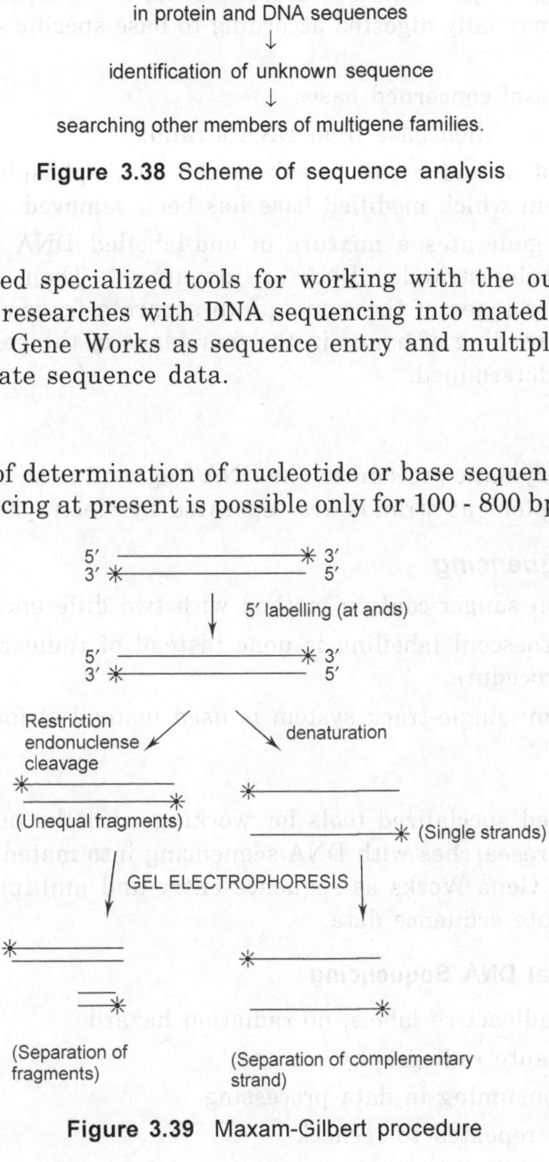

Figure 3.39 Maxam-Gilbert procedure

Maxam-Gilbert procedure: In this technique, the DNA fragment to be sequenced is end-labelled by the addition of 32 P - d ATP either at the 5-ends (by the enzyme polynucleotide kinase) or at the 3-ends (by the enzyme deoxy nucleotidyl transfer) of its both the strands.

This end-labelled fragment is digested with restriction endonuclease generate two fragments of unequal lengths of which only one end would be labelled. These fragments are separated by gel electrophoresis and sequenced separately. Alternatively, end-labelled fragment is denatured and complementary strands are separated through gel electrophoresis and sequenced separately.

The single end-labelled ds or ss DNA samples are subjected to base-specific chemical cleavage at four sites namely, G, C, G + A/C + T. Then, in four separate reaction mixtures, the DNA samples are partially digested according to base-specific sequences by following steps:

(*i*) modification of concerned bases

(*ii*) removal of modified base from DNA strand.

(*iii*) Induction of strand break (break in the sugar-phosphate back-bone) in the position from which modified base has been removed.

Such a cleavage generates a mixture of end-labelled DNA fragments of variable lengths. Digests of double-stranded DNA are denatured. Then, they are subjected to electrophoresis separate lanes of the same gel to separate fragments according to their lengths by sequential reading of bands in the four lanes of the gel by auto-radiography, the base sequence is determined.

Sanger Coulson Method

Also termed as enzymatic procedure. The DNA fragment to be sequenced is denatured and the resulting complement strands are separated by electrophoresis.

Automated DNA Sequencing

It is also based on sanger-coulson method with two differences:

(*i*) labelling flroescenl labelling is done instead of radioactive labelling used in standard procedure.

(*ii*) track system: single-track system is used instead of four track system.

Sequencer

It offers automated specialized tools for working with the output from automated sequences and assists researches with DNA sequencing into mated sequences along with GCG, Mac Vector and Gene Works as sequence entry and multiple sequence alignment editor helps to gene sate sequence data.

Advantage Over Manual DNA Sequencing

(*i*) no use of radioactive labels, no radiation hazard

(*ii*) no need of auto radiography

(*iii*) less time-consuming in data processing.

(*iv*) test can be repeated to recheck

(*v*) fast.

Models for Sequence Analysis

They include:

1. Global alignment
2. Local alignment
3. End free space alignment
4. Gap penalty

To study overview of similarities between two sequences, dotplot matrix is applied. Doat matrix search help to make easy detection of repeats by comparing a sequence against itself. *e.g.*, each member of human Alu 1 middle sequence family is itself made of two sub-repeats and human Alu 1 sequence P27 (Gen Bank K 01153) sequence from approximately 30 ..120 is imperfectly repeated at positions 140 ..260.

Models for Protein Sequences

PAM

BLOSUM are two popular scoring models for protein sequences.

PAM: (percent accepted mutation)

BLOSUM: blocks substitution matrix

PAM

This approach is a scoring system per sequences in which 1% residues have undergone mutation in PAM-1 and 250% in PAM-250 systems.

PAM approach is based on explicit evolutionary model to examine kinds of mutations that occur in closely related protein sequence.

Blocks are locally conserved regions containing sequences at all different evolutionary distances.

PAM 250 amino acid similarity matrix:

Cys	12											
Gly	–3	5										
Pro	–3	–1	6									
Sec	0	1	1	1								
Ala	–2	1	1	1	2							
Thl	–2	0	0	1	1	3						
Asp	–5	1	–1	0	0	0	4					
Glu	–5	0	–1	0	0	0	3	4				
Asn	–4	0	–1	1	0	0	2	1	2			
Gln	–5	–1	0	–1	0	–1	2	2	1	4		
His	–3	–2	0	–1	–1	–1	1	1	2	3	6	
Lys	–5	–2	–1	0	–1	0	0	0	1	0	0	5
	Cys	Gly	Pro	Ser	Ala	thr	Asp	Glu	Asn	Gln	His	Lys

Substitution of as aspartate for GLUTAMATE, both acidic adds 3 to score

Substitution of Lys for nonpolar Pro adds -1 to score.

Generally, the more conservative the replacement the higher the value that will be added to the score.

One PAM unit is defined as amount of sequence divergence corresponding to a 1% anion acid replacement rate.

BLOSUM

Series of matrix are also commonly used.

BLOSUM approach is based an empirical frequencies and PROSITE signatures.

BLOSUM 45 amino acid similarity metrix

Gly	7											
Pro	–2	9										
Asp	–1	–1	7									
Glu	–2	0	2	6								
Asn	0	–2	2	0	6							
His	–2	–2	0	0	1	10						
Glu	–2	–1	0	2	0	0	–1	6				
Lys	–2	–1	0	1	0	–1	1	5				
Arg	–2	–2	–1	0	0	0	–1	1	7			
Ser	0	–1	0	0	1	–1	0	–1	–1	4		
Thr	–2	–1	–1	–1	0	–2	–1	–1	–1	2	5	
Ala	0	–1	–2	–1	–1	–2	–1	–1	–2	1	0	5
	Gly	Pro	Asp	Glu	Asn	His	Gln	Cys	Alg	Ser	Thr	Ala

Table 3.13 Comparing PAM and BLOSUM

	PAM	*BLOSUM*
basis	explicit evolutionary model	empirical frequencies
represents	specific evolutionary distance	blend of distances as seen in database/Prosite
range	identical to completely random	narrower than PAM.

Nucleotide Scoring Matrix

For scoring DNA sequence alignments on scoring similar lines as amino acid scoring matrices, scoring matrices have been developed for nucleotides. Based on Markov transition model, a series of nucleir acid PAM matrices have been developed. But, they provide little Information per aligned nucleotide pair.

DNA matrices about mutations and ambiguous DNA symbols are also available and mutations of transitions are more probable than Tranversions.

MICROARRAYS

Microarrays represent high-density miniaturized arrays of molecular samples. The technology involves a series of probes immobilized on a glass slide as microdots, which are then hybridized with a mixture of test DNA sequences labelled with a fluorochrome.

Preparation

Prepared either by synthesis of oligonucleotide on a DNA chip, or by deposition of available DNA sequences on DNA chip.

Types

1. *DNA microarray*: contain cloned gene sequences, cDNA, ESTs.
2. *Antibody microarray*: contain spots of different antibodies.

DNA Chip

They are of two types:

(*i*) oligonucleotide-based chips.

(*ii*) DNA-based chips.

(*i*) Obigo nucleotide-based chips contain high density of short oligonucleotides (20–25 nucleotides long) of known sequence immobilized within an area of 1.6 cm^2.

(*ii*) DNA-based chips contain high density of cDNA samples (sometimes derived term PCR).

Technique

A fluorescently labeled DNA test molecule whose sequence is to be determined is applied to the chip.

Hybridization occurs between complementary sequences to test DNA molecule and oligonucleotide of the chip and intensity of fluorescence is detected and quantity assay of hybridization intensity is obtained.

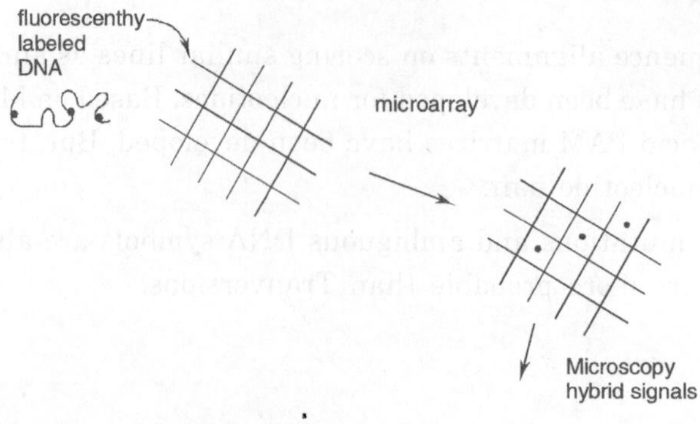

Figure 3.40 Hybridization of chip

Applications of Microarrays

1. To study gene expression pattern, regulator elements, SNP polymorphism.
2. Defection of genetic disease *e.g.,* detection of mutant alleles of gene BRACA1 (breast cancers), cystic fibrosis (CFTR), β-globin (thalassemia).
3. Detection of microorganisms *e.g.,* E.coli, S. cerevisiae.
4. Transcript monitoring.
5. Protomics-protein linkage map, to identify protein of interest.

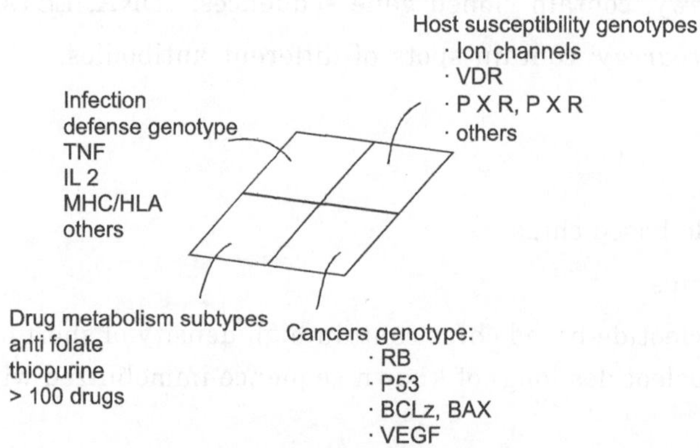

Figure 3.41 Possible design of microarrays for diagnostics

DNA chips hold a great provide to biotechnologists in future.

Table 3.14 Properties of different types of DNA array for expression analysis

Property	*Nylon*	*Glass*	*Affinities gene chips*
Target size	Typical	100 - 300 bp	Typical 20–25 nt
Target source	maintained clone sets		• sequence derived from public and/or private databases

Target Composition	ds DNA fragments		• chemically synthesized single-strained oligonucleotides.
Probe labelling	Radioactive Enzymatic	Dual florescent	Fluorescent
Detection Cost	Auto radiography Low	Confocal scanning moderate	Confocal scanning high

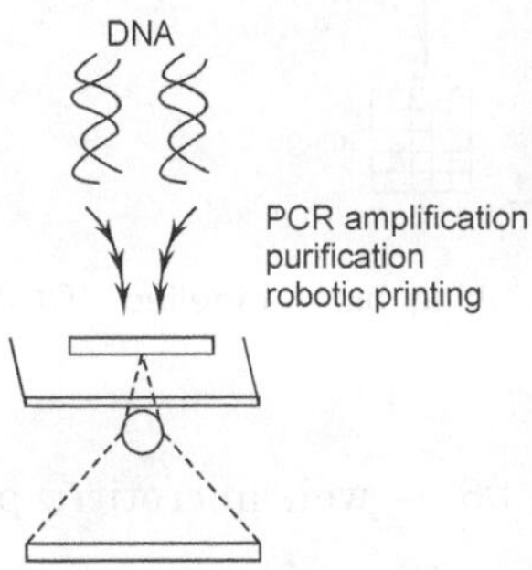

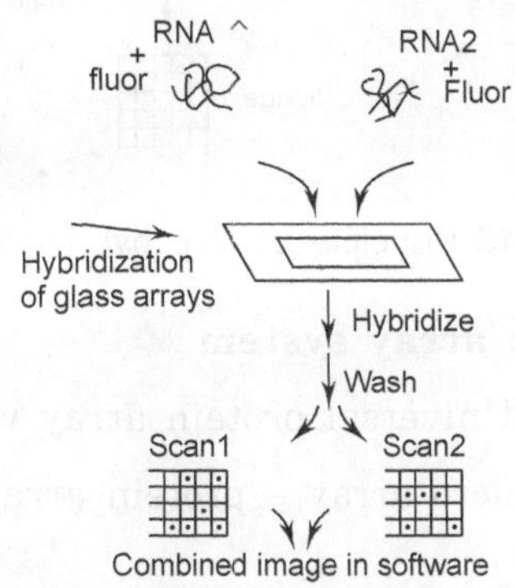

Figure 3.42 Array manufacture

Figure 3.43 Spotted (DNA microarray)

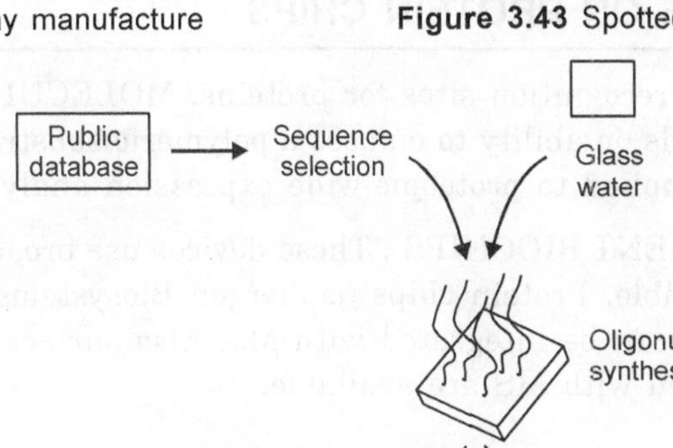

Figure 3.44 Principle of chip manufacture (oligonucleotide chip)

Internet resources for microarrays and oligo chips:

www.clonetech.com

www.resgen.com

www.stratagene.com

www.affymetrix.com

www.operon.com
www.biorobotics.co.uk
www.genomicsolutions.com

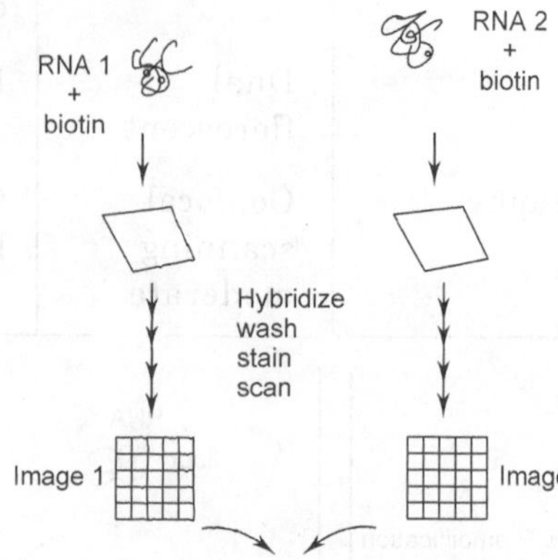

Figure 3.45 Principle of chip hybridization using biotin-labelled cRNA probes

Different protein array system

1. UPA – Universal protein array with 96 — well microtitre plates.
2. Glass micro array – protein arrays on glass slides.

MOLECULAR IMPRINTS OR PROTEIN CHIPS

They contain artificial recognition sites for proteins, MOLECULARLY IMPRINTED POLYMERS - (MIPs) depends on ability to emboss a polymeric substrate with recognition molecules. It is get to be applied to proteome-wide expression analysis on mass-scale

BROAD–CAPTURE AGENT BIOCHIPS : These devices use broad specificity capture agents. Commercially available. Protein chips (ciphergen Biosystems inc) bind different classes of protein and they can be integrated with MS. Also surface plasmon resonance based protein chip integrated with MS are available.

SOLUTION ARRAYS

Next generation of miniature protein array platforms would be based on micro fluidics.

SEQUENCE ANALYSIS OF PROTEINS AND NUCLEIC ACIDS

The sequencing projects rapidly generate very large amounts of data which have to be mined to extract relevant information.

Terminology

Annotation

It means obtaining biological information from unprocessed sequence data.

Structural Annotation. It means identification of genes and other sequence elements.

Functional Annotation. It means determination of their functional rules in the organism.

Rather than focusing on individual genes, nowadays annotation of entire genomes is undertaken. Raw genomic sequence can be annotated by comparison with database of previously cloned genes and ESTS and sophisticated algorithms.

Annotation is achieved by the application of information technology to the management and analysis of biological data, a field known as BIOINFORMATICS.

The science of bioinformatics has three components:

1. Development of new algorithms and statistics for assessing and interpreting large datasets.
2. Using algorithms for analysis and interpretation of nucleotide and amino acid sequences, protein domain structure and protein interactions data.
3. Creation of database that permit efficient access and management of different types of information.

Overview of Sequence Analysis

The first task is to identify any genes present in a long piece of DNA that has been sequenced.

Once a gene has been identified, the nucleic acid sequence is converted into a protein sequence.

It may be possible to identify other proteins with a similar sequence which may help to identify its function.

Also, more information about its function can be obtained by sequence comparisons to identify particular motifs in a protein *e.g.,* ATP-binding or DNA-binding.

Certain Considerations

1. In prokaryotes, gene density is high, protein coding genes lack introns so recognition is relatively easy.
2. In eukaryotes, a gene is harder to recognize since it is composed to large no. of exons and introns.

   e.g., In Human genome, exon is 150 bp intron is several kb complete gene can be hundreds of kb.

Methodology

Includes:

1. Detecting open reading frames
2. Exon/Intron boundaries
3. Identification of function of genes and their products
4. Expression signals
5. Protein structure
6. Protein motifs and domains

7. (*a*) Sequence comparisons
   (*b*) Protein sequence comparison
   (*c*) Protein sequence alignments
   (*d*) Databanks

Open Reading Frames (ORF)

The first task during identification of possible genes in a length of DNA sequence is identification of correct reading frame. Since there are three possible reading frames on each strand of a DNA molecule. The correct reading frame is assumed to be longest frame interrupted by a stop coden (TGA, TAA, TAG). The longer the ORF, more likely it is to be a gene because long ORFs are unlikely to occur by chance.

5′ end: (*i*) N-terminal amino acid of a protein usually is methionine so the presence of an ATG codon might indicate the 5′ end of a gene.

(*ii*) In a mRNA, molecule, the start codon may be flanked by a kozak sequence. (CCGCC AUGG) and finding of this sequence helps to identify 5′ end of gene.

CPG island: Identification of segments with a much higher than average GC content and higher than average frequency of CPG dinucletide is indicative of CPG ISLAND.

Bias towards G or C as the third base in a coden-can also used as final aid. Sophisticated computer programs are also available for it.

Software Programs for Finding Genes

Several sophisticated software algorithms have been devised to handle gene prediction in eukaryotic genomes namely

1. Neural networks *e.g.* GRAIL
2. Rule-based system *e.g.* Genefinder
3. Hidden Markov method *e.g.* GENSCAN HMM Gene.

Exon/Intron Boundaries

Human intron/exon boundaries are surrounded by some recurrent motifs and the most obvious and conserved of these is GU-AG motif. Most introns begin with GU (encoded by GT in the sense strand of DNA) and finish with AG. These combination occurs theoretically with frequency of 1:16. Even computer algorithms are available for predicting intron/exon boundries.

Another evidence can be obtained from screening databanks of ESTs.

Also, Gen Bank database can be searched for matching full length CDNA sequence.

Identification of Function of Genes and their Products

The simplest way to identify function of new genes is to search homologues in the protein databases.

BLAST programs are the fastest sequence alignment tools. Others are SWISS-PORT and TrEMBL.

SOFTWARE PROGRAMS FOR FINDING GENES

Computer software are available to predict the existence of genes in unprocessed genome sequence data. Also, computer-based prediction have advantage of its speed-annotation can be carried out concurrently with sequencing itself-but it has a disadvantage of inaccuracy particularly in complex genome of higher eukaryotes.

Several sophisticated software algorithms have been devised to handle gene prediction in eukaryotic genomes.

Many of currently used gene prediction programs incorporate Markov model to distinguish hexamer usage between coding and non-coding DNA. GRAIL is one of the oldest gene prediction programs and can be used with human, mouse, Arabidopsis, Drosophilia and E. coli sequences. While GENIE has been trained only on human and Drosophila sequences.

Thus gene-prediction algorithms need to be trained with data or else implanted with a set of rules so that the algorithm can recognize key features that distinguish a gene or exon from non-coding DNA, a feature not identical in all organisms.

Algorithms	*Example*	*Principle*
Rule-based system	Gene Finder	Uses an explicit set of rules to make decisions.
Neural Network	GRAIL	Modelled on process of learning in cognitive systems. Uses data training set to build rules for prediction or classification on data sets.
Hidden Markov Model	FGENEH GENE SCAN GENIE Gene Mark HMM HMM Gene	A set of discrete states and transition between those states with associated probability estimates feature.

Gene prediction software	
FGENEH	Gene Builder
GENEID	Wise 2/Genewise
GENIE	BLOCKS.
GEN SCAN	
HMM Gene	
Gene Mark HMM	
GRAIL	
GLIMMER M	

PREDICTION OF STRUCTURE AND FUNCTION OF PROTEINS AND GENES

Identification of Function a New Gene

It is possible to identify the function of new genes or putative genes, by searching homologues in the protein database.

Programs available are

- BLAST tools:
  BLASTP
  PSI-BLAST
- FASTA
- HMMER
- SWISS-PROT
- TrEMBL
- BLAST programs are fastest sequences alignment tools with less sensitivity and FASTA and HMMER are slower but more sensitive.
- SWISS-PROT-database

It is not just a repository of protein sequence, rather a collection of confirmed protein sequences annotated with information such as function and biological role of protein family assignment and bibliography. The data is of very high quality and actively curated (managed).

TrEMBL database has entries in the same format as SWISS-PROT and they are derived from translation of all coding sequences in the EMPL nucleotide sequence database. It is easier to compare amino acid sequences than nucleotide sequences due to redundancy in genetic code.

Secondary Protein Databases

Database	*Features*
BLOCKS	Contain conserved protein regions and their multiple alignments.
PFAM	Contain profiles and alignment for common protein families.
PRINTS	Short protein motif compendium
Pro Dom	Collection of protein domain
PROSITE	Longer protein signature collection
SMART	Curated collection of protein domain.

These secondary databases have been constructed using different analytical methods namely motif recognition, fingerprinting of motifs, domain profiles, hidden Markov models.

InterPro is cross referencing system that permits screening of protein sequence against each of the secondary databases to extract relevant information.

Gene Ontology

Enables the relating of protein function to gross cellular or organism function *e.g.*, central metabolism, cell division, nucleotide replication.

Bioinformatic Tools

(*a*) **Alignment tools**

Local sequence alignment tools

- FASTA
- PatMatch
- BLAST
- ParAlign
- Protein Engine
- Interpro

Multiple alignment tools

- Clustal W
- PHYLI P
- Bionumeric

Multipurpose analysis tool

- Biotech nx 3d

PCR primer designing

- Primer
- Prima

STS sequence search

- Program sts search

SNPs discovery

- SNP pipeline
- Auto SNP
- SEAN
- PHRED
- PHRAP
- CONSED

SSR, mining

- TROLL
- TANDEM REPEAT FINDER
- MSL

(*b*) **Assembly package for large scale genome sequencing**

PHRED

PHRAP

DEMIGLACE

CONSED

(*c*) **EST clustering package**

CORPUS

Paracel EST clustering package

(*d*) **Gene finder**

GRAIL, GENESCAN, GENEWISE, Genefinder, Glimmer MR.

(*e*) **Gene Ontology Consortium**

Known genes in database.

(*f*) **Central repository for biological literature**

PubMed.

Global Analysis of Protein Expression

The entire complement of proteins synthesized by a cell or organism is PROTEOME PROTEOMICS is study of gene products encoded by a genome. Proteomics aims to identify the entire complement of proteins elaborated by a cell under diverse conditions *i.e.*, the protein equivalent of whole genome.

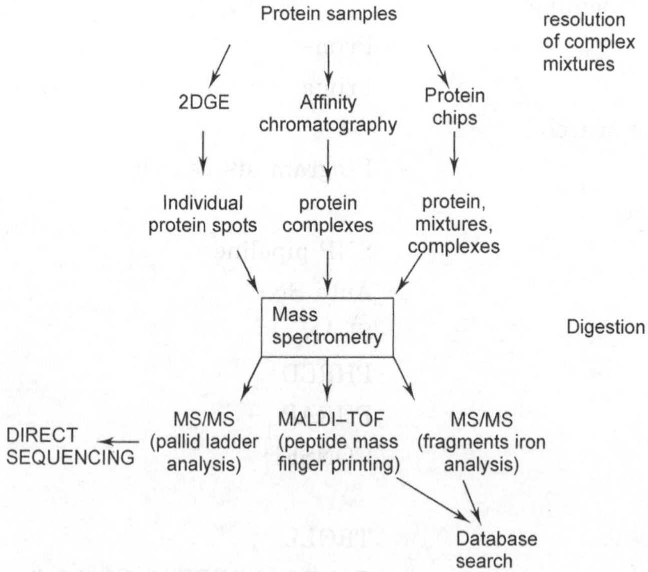

Figure 3.46 Routes of protein annotation in proteomics

Why to Look at Protein Expression?

Since the ultimate product of most genes is a protein, not an RNA molecule, and proteins carry out the actual function of the gene by interacting with cellular and extracellular environment.

There is no one-to-one correspondence between mRNAs and proteins and many genes are under post transcriptional regulation and proteins undergo post-translational modifications which are ultimately associated with protein function. Therefore, direct analysis at the protein level is beneficial and desirable.

Currently, the most widely used technology for proteome analysis is protein separation by 2-dimensional gel electrophoresis (2 DGE), followed by annotation using high-throughput mass spectrometry.

PROTEOMICS

Proteome

The entire complement of proteins synthesized by a given cell is termed as PROTEOME and global study of proteins is PROTEOMICS. The term proteome was coined by a VC Wasinger in 1995.

Since proteins cannot be amplified like nucleic acids analysis of protein expression is challenging. Most widely used technologies for proteome analysis are-protein separation by 2-D electrophoresis and for multi dimensional liquid chromatography followed by mass spectrometry.

2-D Gel Electrophoresis (2 DGE)

This produces a visual display of the proteome.

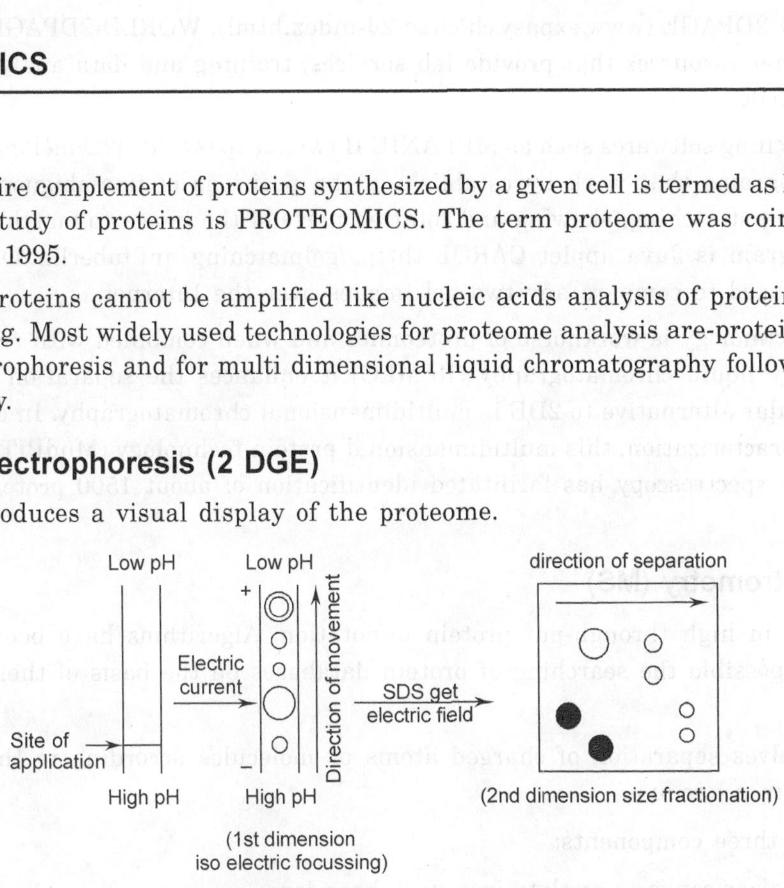

Figure 3.47 2D electrophoresis

IEF: Isoelectric focusing-electrophoresis is carried out in a pH gradient, allowing protein to migrate to its isoelectric point. Size fractionation is done in second dimension on the basis of molecular mass using SDS (sodium dodecyl sulfate).

After fractionation, staining of gel is carried out by silver nitrate, coomassie brilliant blue dye. For proteomics applications, these agents lack sensitivity to defect scarce proteins and newer sensitive fluorescent stains known as SYPRO dye are available to produce fingerprint of proteins of the cell.

Multiplexed Analysis

Multiplex analysis allows expression of protein profiles on single gels followed by their calculations using algorithms *e.g.*, MELANIE II, CAROL are gel-matching software.

Multidimensional Liquid Chromatography

Liquid chromatography (LC) method using multidimensional technology have replaced 2 DGE. Also, proteins separated in liquid phase do not require staining for their detection. LC columns are directly coupled to mass spectrometer and thus automating the peptide mass profiling.

WORLD-2DPAGE (www.expasy.ch/ch2d/2d-index.html). WORLD-2DPAGE sites, have links to further resources that provide lab services, training and data analysis software relevant to 2DE.

Gel matching softwares such as MELANIE II (www.expasy.ch/ch2D/melanie) are freely available programs that work by establishing the positions of unambiguous landmark spots and then stretching, skewing and rotating parts of the image to match other spots. Another program is Java applet CAROL (http://gelmatching. inf.fuberlin.de/carol.html). This can be used to compare any two gel images over the Internet.

2 DE technology is workhorse of proteomics and when combined with reverse phase microcapillary liquid chromatography (RPMLC) it enhances the separation of proteins. Another popular alternative to 2DE is multidimensional chromatography. In case of yeast proteome characterization, this multidimensional protein technology (MudPIT) along with tandem mass spectroscopy has facilitated identification of about 1500 proteins in yeast proteome.

Mass Spectrometry (MS)

It helps in high through-put protein annotation. Algorithms have been developed which made possible the searching of protein databases on the basis of their molecular mass.

MS involves separation of charged atoms or molecules according to their mass-to charge ratio in a vacuum.

MS has three components:

1. Ionizer-converts analyte into gas phase ions
2. Mass analyzer-separates the ions according to their mass, charge ratio (m:z)
3. an ion detector.

   The data obtained can be used to search protein databases for identifying particular proteins.

MS Resources
www. expasy.ch/tools/
proteome
www.narrador. embl_heidelber.de
www. seqgnet_dl.ac.
uk/Bioinformatics
http=//prospector.ucsf.edu

Strategies of Protein Annotation

Two major strategies are:

- Peptide mass finger printing.
- Fragment ion searching.

Peptide Mass Finger Printing

It is carried out by using MALDI-TOF using gel digestion with a sequence specific protease like trypsin to obtain mass fingerprint using MALDI-TOF. The fragments generate by protease digestion are analysed by MS for determination of their molecular masses and data thus obtained are used to search protein databases. A number of computer algorithms have been developed to correlate MS determined peptide masses with virtual peptide masses derived from protein databases.

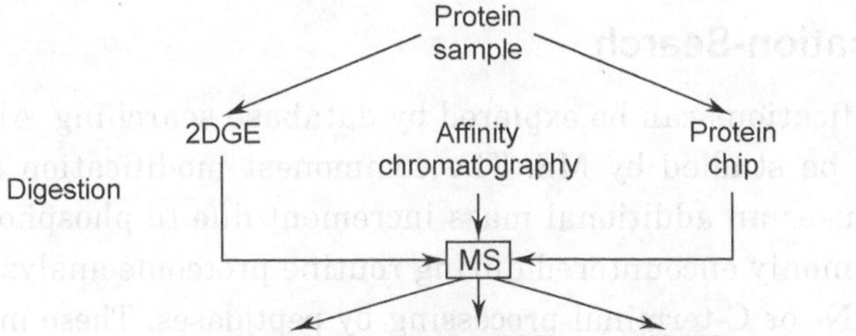

Figure 3.48 Current route of protein annotation in proteomics

Fragment Ion Searching

Here, fragmentation is achieved by Tandem mass spectroscopy (MS/MS) either with quadrupole or TOF analyzers or a mixture, separated by collision cell to induce fragmentation. Then, data of peptide mass and mass of its fragment ionsis searched and matched with available databases and ESTs.

Table 3.15 Protein identification programs

Program	*Basis*
Mascot www.matrixscience.com	uses MOWSE algorithm
ProFound http://prowl.rockfeller.edu	uses Z-score
Protein Prospector (MS-Fit) http://prospector.ucsf.edu	uses MOWSE score

MOWSE = Molecular Weight Search algorithm

Table 3.16 Mass Spectrometry Resources on NET

www.expasy.ch/tools/#proteome
http://prospector.ucsf.edu
www.seq net.dl-ac.uk/Bioinformatics/
www.narrador-embl-heidelberg.de/GroupPage/ Pagelink/peptidesearchpage.html

Protein Modification-Search

Protein modifications can be explored by database searching. Also, post translational modifications can be studied by MS. The commonest modification is phosphorylation of proteins which causes an additional mass increment due to phosphogroup (80 Da). Other modifications commonly encountered during routine proteome analysis include acetylation, glycosylation and N- or C-terminal processing by peptidases. These modifications also cause mass change that can be analyzed by MS.

Also, protein interaction can be exploited for biotechnology applications including therapeutic purposes and drug discovery.

Protein Arrays and Protein Chip

Protein arrays are emerging as a useful closed system for proteome analysis. These are miniature devices in which proteins or molecules that recognize proteins, are arrayed on the surface.

Comparison of arrays

In concept, protein arrays are no different to DNA arrays, but they suffer from several practical limitations.

Table 3.17 Comparison of arrays

	DNA Array	*Protein Array*
Amplification	Nucleic acid sequences can be amplified by PCR.	No amplification procedure exist for protein.
Sequences	Made up of 4 nucleotides	No such sequence.
Principle of molecular recognization.	hybridization between complementary base pairs. Single complex pro be used.	Recognization parameters vary widely same probe cannot be used.
Labelling	Labels are incorporated evenly does not interfere with hybridization	Labels are much more variable. Labelling of protein interfere with protein binding.

Applications of protein microarray

Various protein microarrays available are

1. Antibody (Ab) arrays (microimmoassays)
2. Antigen (Ag) arrays (reverse microimmoassays)
3. General protein arrays
4. Arrays of specific capture agents

Table 3.18 Different arrays

Array	*Application*
Ab array	Detection of Ab against infection cytokines.
Ag array	Used for reverse immunoassay.
General protein array	To study protein-protein interactions, protein arrays for yeast proteome protein functions, etc.
Arrays of specific capture agents.	Include aptamers, singlestranded nucleotides, molecularly imprint, biochips.

Molecular Imprints

Though they do not fit under umbrella of array, but contain molecularly imprinted polymers (MIP) which have artificial recognition sites for proteins.

Broad-Capture Agent Biochips

These devices use broad-specificity capture agents and are marketed as Protein chips by Ciphergen Biosystems Inc. which doubles itself as a modified MALDI plate. After washing, this chip is coated with a matrix solution and analyzed by TOF-MS. Also, SELDI (surface-enhanced laser desorption and ionization) provides more uniform mass spectra than MALDI for protein quantification.

Solution Arrays

This is a microfluidic devices and are the next generation of highly sensitive miniature protein array platforms.

SUMMARY

Bioinformatics has emerged as a scientific discipline that encompasses the application of computing science and technology to analyze and manage biological data. As sequence data began to accumulate rapidly more powerful sequence analysis software and algorithm were developed. The mainstay of bioinformatics is that nucleic acid and proteins can be transformed into sequences of digital symbols, which allowed bioinformatics to flourish.

Genomics is a science of mapping sequences and analysing genome. This unit has given an overview of techniques of genome sequencing, gene mapping, sequence analysis, DNA sequencing and microarrays.

Genomics offer sequencing, mapping and analysis of genome. With the help of computer-based techniques, human genome was sequenced. Now it is possible to identify function of genes from protein databases.

Since proteins cannot be amplified like nucleic acid, analysis of protein expression is challenging 2 DGE; MS and protein chips are most widely used technologies for proteome analysis.

REVIEW QUESTIONS

1. What is bioinformatics and why to study it?
2. How is large scale molecular biology data generated?
3. What is the scope of bioinformatics in IT?
4. What are EMBL, NCBI?
5. What is GenBank?
6. Discuss computational representation of molecular data storage technique.
7. What is phylogenetic analysis?
8. What are the methods of evaluating phylogenies?
9. Define
   - genome
   - genomics
   - EST's
   - Genes
   - Human genome maps.

10. Describe random shotgun sequencing.
11. What are applications of mapping?
12. What are the computer tools for sequencing?
13. What is SNP?
14. Short note - DNA microarrays.
15. Define
    - PAM
    - BLOSUM
16. Give applications of DOT Matrices.
17. What is cell? What are different types of cell?
18. Describe brief structure of protein.
19. Describe brief structure of nucleic acid.
20. What is central dogma of molecular life?
21. Discuss the link of bioinfomatics and genomic revolution.
22. How are amino acid sequence compared with database?
23. Short note
    - SWISS-PROT
    - PRIL.
24. Discuss origin and evolution of macromolecules in the cell.
25. What are the possible precursors of biomolecules?
26. What is evolution?
27. Discuss evolution of mitochondria and chloroplast.
28. What is molecular evolution?
29. What is genome evolution?
30. What are the applications of molecular phylogenetics?
31. Give an account of role of genomics, computational biology and personalized patient healthcare.
32. How a biologist visualizes and analyzes complex phylogenic data set?
33. What are different types of network?
34. What are different models for network?
35. Give topological structures of biological networks.
36. What are practical significance for analyzing networks.
37. Enumerate software for network.
38. What are neural networks?
39. How neural networks predict secondary structure of protein?
40. What are consensus networks?
41. What are neural networks?
42. Give an account of ORF.
43. Give an exon/intron boundaries.

44. What software are available for finding function of a gene?
45. Prepare a list of software programs for finding a gene.
46. What programs are available for prediction of structure and function of a gene?
47. What is secondary protein database?
48. What is massspectrometry? Enumerate its uses.
49. What is shot gun sequencing?
50. Discuss methods of genome sequencing.
51. Discuss different methods of proteome analyses.
52. What is protein chip?
53. What is MIP?
54. Discuss protein annotation.
55. Give a flow sheet for visual display of protein.
56. Describe distance method of predicting phylogenetic analysis.
57. What are methods of evaluating phylogenies?
58. Give outline of information expression.
59. What are levels of protein structure?
60. Give an account of evolution of protein structure.
61. Describe protein visualization tools.
62. How will you predict protein structure, discuss?
63. Give models of structure prediction.
64. How the protein structure can be predicted?
65. How a 3D structure of a protein is derived?
66. Give an account of protein databases?
67. What is composite protein sequence?
68. What do you understand by central dogma of molecular biology?
69. Give an account of gene.
70. Explain the meaning of bioinformatics.
71. Outline the interaction of displines contributing to the field of bioinformatics.
72. Describe computer network.
73. Give an account of database.
74. What is biological basis of life?
75. Discuss how life evolved on earth.
76. Explore role of network in biological sciences.
77. Give models for network.
78. Outline significance of analysis of networks.
79. Enumerate software's for network.
80. What is the use of consensus network?
81. What are visualization tools for protein structure?
82. What is biodiversity and give its types?

83. Give main reasons for loss of diversity.
84. What is phylogenic analysis?
85. What are different models of sequence evolution?
86. Give a comparative account of structural and functional genomics.
87. What is random shotgun sequencing?
88. What is gene prediction?
89. Give an outline of sequence analysis of proteins and nucleic acid?
90. Compare Maxam-Gilbert and Sanger's technique of sequencing.
91. What are models for sequence analysis?
92. Outline the process of mapping.
93. What are computer tools for mapping?
94. What are protein chips?
95. What are solution arrays?
96. What are microarrays?
97. Enlist applications of microarrays.
98. List out fields of biological Sciences where computers and engineering have a key role.
99. Prepare a list of software programs for finding genes.
100. What is a proteome?
101. How will you produce a visual display of proteome?
102. Prepare an outline of alternative techniques to 2 DGE.
103. Give an overview of MS.

Chapter 4

SCIENTIFIC WRITING

Do not let me tell you how to write a paper, let me try to improve Your Writing!

SCIENTIFIC PAPER

What is a Scientific Paper

A scientific paper is **not** a technical report or term paper. It is a paper worth writing only if it has general implications for knowledge. One should think of his role as guiding future efforts of scholars since others will come after you with newer data and better models!

Need to Write Scientific Papers

Scientists are motivated for writing papers two ways namely, to understand the world and to get credit for it. In academic and public sectors, scientific papers are means of expansion of human knowledge. PUBLISH or PERISH should be the rule for scientists working as individuals professional survival: you do not publish, you are out.

Determinants of Quality of Scientific Paper

Nowadays, quality of a scientific paper is measured by citation index. It depends on:

(*i*) originality and importance of ideas.

(*ii*) effectiveness of communication to flag new ideas.

(*iii*) means of communication: role of advertising, presentation, communications at meeting, e-mail exchanges, citations etc.

View Writing of Paper as a Part of Your Research

Remember writing of paper is not description of work, IT IS THE WORK.

Suggestions:

(*i*) Start writing paper as soon as possible: view it as a tool of your research.

(*ii*) Write an "introduction" as you engage into your research:
Try to highlight

- What you are trying to do?
- Why it is important?
- What has been done earlier?

(*iii*) Write the "methods" when you think they are mature/materializing.

Golden rule—any difficulty in writing means there is a problem with the methods.

(*iv*) Write "results" and "discussions" after spending enough time on analysing and interpreting.

(*v*) Spend little bit of time daily with your evolving paper. Try to be a critical reader or reviewer to bring out the best out of it.

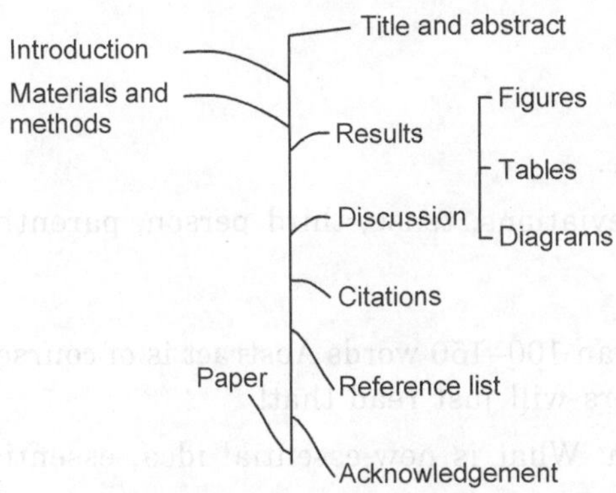

Figure 4.1 Parts of a scientific paper

Finally, Preparing Paper for Submission

Very few will read your paper in a thorough and deliberate way, from beginning to end. Remember you have to market your paper for the casual readers!

1. **Title and Abstract**—are for search engines most readers won't go beyond that!
2. **Results:** Figures + Captions and Table + Footnotes:
   (*i*) They must be self-contained. A lot of readers go through these without reading the text and some look for quick explanation in text.
   (*ii*) Make figures attractive.
3. Remember that the take-home message of your paper should be "in your face", *i.e.*, in abstract, introduction and conclusions.

Make sure that everyone gets the message!

GUIDELINES FOR WRITING A SCIENTIFIC PAPER

Writing an effective paper is not easy. A good rule of thumb is to write as if your paper will be read by a person who knows about the field in general but doesn't already know what you did. You should read some scientific papers that have been written in a format which you plan to use and then plan to write a scientific paper.

Typical Outline of a Paper

Style and Format of a Paper:

Abstract.

Introduction.

Materials and Methods.

Results.

Tables and Figures.

Discussion.

Citations.

Reference lists.

Genetic nomenclature.

Format : flow, abbreviations, tense, third person, parenthesis, proof reading.

Abstract

Typically not more than 100–150 words Abstract is of course the most important part of the paper—many readers will just read that!

- Try to focus on: What is new-essential idea, essential number.
- Try to write one fact/idea per sentence.
- Try to give everything that you want the casual reader to remember!

The abstract must not contain reference. Avoid use of "in this paper" in the abstract.

Introduction

(Brief!).

Introduction lets reader to know what this paper is about.

Points to remember :

(*i*) introduce problem.

(*ii*) outline solution.

(*iii*) also include a clear statement why the problem is important.

How to Write

Begin with a mini-review and finish the introduction by saying what your paper is about.

Direct Approach

1st paragraph

- state the problem succinctly.
  - do not encumber with too many references.
  - tell in one sentence what your paper is about at the end of first para.

2nd and following paragraph

- you have already told the reader what your paper is about.
- give – the background information.
  – what people have done before.
- limitations etc. (give references).
- Last paragraph: elaborate on what you will be doing in your paper.

Methods

Write this as soon as you think that your methods are mature. The writing process will make you check whether your method is really mature. Provide useful reference for future modelers to use.

Results

Start by presenting your results (Figure X shows....) and then discuss what they mean. Logically linear flow of thoughts is essential. Write one theme per paragraph.

1st sentence lays out the theme and the last one provides link to the next paragraph. It should be between 1/2–1 page.

Focus on what you can say with confidence.

Comparison of Model (Results) with Observations

Comparisons with observations should have a clear purpose in terms of learning.

Conclusions

Most papers need a conclusions section. A default approach is to treat it as an extended abstract. But, this is also an opportunity to be **reflective about what you learned**, what uncertainties are remaining, links to other problems, etc.

1st para — focus on what you did.

Following paras — one major finding per para.
1st sentence states finding, following sentence elaborates.

Final para — it should have some forward-looking perspective.

Please do not let your paper finish on a whimper!

References (Bibliography)

Important Points

- Be serious about search and reading papers. Devote a bit of time to this each day.
- Never cite a paper for which you have not read at least the relevant part.
- Cite papers in a context that makes it clear what the paper did, otherwise the reference is useless.
- If you are not clear on what the cited paper did, then re-read it.
- Do not cite textbooks.
- There is nothing wrong in citing yourself or your group extensively. But do not ignore what others have done!
- Reference should be helpful to the reader, but, not of historical interest!

→ Remember that extensive referencing is the scholarly and ethical thing to do.

→ Follow the Universal guidelines of citation authority or guidelines of the journal intended for submission Don'ts.

Avoid use of et al. in a bibliography unless list is very long (5 or more authors).

Acknowledgements

- Acknowledge your funding source. List the grant number. Write text like "This work was supported by the National Science Foundation under grant EIA NN—NNNNN".
- Generally, anonymous reviewers don't get acknowledged, unless they really provided an exceptional level of feedback or insight.

Things to Avoid

1. Avoid too much motivational material, unnecessary details.
2. Avoid spelling errors:
    - spelling checkers are also available.
    - ask your colleague to edit your spelling.
    - consult a dictionary such as **Merriam Webster** (online).
3. Avoid text in arial, unusual fonts. Use Times Roman.

REVIEW ARTICLES

Review

Review articles are very popular and readers like reviews because they are part of the solution to the problem of keeping up, with the ever expanding literature.

Most commonly, reviews are written by invitation from editor of a traditional journal. Sometimes, there are journals and magazines entirely devoted to review articles, and again most of them are obtained by invitation.

Characteristics of Good Reviewer

Reviewer is generally an expert in the chosen field. However, to produce a good piece of work, considerable time and access to extensive library search are needed.

Selection of Topic for a Review

Usually subjects are suggested by person assigning/inviting the review. Sometimes author himself approaches an editor for writing a review on his own topic. Considerable experience and authority are required to write a review article.

Searching Material for Review Article

In the days of computer literature searching, it is easier to search the essential references for the article. However, reviewer must visit the library because sometimes related articles that are not revealed by computer search can be picked up. Care should be taken regarding incorporating unpublished observations and personal communications, since these cannot be verified by the reader.

Contents of Review

The review contents should be in the following order:

(*i*) what is the problem
(*ii*) background
(*iii*) basic science
(*iv*) methodology
(*v*) animal studies
(*vi*) human studies
(*vii*) discussion
(*viii*) conclusion
(*ix*) recommendations
(*x*) future prospects

In addition, review should contain a glossary of terms. Also, an abstract or summary is desired by certain journals.

Layout of Review

While writing a review, one should adhere to instructions for authors of a particular journal. It should be typed on A4 paper, double spaced, should have 300 words per page.

Also, it should be supported by appropriate references to address its contentious issues using key publications and items. Also, it should be supported by tables and figures. And if tables or figures are to be reproduced from any copyright material, then written permission must be obtained from the copyright holder.

Care should be taken regarding mis-spelling, errors in the text. Typeface used should be serif typeface (*e.g.*, Times Roman) and most journals accept manuscript online, by e-mail or computer disk (CD), but still some journals request 2–3 copies of printed version. Also, one should keep a copy of what is actually sent to the journal for making changes in the future.

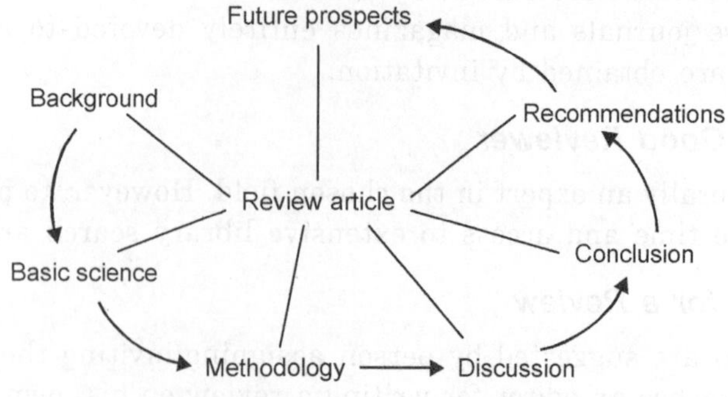

Figure 4.2 Components of review article

References quoted in bibliography should be according to style and format required by requesting journal. *e.g.*, Vancouver style.

A good review should help the reader to discern the relevant pros and cons easily and have the key references for confirmation and further information.

REPORTS

Research report is considered a major component of the research study for the research task. The purpose of research is not well served until the report has been presented and/or written.

Steps in Writing Report

1. Logical analysis of the subject matter.
2. Preparation of final outline.
3. Preparation of rough draft.
4. Preparation of final draft out of rough draft.
5. Preparation of bibliography.
6. Writing the final draft.

It must be kept in mind that every report should be an attempt to solve some intellectual problem and must contribute to the solution of a problem. Also, it should add to the knowledge of both the researcher and the reader.

Layout of Research Report

Aim of writing a research report is that anyone reading the research report must be conveyed enough about the study. It should comprise

1. preliminary pages.
2. main text.
3. end matter.

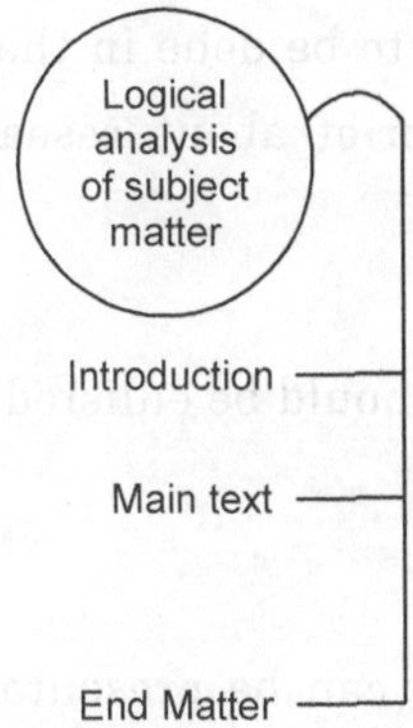

Figure 4.3 Research report layout

Preliminary pages

They should carry

- Title date.
- acknowledgement in form of Preface (forward).
- table of contents.
- list of tables and illustrations.

Main text

It provides outline of research report along with all details

(*i*) **Introduction—**highlighting why the problem was considered worth investigating alongwith background and relevant research of others, hypothesis of study, if any and methodology adopted should be explained in detail : how study was carried out, basic design of study, details of experimental manipulation; instructions/ questionnaire if any, details of sample used: who were the subjects, their number, selection criteria, statistical analysis adopted. Also scope of the study should be explained.

(*ii*) Statement of findings and recommendations.

(*iii*) **Results—**findings of the study should be presented in detail in the form of tables, charts.

(*iv*) **Implications** drawn from the results:

(*a*) inference drawn from the study.

(*b*) generalizations of this inference.

(*c*) relevant questions that still remain unanswered or few questions by the study alongwith suggestion for kind of research that would provide answers for them.

The report should finish with a short conclusion that summarises and recapitulates the main points of the study.

Also, a forecast of probable future of the subject and an indication of kind of research that needs to be done in that particular field is also essential.

(*v*) **Summary.** Summary in brief about research problem, major findings and major conclusions drawn.

End matter

At the end of report, appendices should be enlisted. Bibliography of sources consulted should also be given.

Types of Report

Results of research investigation can be presented in a number of ways *viz.*:

1. Technical report.
2. Popular report.
3. Article.
4. Monograph.
5. Oral presentation.

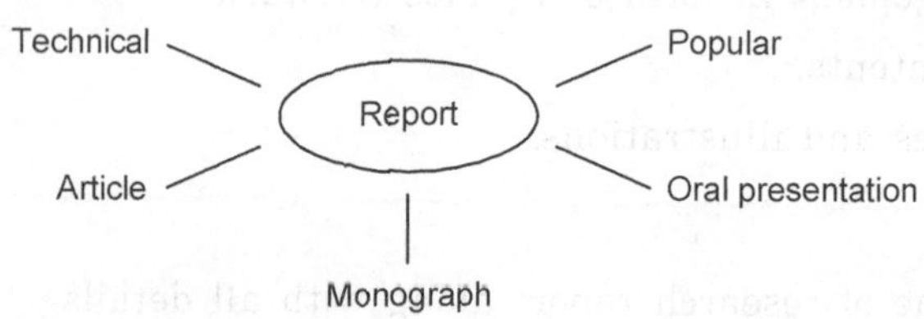

Figure 4.4 Ways of Report—presentation

Technical Report

It is used whenever a full written report of the study is required whether for record-keeping or for public dissemination.

Outline

(*i*) **Summary of results:** in 2–3 pages.

(*ii*) **Nature of study:**

- objective.
- formulation of problem.
- hypothesis.
- type of analysis data required.

(*iii*) **Methods employed:** details of sample design

(*iv*) **Data:**

- discussion of source, characteristics, limitation of data collected.
- in case of survey, description of details of data collection.

(*v*) **Analysis of data and presentation** of findings—in form of tables and charts.

(*vi*) **conclusions.**

(*vii*) **bibliography.**

(*viii*) **technical appendices.**

(*ix*) **index.**

Popular Report

Popular report is used if research results have policy implications. Technical details are minimized. It requires attractive layout with many subheadings and emphasis on practical aspects and policy implications.

Oral Presentation

At time, oral presentation of the results of the study is considered effective, particularly in cases where policy recommendations are indicated by project results.

Use of slide, wall charts and blackboards are used.

Thus, report-writing is an art which is learnt by practice and experience.

THESIS AND DISSERTATION

Students enrolled for an honours degree, a postgraduate degree or a doctoral degree are almost invariably required to submit a thesis or dissertation. The terms "Thesis" and "Dissertation" are often used interchangeably. However in Indian University, thesis is considered as higher than the dissertation on the basis of the fact that for the Ph.D. degree, the requirement of thesis is imposed; and for the lower degrees of MA/MSc, MEd, MPhil, the requirement is that of a dissertation.

The thesis is divided into three broad sections:

(*i*) Preliminary section.

(*ii*) Main body.

(*iii*) Reference section.

Subsections of Thesis

The main body of thesis is divided into different sub-sections such as:

(*i*) introduction.

(*ii*) review of literature.

(*iii*) design of study.

(*iv*) presentation and analysis.

(*v*) summary.

(*vi*) conclusion.

The reference section includes bibliography, appendices and index in a proper form.

Qualities of a Good Research Thesis

Before writing the thesis a good deal of planning is necessary. It facilitates thesis writing with proper emphasis on different aspects.

A good thesis must have clarity of both thought as well as language to help the reader to grasp the ideas of the researcher easily. Also, presentation of report is also a vital factor. The thesis should neither be too voluminous nor too concise.

There should be chapters, sections, sub-sections, headings, sub-headings, tables and diagrams.

There is no unique and universally accepted method of writing the thesis. The thesis must be written in drafts one after the other. Ideas and sentences are to be re-aligned and the material must be carefully re-examined and re-edited.

Summary of Thesis

Along with the thesis, a summary is prepared, soft-bound separately and submitted.

The summary is sent to the evaluators in advance to obtain their consent to examine the full thesis.

Summary should consist of a brief review of all that has been done and found in the thesis. Summary is a statement in brief of theoretical rationale, hypothesis, procedures and results and is the most widely read part of any thesis.

HOW TO WRITE REFERENCES BIBLIOGRAPHY OF RESEARCH PAPER: VANCOUVER STYLE

NOTE:

- A list of references **contains details only of those works** cited in the text.
- A **bibliography** lists sources **not cited in the text** but which are relevant to the subject and were used for background reading.
- **Before** you compile your bibliography/reference list **check with your lecturer/tutor** for the bibliographic style **preferred** by the Academic Department.
- A citation is an acknowledgement in your text of references that support your work. It is in the form of a number that correlates with a source in your reference list.
- There are many ways of setting out bibliographies and reference lists. The following are examples of **one style–the Vancouver System**. It is commonly used in medical and scientific journals.
- Your **reference list** should identify references cited (*e.g.*, book, journal article, pamphlet, internet site, cassette tape or film) in sufficient detail so that others may locate and consult your references.

- Your **reference list** should appear at the end of your essay/report with the entries listed numerically and in the same order that they have been cited in the text.
- If you have cited sources from the Internet, these should be in your reference list.
- The **bibliography** is a *separate list* from the reference list and should be arranged **alphabetically** by author or title (where no author is given) in the Vancouver Style.
- **Punctuation marks** and **spaces** in the reference list and citations are very important. Follow the punctuation and spacing exactly in the examples given.

Indicating References in the Text of Your Essay

It is important to BE CONSISTENT when you are referencing.

- In the Vancouver Style, citations within the text of your essay/paper are identified by Arabic numbers in round brackets. This applies to references in text, tables and figures, *e.g.,* (2) this is the style used by the referencing software Endnote.
- The identification of references **within the text** of your essay/paper may vary according to the preferred style of the journal or the preferred style of the department or lecturer. For example **superscript** may be preferred when referencing.
- The Vancouver System assigns a number to each reference as it is cited. A number must be used even if the author(s) is named in the sentence/text.
Example: Smith (10) has argued that....
- The **original number assigned** to the reference is reused each time the reference is cited in the text, regardless of its previous position in the text.
- When **multiple references** are cited at a given place in the text, use a **hyphen** to join the first and last numbers that are **inclusive**. Use **commas** (without spaces) to separate **non-inclusive** numbers in a multiple citation *e.g.*, 2, 3, 4, 5, 7, 10 is abbreviated to (2-5, 7, 10) **Do not** use a hyphen if there are no citation numbers in between that support your statement *e.g.*, 1-2.
- The placement of citation numbers within text should be carefully considered, for example a particular reference may be relevant to only part of a sentence. As a general rule, reference numbers should be placed outside full stops and commas, inside colons and semicolons; however, this may vary according to the requirements of a particular journal.

Examples:

There have been efforts to replace mouse inoculation testing with in vitro tests, such as enzyme linked immunosorbent assays (57,60) or polymerase chain reaction, (20-22) but these remain experimental.

Moir and Jessel maintain "that the sexes are interchangeable". (1)

Citing a Book

The essential details required are (in order):

1. **Name/s** of author/s, editor/s, compiler/s or the institution responsible.
    - Where there are 6 or less authors you must list all authors.
    - Where there are 7 or more authors, only the first 6 are listed and add "et al" (et al means "and others").
    - Put a comma and 1 space between each name. The last author must have a full-stop after their initial(s).

    Format: surname (1 space) initial/s (no spaces or punctuation between initials) (full-stop OR if further names comma, 1 space)

    Example 1.1: Smith AK, Jones BC, editors.

    Example 1.2: Smith AK, Jones BC, Bloggs TC, Ashe PT, Fauci AS, Wilson JD et al.

    Example 1.3: The Cardiac Society of Australia and New Zealand.

    Example 1.4: When no author is given "Anonymous" or "Anon" is unnecessary. Us the title of the article or book.

2. **Title** of publication and subtitle if any
    - Do not use italics or underlining.
    - Only the first word of journal articles or book titles (and words that normally begin with a capital letter) are **capitalised.**

    Format: 1: title (full-stop, 1 space)

    Example 2.1: Harrison's principles of internal medicine.

    Example 2.2: Physical pharmacy: physical chemical principles in the pharmaceutical sciences.

    Example 2.3: Pharmacy in Australia: the national experience

3. **Edition,** if other than first edition.
    - Abbreviate the word edition to:- ed. (Do not confuse with editor.)

    Format: edition statement (fullstop, 1 space)

    Example 3.1: 3rd ed.

4. **Place of publication**
    - If the publishers are located in more than one city, cite the name of the city that is printed first.
    - Write the place name in full.
    - If the place name is not well known, add a comma, 1 space and the state or the country for clarification. For places in the USA, add after the place name the 2 letter postal code for the state. This must be in upper case *e.g.*, Hartford (CN): (where CN=Connecticut). For more information see: <http://www.usps.com/ncsc/lookups/usps_abbreviations.htm>.

Format: place of publication (colon, 1 space)

Example 4.1: Hartford (CN):

Example 4.2: Texas (NSW):

Example 4.3: Kyoto (Japan):

5. **Publisher**

   - The publisher's name should be spelt out in full.

   Format: publisher (semi-colon, 1 space)

   Example 5.1: Australian Government Publishing Service;

   Example 5.2: Raven Press;

   Example 5.3: Williams & Wilkins;

6. **Year of publication.**

   Format: year (full-stop, add 1 space if page numbers follow)
   Example 6.1: 1999.

   Example 6.2: 2000. p. 12-5.

7. **Page numbers** (if applicable).

   - Abbreviate the word page to "p.".
   - NOTE: do not repeat digits unnecessarily–abbreviate.

   Format: p (full-stop, 1 space) page numbers (full-stop).
   Example 7.1: p. 122-9.

   Example 7.2: p. 1129-57.

   Example 7.3: p. 333,338,340-5. (when article not on continuous pages)

8. **Series title and individual volume (if any).**

   - Put in brackets.
   - Abbreviate the word volume to "vol".

   Format: (Series title (semi-colon, 1 space) vol (1 space) volume number) full-stop outside brackets
   Example 8.1: (Annals of the New York academy of sciences; vol 288).

Examples of Citing Books

- **One to six authors**

  Getzen TE. Health economics: fundamentals of funds. New York: John Wiley & Sons; 1997.

Explanation of above citation:

Author	**TITLE**	
↓	↓	
Getzen TE.	Health economics: fundamentals	
New York:	and flow of funds.	1997.
	John Wiley & Sons;	
↑	↑	↑
PLACE OF PUBLICATION	**PUBLISHER**	**YEAR OF PUBLICATION**

Lodish H, Baltimore D, Berk A, Zipursky SL, Matsudaira P, Darnell J. Molecular cell biology. 3rd ed. New York: Scientific American; 1995.

- **More than six authors**

  Give the first six names in full and add "et al". The authors are listed in the order in which they appear on the title page.

  Fauci AS, Braunwald E, Isselbacher KJ, Wilson JD, Martin JB, Kasper DL, et al, editors. Harrison's principles of internal medicine. 14th ed. New York: McGraw Hill, Health Professions Division; 1998.

- **Editor/s**

  Follow the same methods used with authors but use the word "editor" or "editors" in full after the name/s. The word editor or editors must be in lower case. (Do NOT confuse with "ed." used for *edition.*)

  Millares M, editor. Applied drug information: strategies for information management. Vancouver (WA): Applied Therapeutics, Inc.; 1998.

- **Sponsored by institution, corporation or other organisation (including PAMPHLET)**

  Australian Pharmaceutical Advisory Council. Integrated best practice model for medication management in residential aged care facilities. Canberra: Australian Government Publishing Service; 1997.

  Example of pamphlet (if available include additional information e.g., place of production, printer):

  Pharmaceutical Society of Australia. Medicines and driving [pamphlet]. Pharmaceutical Society of Australia; 1998. DR-7.

- **Package insert (leaflet supplied with medicine):**

  Lamasil [package insert]. East Hanover (NJ): Sandoz Pharmaceuticals Corp; 1993.

- **Edition (other than first)**

  Blenkinsopp A, Paxton P. Symptoms in the pharmacy: a guide to the management of common illness. 3rd ed. Oxford: Blackwell Science; 1998.

- **Chapter or part of a book to which a number of authors have contributed**

  Porter RJ, Meldrum BS. Antiepileptic drugs. In: Katzung BG, editor. Basic and clinical pharmacology. 6th ed. Norwalk (CN): Appleton and Lange; 1995. p. 361-80.

- **Dictionary and similar references**

  Stedman's medical dictionary. 26th ed. Baltimore: Williams & Wilkins; 1995. Apraxia; p. 119-20.

  Note: Include the Definition looked up–in this case "Apraxia"

- **Book in a Series**

  Bennett GL, Horuk R. lodination of chemokines for use in receptor binding analysis. In: Horuk R, editor. Chemokine receptors. New York (NY): Academic Press; 1997. p. 134-48. (Methods in enzymology; vol 288).

  Chemokine receptors = name of the book

  Methods in enzymology = title of the series

- **Encyclopaedia**

  Hanrahan C. Valerian. In: Krapp K, Longe JL, editors. The Gale encyclopedia of alternative medicine. Michigan: Gale Group; 2001. vol 4 p. 1768-70.

- **Legal Material**

  Note: (s = section of act, r = regulation)

  Pharmacy Act 1976 (old)

  Airlines Equipment Amendment Act 1981 (Cwlth), s. 19(1)(a)(ii)

  Public Service Regulations (Cwlth), r.83(2)(a)(ii)

Citing A Journal Article

The essential details required are (in order):

1. **Name/s** of author/s of the article.

   See step 1 of "Citing a book" for full details.

2. **Title of article.**

   See step 2 of "Citing a book" for full details.

   Example 2.1: Validation of an immunoassay for measurement of plasma total homocysteine.

3. **Title of journal (abbreviated).**

   - Abbreviate title according to the style used in Medline. A list of abbreviations can be found at:

     http://www.ncbi.nlm.nih.gov/entrez/query.fcgi?db=journals

   - Note: no punctuation marks are used in the abbreviated journal name–just spaces.

   Format: journal title abbreviation (1 space)

Example 3.1: Bol Soc Dent Guatem Example 3.2: J Mol Biol

4. **Year (and month/day if necessary/available) of publication.**

- Abbreviate the month to the first 3 letters.

Format: year (1 space) month (1 space) day (semi-colon, no space) OR year (semi-colon, no space)

Example 4.1: 1996 Jun 1; 12(5): 127-33.

5. **Volume number (and issue/part–).**

   - *If the journal has continuous page numbering through volume's issues, the month/day and issue information may be omitted.

Format: volume number (no space) issue number in brackets (colon, no space) *OR* volume number (colon, no space)

Example 5.1: 1996;12(5):127-33. or 1996; 12:127-33

6. **Page numbers**

NOTE: do not repeat digits unnecessarily

Format: page numbers (full-stop)

Example 6.1: 531-5

Examples of Citing Journals

NOTE SOME JOURNALS MAY HAVE:

- A day, month and year.
- A month and year.
- A season and year e.g., Autumn 2001.
- Only a year.

Russell FD, Coppell AL, Davenport AP. In vitro enzymatic processing of radiolabelled big ET-1 in human kidney as a food ingredient. Biochem Pharmacol 1998 Mar 1;55(5): 697-701.

Explanation of above citation:

AUTHORS ↓ — TITLE OF ARTICLE ↓

Russell FD, Coppell AL, Davenport AP. In vitro enzymatic processing of radiolabelled big ET-1 in human kidney as a food ingredient. Biochem Pharmacol 1998 Mar 1;55(5):697-701.

↑ TITLE OF JOURNAL — ↑ PUBLICATION YR/MO/DAY — ↑ VOLUME/ ISSUE NO. — ↑ PAGE NO.S

NOTE: Choose an option and be consistent

Option 1: Month and day (if available) may be omitted only if continuous paging through issues.

Option 2: Month/day (if available) and issue number (if available) are important if the pages in the journal are non-continuous

Option 3: Continuous page numbers (most journals have this)-may omit month/day and issue number. Example below.

Russell FD, Coppell AL, Davenport AP. In vitro enzymatic processing of radiolabelled big ET-1 in human kidney as a food ingredient. Biochem Pharmacol 1998;55:697-701.

No author given in article

Coffee drinking and cancer of the pancreas [editorial]. BMJ 1981;283:628.

Journals with parts and/or supplements

Examples:

Volume with supplement:

Environ Health Perspect 1994;102 Suppl 1:275-82.

Issue with supplement:

Semin Oncol 1996:23(1 Suppl 2):89-97.

Volume with part:

Ann Clin Biochem 1995; 32 (Pt 3):303-6.

Issue with part:

N Z Med J 1994;107(986 Pt 1):377-8.

Issue with no volume:

Clin Orthop 1995;(320):110-4.

No issue or volume:

Curr Opin Gen Surg 1993:325-33.

Citing Conferences

Treat the proceedings of a conference like a book, adding pertinent information about the conference and cite a presentation from the proceedings like a work in a collection of pieces by different authors:

Conference Papers

Bengtsson S, Solheim BG. Enforcement of data protection, privacy and security in medical informatics. In: Lun KC, Degoulet P, Piemme TE, Reinhoff O, editors. MEDINFO 92. Proceedings of the 7th World Congress on Medical Informatics; 1992 Sep 6-10; Geneva, Switzerland. Amsterdam: North-Holland; 1992. p. 1561-5.

Conference Proceeding

Kimura J, Shibasaki H, editors. Recent advances in clinical neurophysiology. Proceedings of the 10th International Congress of EMG and Clinical Neurophysiology; 1995 Oct 15-19; Kyoto, Japan. Amsterdam: Elsevier; 1996.

Citing A Newspaper Article

The details may vary depending on the layout of the newspaper *e.g.*, section may not be relevant.

Format: Author if given (full-stop, 1 space) **Title of article** (full-stop, 1 space) **Name of newspaper** (1 space) **Date of edition** (year Month Day) (semi-colon, no space) **Section** if applicable (section abbreviated to Sect.) (colon, no space) **Page/s** (1 space) **Column number** in round brackets (column abbreviated to col.) (full-stop)

> Lee G. Hospitalizations tied to ozone pollution: study estimates 50,000 admissions annually. The Washington Post 1996 Jun 21; Sect. A:3 (col. 5).

Citing Multimedia Material

The details required are the same as for a book, with the form of the item indicated in brackets after the title and edition statement.

> Get the facts (and get them organised) [videocassette]. Williamstown (Vic): Appleseed Productions; 1990.

Citing Internet and Other Electronic Sources

- This includes software and Internet sources such as web sites, electronic journals and databases.
- These sources are proliferating and the guidelines for citation are developing and subject to change.
- The following information is based on the recommendations of the National Library of Medicine.
- The **basic form** of the citations **follows the principles listed for print sources** (see above).

In the case of sources that may be subject to alteration it is important to acknowledge the **DATE THE INFORMATION WAS CITED.** This is particularly true for web sites that may disappear or permit changes to be made and for CD-ROMS that are updated during the year.

Journal on the Internet

NOTE: Follow the same procedure for citing print journals as for electronic journals regarding date, volume pages and journal title

Format: Author/s (full-stop after last author, 1 space) **Title of article** (full-stop, 1 space) **Abbreviated title of electronic journal** (1 space) **[serial online]** (1 space) **Publication year** (1 space) **month(s)** - if available (1 space) **[cited year month (abbreviated) day]** -in square brackets (semi colon, 1 space) **Volume number** (no space) **Issue number** if applicable in round brackets (colon) **Page numbers or number of screens** in square brackets (full-stop, 1 space) **Available from** (colon, 1 space) URL: **URL address underlined.**

Examples:

Morse SS. Factors in the emergence of infectious disease. Emerg Infect Dis [serial online] 1995 Jan-Mar [cited 1999 Dec 25]; 1(1):[24 screens]. Available from:URL:http://www/cdc/gov/ncidoc/EID/eid.htm

Garfinkel PE, Lin E, Goering P. Should amenorrhoea be necessary for the diagnosis of anorexia nervosa? Br J Psych [serial online] 1996 [cited 1999 Aug 17]; 168(4):500-6. Available from: URL:http://biomed.niss.ac.uk

WWW Site

(If the author is not documented, the title becomes the first element of the reference.)

Format: Author (full-stop after last author, 1 space) **Title** (full-stop, 1 space) **[Online]** (full stop, 1 space) **Publication Year** (1 space) **[cited year month (abbreviated) day]** (semi colon) **Number of screens in square brackets or pages** (full-stop, 1 space) **Available from** (colon, 1 space) URL: (no space) **URL address underlined**

NOTE:
- The number of screens is NOT necessary. Put a semi colon and 1 space after the cited date if no pages or screen numbers are listed.
- When the date is approximated, indicate that by following the date with a question mark and inserting the statement in square brackets. *e.g.*, [2001?]

Examples:

National Organization for Rare Diseases [Online]. 1999 Aug 16 [cited 1999 Aug 21]; Available from: URL:http://www.rarediseases.org/

Royal College of General Practitioners. The primary health care team. [Online]. 1998 [cited 1999 Aug 22];[10 screens]. Available from: URL:http://ww.rcgp.org.uk/informat/publicat/rcf0021.htm

Zand J. The natural pharmacy: herbal medicine for depression [Online]. [1999?] [cited 2001 Aug 23];[15 screens]. Available from: URL:http://www.healthy.net/asp/templates/Article.asp?PageType=Article&Id=920

Web Based/Online Databases

[Basic Format:]

Author/editor, (full stop, 1 space) **Title** (full stop, 1 space) **[type of medium = Online]** (full stop, 1 space) **Publishing details** if available. **Available from:** (1 space) **Title and publishing details of the database if available, [cited date]** (full stop)

Kirkpatrick GL. Viral infections of the respiratory tract. In: Family Medicine. 5th ed. [Online]. 1998. Available from: Stat!Ref. Jackson (WY): Teton Data Systems; 2001. [cited 2001 Aug 31].

This is a chapter within an online book. Publication comes out quarterly therefore needs a cited date.

CD-ROM

[Basic Format:] Follow Book format:

- add [type of medium] after the title (full stop, 1 space) - Note: [type of medium] can be:-[CD ROM], [serial on CD-ROM] or [book on CD]
- add Version number (if available) after type of medium (full stop, 1 space)

  Clinical pharmacology 2000 [CD-ROM]. Version 2.01. [cited 2001 Aug 7]; Gainsville (FL): Gold Standard Multimedia; 2001.

  Note: this publication comes out quarterly therefore it needs a cited date.

Books on CD-ROM

Examples:

The Oxford English dictionary [book on CD-ROM]. 2nd ed. New York (NY): Oxford University Press; 1992.

Paracetamol. Martindale's: *the extra pharmacopoeia. In: International Heatthcare Series* [CD ROM], [cited 1998 Sep 3]; Englewood (CO): Micromedex; 1998.

Journal on CD-ROM

Format: Author/s (full-stop, 1 space) **Title of article** (full-stop, 1 space) **Abbreviated title of journal** (1 space) **[serial on CD-ROM] Year** (semi-colon, no space) **Volume** (colon, no space) **Pages** (full-stop)

Example:

Gershon ES. Antisocial behavior. Arch Gen Psychiatry [serial on CD-ROM]. 1995;52:900-901.

Other Software

Format: Title (1 space) **medium in square brackets** [*e.g.,* computer program, computer file] (full-stop, 1 space) **Version** (full-stop, 1 space) **Place of production** (colon, 1 space) **Producer** (semi-colon, 1 space) **Year** (full-stop).

Example:

Epi Info [computer program]. Version 6. Atlanta (GA): Centers for Disease Control and Prevention; 1994.

ADDITIONAL NOTES ON THE VANCOUVER STYLE

☞ TABLES

- Each table should be given a brief title.
- Number each table in the text in consecutive order.
- Explanatory matter is placed in footnotes, not in the heading.

☞ ILLUSTRATIONS and FIGURES

- Number each figure in the text in consecutive order.
- The original source should be acknowledged.
- The legends should be labelled with numerals corresponding to the figures etc.

☞ MEASUREMENT

- Length, height, weight and volume should be reported in metric units.
- Temperatures should be in degrees Celsius.
- Blood Pressure measured in mm of mercury.
- All haematological and biochemistry measurements stated in SI units.

☞ ABBREVIATIONS and SYMBOLS

- Use only standard abbreviations. Consult the following for abbreviations:

Committee on Form and Style of the Council of Biology Editors. CBE style manual. 3rd ed. Washington: American Institute of Biological Sciences; 1972. (5th ed. Available at PAH)	Z250.6.B5C6 1972 SS&H
Iverson C, Flanagin A, Fontanarosa PB, Glass RM, Glitman P, Lantz JC, et al. American Medical Association manual of style: a guide for authors and editors. 9th ed. Baltimore, MD: Williams and Wilkins; 1998.	Ref R119.A533 1998 Biol
O'Connor M, Woodford FP. Writing scientific papers in English: an ELSE-Ciba Foundation guide for authors. Amsterdam: North-Holland; 1975.	T11.O2 1975 Biol/PSE/SS&H/Gatton/ HML/PAH

A SAMPLE REFERENCE LIST

- The following are examples of entries in a bibliography or list of references.
- A list of references contains details only of those works cited in the text.
- The references are listed in the same numerical order as they appear in the body of the text

1. Getzen TE. Health economics: fundamentals and flow of funds. New York (NY): John Wiley & Sons; 1997.
2. Millares M, editor. Applied drug information: strategies for information management. Vancouver, WA: Applied Therapeutics, Inc.; 1998.
3. Australian Government Publishing Service. Style manual for authors, editors and printers. 5th ed. Canberra: Australian Government Publishing Service; 1994.

4. Australian Pharmaceutical Advisory Council. Integrated best practice model for medication management in residential aged care facilities. Canberra: Australian Government Publishing Service; 1997.
5. Bennett GL, Horuk R. lodination of chemokines for use in receptor binding analysis. In: Horuk R, editor. Chemokine receptors. New York (NY): Academic Press; 1997. p. 134-48. (Methods in enzymology; vol 288).
6. Coffee drinking and cancer of the pancreas [editorial]. BMJ 1981;283:628.
7. Morse SS. Factors in the emergence of infectious disease. Emerg Infect Dis [serial online] 1995 Jan-Mar [cited 1996 June 5]; 1(1):[24 screens]. Available from: URL:http://www.cdc.gov/ncidoc/EID/eid.htm
8. Iyer V. Farquhar C. Jepson R. The effectiveness of oral contraceptive pills versus placebo or any other medical treatment for menorrhagia. (Cochrane Review) In: The Cochrane Library, Issue 4, Oxford: Update Software; 1998.
9. Standard 6: Preparation of cytoxic drug products. In: Australian pharmaceutical formulary and handbook. 17th ed. Parkville, Vic: Pharmaceutical Society of Australia. 2000. p. 101-8.
10. Ampicillin. In: Australian medicines handbook 2000. Adelaide (SA): Australian Medicines Handbook. 2000. p. 5-35-6.0

Further information can be obtained from:

- Australian Government Publishing Service. Style manual for authors editors and printers. 5th ed. Canberra: Australian Government Publishing Service; 1994.
- International Committee of Medical Journal Editors. Uniform requirements for manuscripts submitted to biomedical journals. Med Educ 1999; 33:66-78.
- Iverson C, Flanagin A, Fontanarosa PB, Glass RM, Glitman P, Lantz JC, et al. American Medical Association manual of style: a guide for authors and editors. 9th ed. Baltimore: Williams & Wilkins; 1998.
- Li X, Crane N. Electronic styles: a handbook for citing electronic information. Medford (NJ): Information Today; 1996.

SUMMARY

Writing scientific paper, research report or presenting a research data for oral presentation is an art which comes with careful planning, practice and experience. This unit aims to make the reader conversant with basic features of planning and writing their research articles, reports.

REVIEW QUESTIONS

1. What is a scientific paper?
2. How will you rate a scientific paper?
3. What do you mean by uniform guidelines for submission of an article?
4. Give details of style and format of scientific paper.

5. How will compute your observations?
6. What should be the layout of the report?
7. How to plan and write a dissertation?
8. What is a scientific document?
9. What are the qualities of a good research paper?
10. What is the layout of a review?
11. What are the ways in which results can be computed?
12. What are different types of reports?
13. Plan a 'research plan' and give the proposed layout of the same.
14. If you are given a review article on "role of biotechnology in cardio vascular disease", write the points of its contents.
15. In the same topic given above. What recommendations and future prospects would you write.
16. How will you write your research paper?
17. Give outline of a paper.
18. Suppose you have to subunit a technical report on gene cloning, give the layout of same.
19. If you have to present an oral presentation on "diagnostic uses of biotechnology", write layout of the presentation.
20. Suppose an MPhil student is assigned a dissertation on "gene mapping for a genetic disease". Write the headings for its synopsis (research plan).

Chapter 5

SCIENTIFIC LITERATURE

WRITING AN ABSTRACT FOR A SCIENTIFIC MEETING

Scientific programme includes a limited spaces for presentation of abstracts, either as oral communications or posters.

Preparation of Abstract

One should follow the instructions for writing an abstract. It should have the following headings:

(*i*) Title.

(*ii*) Authors—name of author; name and address of affiliated institution, telephone number, e-mail address.

(*iii*) Background.

(*iv*) Aim of study.

(*v*) Study design.

(*vi*) Results.

(*vii*) Discussion.

(*viii*) Conclusion and implications.

Writing an abstract is only the first phase. Next is to convert it into an oral presentation or a poster.

USING THE COMPUTER IN RESEARCH

Computer has become an essential tool in biotechnology research. It may be used for routine jobs of word processing and data collection and analysis. Also when connected to internet, it may be used for searching biomedical (biotechnology) literature, accessing information about nucleic acid and protein sequences, predicting protein structure, seeking research methodology and searching databases of genome program.

Title

Authors
Affiliation

Abstract

Background
Aim
Methods
Results
Discussion
Conclusion (100–400 words)

Figure 5.1 Preparation of abstract for oral presentation.

Computer and Internet

By using computers one can greatly broaden it use to some of the following:

(*i*) Searching the biomedical literature for pertinent books and journal articles.

(ii) Accessing biological databases that provide nucleic acid and protein sequences and structures.

Once connected to internet, many programs are available as **free ware**, softwares are provided without charge by its creator.

Basic Facilities Available for Use on Internet for Researchers

e-mail (electronic mail)

One can communicate by e-mail. Messages containing text, files, and graphics may be sent to anyone who has a computer with an internet link and e-mail address. Communications among scientists is now done primarily by e-mail. Also, one can join list server discussion groups such as USE NET.

World Wide Web (www or web)

It has become most rapidly growing component of the internet since its launching in 1992. It permits transfer of data as pages in multimedia form consisting of text, graphs, audio and video. The pages are linked together by hypertext pointers so that data stored on computers in different locations may be retrieved via network by one's computer. To access all the resources on web, one needs a **browser** (that reads hypertext and displays web pages on computer) and common web browsers are: Internet Explorer, Netscape Navigator.

To access web, web browser is activated and on screen home page will be displayed. The dialogue box on this page asks for "address", "netsite", "location" or "URL" (Uniform Resource Locater), Type in the web page address which is usually in the form http:// w.w.w.—The home page, with instructions on the use of the website will be displayed on the screen. One important feature to be noted is that some words on the page are highlighted. If any one of these words are clicked by mouse, the computer gets connected to another, related, webpage that provides information on the hyperlink.

Web addresses that are useful for biotechnology research are given at the end of Unit. Millions of new Web sites are created every year and to access these new sites, one needs the help of a SEARCH ENGINE, a searchable directory that organizes Webpages by subject classification. Major search engines include Yahoo, Google, Netscape Search, Scirus, etc. As one "surfs the web" one may find sites of interest. They can be saved and reviewed at a later date.

Applications of Web

It is not necessary to have a complete understanding of internet in order to tap into its vast resources. The fundamental concept provided here would allow a junior researcher in Biotechnology to take advantage of two essential activities :

(*i*) biotechnology and molecular biology literature.

(*ii*) using web directories and biological databases.

THE LITERATURE

Researchers do not spend all their working time in the laboratory and an important component of their research project is a search of biotechnology literature. The library should be considered a tool for experimental biotechnology in the same way as any scientific instrument.

The library is used in all stages of research. Before an investigator can begin experimentation, a research idea must be generated. A research project usually begins in the form of a question to be answered or problem to be solved.

For the ease of solution, a major project can be subdivided into questions that may be answered by experimentation. Before the laboratory work starts, the researcher must have a knowledge of the past and current literature dealing with the research area. Thus, one can reduce the project to two questions:

What is the current state of knowledge in the area?

What are the significant unknowns?

Answers to these questions can be achieved only after developing a familiarity with the literature. Not only the knowledge of literature is essential but also knowledge of techniques and laboratory procedures are required.

Experimental details can be available in good methods books and journals. Finally, while performing experiments, the researcher often needs lots of information. Various handbooks, encyclopedias, websites are available for this purpose. The beginning researcher in biotechnology will not be expected to proceed through all of these stages in the design of an experiment.

Thus, a familiarity with the literature increases the understanding of the experiment and may aid in the development of more effective methods. With this background, when you do begin a research program, you will be able to use the library to the fullest advantage.

The molecular biology literature is massive and rapidly expanding. It is almost a full-time job just to maintain a current awareness of a specialized research area. Since biochemistry, biological sciences, biotechnology, molecular biology, physical sciences, and basic medical sciences are overlapping; one should not be hesistant to explore these overlapping literature while planning a research project.

TextBooks

The student's first exposure to biotechnology is probably a lecture course accompanied by reading of a general textbook of biotechnology.

By providing an in-depth survey of biotechnology, textbooks provide building a strong foundation of important principles and concepts.

Reference Books and Review Publications

More specialized and detailed biotechnology information that is not offered by textbooks, could be available is reference books.

Reference works range from general surveys to specialized series. The best works are multivolume sets that continue publication of volumes on a periodic basis. Each volume usually covers a specialized area with articles written by recognized authorities in the field. It should be noted that reference articles of interests to biotechnologists are often found in publications that are not strictly biotechnology.

Research Journals

The core of the biotechnology literature consists of research journals. It is essential for a researcher to maintain a knowledge of recent advances in his or her research field and related areas.

Scores of research journals are published with the intent of keeping researchers upto date. With the expansion of scientific information has generated the need for efficient storage and use of research journals. Many publishers are now providing journals informs such as microcards, microfilm, microfiche, floppy and more recently CD-ROM disks and DVDs and online. Now a days most journals can be subscribed online, also they provide e-mail alerts for content of tables, or articles of specific interest free of cost.

Some research journals have achieved an especially excellent reputation and articles therein are considered to be of the highest quality. A number of citation or indexing authorities index and grade the journals e.g., Index medicus, Index Copernicus, Excerpta Medica, Current Contents.

METHODOLOGY REFERENCES

The active researcher has a continuing need for new methods and techniques. Several publications specialize in providing details of research methods and many research methods are now available on the web.

Some of the useful Journals are

Science	Science Now, STKE	www.science.com
Nature	Nature Biotechnology,	www.nature.com
	Nature Reviews,	
	Nature Genetics,	
	Nature Review Genetics	

Genome Research

Bioinformatics

Targets

Proc Natl Acad Soc USA

Am J Hum Genet

J Mol Biol

Mol Cell Biol

J Clin Invest

Hum Hered

Nucleic Acid Research

Blood

NEJM

Cell

Current Opinion Cell Biology

Trends Genetics

Trends Biotechnology

Trends Molecular Biology

Trends Molecular Medicine

A Practical Guide to Molecular cloning

Methods Enzymology

Journals in Biotechnology and Genomics

Annual review of Biochemistry

Annual review of genomics and human genetics

Bioinformatics of Genetics

Current genomics

Current opinion in — Cell

Cell — Biotechnology

Gene — Genetics and development
Genetics
Genome research
Genomics
Molecular Genetics and Genomics
Nature biotechnology
Nature Genetics
Nature
Nature review genetics
Nucleic acid research
PNAS (Proceeding of National Academy of Sciences)
Protein Engineering
Science
Trends in Biotechnology
World Journal of Microbiology and Biotechnology

News Letters

- Biotechnology and Development Monitor.
- Genetic Engineering News.
- Genomics and protenomics.

Books of Molecular Biology and Biotechnology

1. Molecular Cell Biology : Lodish, Baltimore, Darnell (Freeman Publication)
2. Principles of Genetics : Snustad, Simmons (John Wiley & Sons, Inc)
3. Principles of Genome Analysis and Genomics : Primrose, Twyman (Black well publishing)
4. From genes to genomes : Dale, Schantz (Wiley)
5. Gene Cloning—an introduction : Brown (Oxford, UK)
6. Molecular Biotechnology : principles and applications of recombinant DNA (Am. Society for Microbiology, USA)
7. Genes VII: Lewin B : Oxford University Press, Oxford

Websites and Clinical Database

Online Mendelian Inheritance in Man (OMIM)

http://www3.ncbi.nlm.nih.gov/omim/

Genetic Interest Group

www.gig.org.uk

Genome database

www.gdb.org

Human Genome Bioinformatics

www.gene.ucl.ac.uk

Human Gene Mutation Database

www.uwcm.ac.uk/uwcm/mg/hgmdo.html

C. Elegans Genetics and Genomics

http://elegans.swmed.edu/genome.shtml

Yeast Genome Projects

http://mips.gsf.de/genre/project/yeast/index.jsp

Dolan DNA Learning Centre at Cold Spring Harbor Lab

www..dnalc.org

Vanderbilt University Medical School

http://peds.mc.vanderbilt.edu/VCHWEB_1/Medical-Genetics.html

The Human Cytogenetic Database (HCDB)

Schinzel A. Oxford Medical, Oxford University Press, Oxford.

European Bioinformatics Institute

www.ebi.ac.uk

National Centre for Biotechnology Information (NCBI)

www.ncbi.nlm.nih.gov

DNA Data Bank of Japan

www.ddbj.nig.ac.jp/

Swiss Institute of Bioinformatics (SIB)

www.isb-sib.ch/

Sanger Centre

www.sanger.ac.uk

The Institute for Genomic Research

www.tigr.org

COMPUTER-BASED SEARCHES AND OTHER AIDS TO LITERATURE

Abstracts

As one studies and works in biological sciences such as Biotechnology, he would often need to complete a thorough literature search on some specialized area or topic. It is not practical to survey the hundreds of books, journals and reports that may contain information related to the topic.

There are number of publications that provide brief summaries of published articles, reviews and patents namely, Chemical Abstracts, Biological Abstracts, Excrepta Medica, Current contents gives selected titles of articles in relevant fields.

The computer revolution has reached into biomedical literature and most college and University libraries are now getting subscription to computer bibliographic search services and online subscription for journals. One such service for bibliography is STN International that allows direct access to some of the World's largest scientific databases *e.g.*, BIOSIS Previews/RN (produced by Bio Sciences Information Services): covers original research article reports, reviews, US patents in biology and biomedicine); CA (Chemical Abstracts Service), MEDLINE AND MEDLARS (US National Library of Medicine and Index Medicus respectively): cover all areas of biomedicine. These networks provide on-line service and their databases can be accessed on net.

Web Directories, Tools and Databases

A wide variety of databases are currently available including genome sequence, bibliography, nucleic acid sequence, protein sequence and structure, metabolic pathways and even useful software programs for exploring structures and sequences.

Some of these are hyperlinked to the database sites. Several software programs are available which are hyperlinked to database sites namely.

Chime (protein structures on moving 3D coordinates)

Entrez (NCBI) (cross-referencing database)

GenBank (NCBI) (Database of gene sequences)

BLAST (searching for similar protein and nucleic acid sequences)

All these databases are readily available, free of charge, on the Web.

SUMMARY

As one studies and works in field of biological sciences, he or she needs a thorough literature search on specialized topics. Various search engines make it easy to survey literature on specific topics on internet and large scientific databases are available on net. Also, tools of research, online journals and public scientific databases make the research easier and one should be conversant with latest computer modalities to be successful.

REVIEW QUESTIONS

1. How to write an abstract?
2. Give an account of role of computers in research.
3. What is indexing, citation?
4. What is an online journal?
5. What are search engines?
6. Describe data base?
7. Prepare a web directory for literature, tools of biomedical science and database.
8. What do you mean by abstract citation?
9. How will you plan an abstract for scientific meeting ?
10. How will you write an abstract for oral presentation ?
11. Enumerate applications of web in research.
12. List famous search engines for biological research.
13. What are components of research literature ?
14. What is citation and indexing of journal ?
15. Find out useful publications in biotechnology.
16. List the website and clinical database in biomedical fields.

Chapter 6

FUNDING AGENCIES

SCIENCE FUNDING ORGANIZATIONS

Biotechnology companies especially those profitable today, face a coming decade that may be even painful than the past decade was for global pharma, when many saw their valuations cut in half, not to mention all restructuring and management havoc. Most biotech companies achieved their success behind just one or two block busting drugs that are priced boldly and marketed aggressively. In spite of billions in R and D, large pharma have failed to produce much in the way of next round of innovations. It seems increasingly clear that once a biotechnology company reaches a certain size, it, like its large pharma counterparts, becomes unable to get much out of its heavy R&D spending.

Since life science product life cycles are short, so companies should extract as much value from their products as possible and this is possible by R and D and careful planning and adequate knowledge of R and D funding and skill to draw funding help in survival of company.

International Funding Agencies

Organization	*Funding Offered*
1. Alexander Von Humboldt foundation	Research Fellowships and research awards for scholars and scientists of all nationalities not resident in Germany.
2. Arnold and Mabel Beckman F.	Supports basic scientific research in USA in fields of Chemistry, Biochemistry, Medicine.
3. Caledonian Research F.	Encourages academic research in Biomedicine.
4. Dalmo Giacometti F.	Pvt. Foundation which supports genetic research and biotechnology.
5. Grants Net	Research funding information from American Association for the Advancement of Science.

6. Swiss National Science F.	Supports scientific research at Swiss Universities, awards fellowships to young scientists.
7. US Civilian R and D F.	Promotes scientific and technical collaboration between US and Countries of Former Soviet Union.
8. Wallace Genetic F.	Supports interests including agriculture research, preservation of farmland, ecology, plant genetic research.
9. Whitaker F.	Private Funding source for biomedical engineering research and education in US.

National Funding Agencies

1. ICMR—Indian Council for Medical Research
2. CSIR—Centre for Scientific and Industrial Research
3. DBT—Department of Biotechnology
4. DST—Department of Science and Technology
5. UGC—University Grants Commission

From time to time, call for proposals, grants are available with the funding agencies. Also, global collaborations are available for funding a research proposal.

BASIS AND TECHNOLOGY FOR STARTING A NEW PROJECT

In life science business environment, new product development is swift, competition is fierce, and market place has multiple distribution channels. To make their position, life science companies need reliable information about their markets regarding researchers, activity of competitors, and quantification impact of business decisions and goals.

Market Survey

Project management is essential to Biotechnology business. Biotechnology companies have a significant challenge ahead of them. They are very much concerned about cost containment and investor confidence, but at the some time they have to comply with regulations and aggressively pursue quick market entry. Without a solid project management infrastructure, it's unlikely that many companies will be able to address these concerns effectively.

Marketing Strategies for Biotechnological Products

Market Launch

Not all products entering the consumer's market undergo same regulatory oversight. Nor all the markets are the same—*e.g.*, one can distinguish domestic and export markets, professional users (such as farmers and doctors) and nonprofessional consumers.

Market Surveillance

Government enforce standards (*e.g.*, food quality, purity of pharmaceuticals and sometimes also directly influences the market. When problems are discovered, government not only wishes to communicate with industry, but also with consumers.

Methodology for Starting a New Project

Basic components of marketing are:

- Market survey.
- Futuristic estimates.
- Indigenous and
- Imported technology.

Marketing Research

Define the problem and research objection

↓

develop research plan

↓

collect the information

↓

analysis the information

↓

present the findings

↓

make the decision

Figure 6.1. Marketing Research Process: Flow Chart.

Marketing Research System

Marketing research is defined as the systematic design, collection, analysis and reporting of data and findings relevant to a specific marketing situation facing the company.

A company can obtain marketing research in a number of ways.

Most large companies/establishments have their own marketing research departments, which often play crucial roles within the organization.

Market Survey

Before starting a new project or as a follow up approach, surveys are undertaken to learn about people's knowledge, beliefs, preferences and satisfaction and to measure these magnitudes in the general population. Also, market for the intended product is surveyed.

Analysis should ensure that the company achieves the sales, profits and other goals established in its plan. The main tools are sales analysis, market share analysis, marketing expense-to-sales analysis and financial analysis of the marketing plan.

Technology

Technology is a sort of knowledge or skill used for employing and controlling factors of productions.

Types

1. **Product Technology**—information that specifies a product's features and uses.

2. **Process Technology**—knowledge used in processing or manufacturing of a product.
3. **Management Technology**—managerial skills required for running a business.

Technology is a strategic assets. Technology can be developed through R and D activities.

Features of Technology

It should be:

1. cost-effective.
2. properly located.
3. has low cost of production.
4. ensuring better quality product to meet customer's preferences

It is not only the cost involved in R and D, but also it is how far the cost of product diminishes, and how far the quality of the product improves that should be considered. If a new product is designed not keeping in the mind the capabilities of the production department, the attempt will be a failure. Many international firms have created cross-functional teams comprise of:

- R and D department.
- production department.
- marketing department.

Acquisition of Technology Through Purchase

In developing countries where funds are too limited to undertake R and D, import of technology is frequent, although firms located in industrialized countries too purchase technology.

There are two ways of technology transfer:

(*i*) point-to-point technology transfer.

(*ii*) diffusion of technology.

(i) Point-to-point technology transfer

It is transfer of technology along with complete secrecy.

(ii) Diffusion of technology

In this type same technology is transferred to many recipients and secrecy is not maintained.

Policy Towards Acquisition of Technology

Different countries have different policies of acquisition of technology. It could be policy with minimum restrictions that allow continuous flow of technology, and gives no. of incentives.

On the contrary, strategy could be to reduce gradually reliance on imported technology thereby encouraging R and D within the country.

Problems in Technology Transfer

- difficulty in maintaining technology secrecy.
- cost of technology is exorbitant.
- developer does not generally like to transfer the latest technology.
- government restrictions on the transfer.

Outsourcing

To reduce the cost and increase the speed and productivity of all phases of R and D, outsourcing of certain R and D activities overseas can streamline the operations offshoring components of discovery, research and clinical trial offers unique opportunities, especially in terms of access to study subjects, trained personnel, lower-cost infrastructure, and labor pools. However, emerging opportunities in overseas are not without significant potential risks, and companies considering this route should keep a close eye on contract and licencing terms, quality control measures, regulatory issues and time lines.

SUMMARY

Due to fierce competition and short life-cycle of biotechnology products, a reliable information of market is essential. When a new product is to be designed, careful project should be planned following market survey, technology survey and cost-investment planning to be successful.

REVIEW QUESTIONS

1. What the sources of funds?
2. List out the international funding available.
3. Name the Indian agencies for offering funding.
4. Are global collaborations for funding available?
5. What do you understand by market surveilliance?
6. What is project management?
7. Discuss importance of project management.
8. How a product is launched?
9. What do you understand by marketing research?
10. What is outsourcing of R and D?
11. What is technology transfer?
12. What are different types of technology transfer?
13. What are the benefits of outsourcing?
14. What are the dangers of outsourcing?
15. What are the components of market survey?
16. Outline the marketing strategies 'biotech products'?
17. How to launch a products?

18. What is technology transfer?
19. Make a list of possible areas of biotechnology where outsourcing is possible.
20. Prepare a list of international science funding agencies.
21. Prepare a list of funding agencies in India.
22. What do you understand by term market survey?
23. Discuss need project management.
24. Outline the process of marketing research.
25. How will you carry out a market survey for your intended biotech product?
26. What are the different types of technology transfer?
27. What should be components of a cross-functional team of biotechnology company?

Chapter 7

PREPARATION OF R & D PROJECTS FOR FUNDING

ORGANIZATION OF RESEARCH PROJECT

1st step in research project is generation of research idea. This idea develops only after extensive reading and studying the relevant literature.

A research project usually begins in the form of a problem to be solved. For ease, this problem project should be divided into questions that may be answered by experimentation.

Key Questions for a Project

— What is the current state of knowledge in the area?

— What are the significant unknowns?

— What will be the possible outcome of project?

Basic Requirements for Project

— Knowledge of literature for design of experiment.

— Knowledge of techniques and laboratory procedures.

— Knowledge of relevant information of related parameter.

Core Capabilities Required in Field of Genomics

— Collection of comprehensive data set using technologically advanced laboratory tools.

— Searching for subtle relationships within them by using computationally sophisticated analytical methods.

CERTAIN CONSIDERATIONS

It is of considerable strategic importance to manage a balance between benefits of technology against a typically short-life and substantial cost of new technology. Projects in genomics (biotechnology) requires co-ordination between researchers concerned with collection, storage and distribution of data.

It requires biomedical scientists, software engineers, professionals carrying out computational analysis of data *i.e.*, from mathematics, statistics, computer science.

Organization

Most biomedical research is served well by traditional model of individual laboratories led by a single principal investigator. However, genomic/biotechnology/molecular biology research often requires multiple investigators.

Team

The interdisciplinary research team should be comprised of:

- scientists.
- academicians.
- business leaders.
- members of public.

Suggested Themes

- New Pathways to Discovery.
- Research Teams of Future.
- Re-engineering Clinical Research Enterprise.

Focus Areas

- Development of tools.
- Technology.
- Network and Resources.
- Generation of funds from:
  - — Business houses.
  - — Government.
  - — Private enterprises : Pharmas.
  - — Creation of chair/seat.
  - — Generating resources from patenting, tradement to sustain research.

MODERN MODELS OF TEAM WORK

They include the following three models:

Outsourcing

The simplest and traditional approach is to increase the scale and disciplinary focus of individual labs collaborating with other research groups. *i.e.*, Outsourcing of capabilities which require little organizational change.

Insourcing

This model retains disciplinary focus of labs led by individual principle investigators but brings new capabilities in-house through 'core-labs'. Their goal is to assist other researchers and are often run by staff scientists (research fellows) rather than by faculty and trainees. This setting is more successful when the services offered are a commodity—well defined and technologically nature.

Integration

This model pays less attention to traditional barriers between individual labs and disciplines. Members of this team interact as partners rather than being under sole leadership of a single faculty member. Here the goal is to fully integrate the capabilities and disciplines to solve a particular set of problems.

Thus teams can be constructed in many different ways, each with its own capabilities and requirements for success.

THREE COMMON CHARACTERISTICS OF SUCCESSFUL TEAM

Clear Compelling Mission

Mission must be larger than an individual. Example of **Human Genome Project,** in which a large number of investigators from different disciplines (biology, mathematics, and engineering) together tackled a daunting scientific challenge, created new technologies, and organizational structures, shared data to an unprecedented degree and as the project matured, analysed and published the results collaboratively.

Selection of Team Members

People who commit to success of the group should be selected for the team.

Leader of Multidisciplinary Team

He must be skilled at motivating and facilitating the work of others.

Unfortunately such characteristics do not map onto the organizational model. In biomedicine, individuals tend to rewarded than teams; successful faculty members enjoy tenure, space and resources to advance their ideas and substantial salaries, but team members (typically trainees and technical staff) have little in the way of all these luxuries!

ORGANIZATION OF A RESEARCH PROJECT

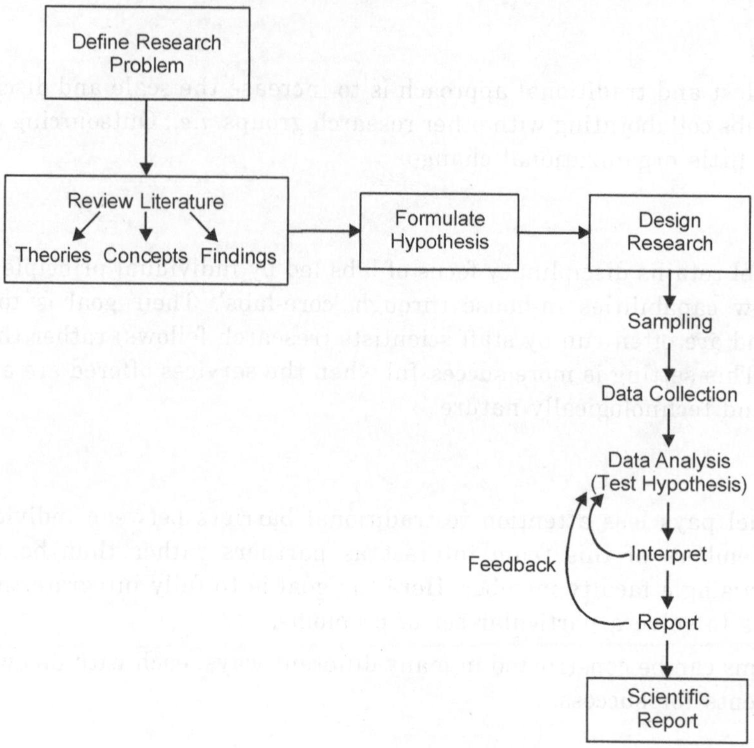

Figure 7.1 Flow chart of Research Process

Research

Research refers to a search for knowledge. It is also defined as a scientific and systematic search for pertinent information on a specific topic.

PURPOSE of research is to discover answers to questions through application of scientific procedures.

Research Methodology

This is a way to systematically solve the research problem. It not only includes research methods, but also use of logic behind the methods that are used in the context of research study, reasons for using a particular technique and not the other so that research results are capable of being evaluated either by researcher himself or by others.

RESEARCH PROCESS

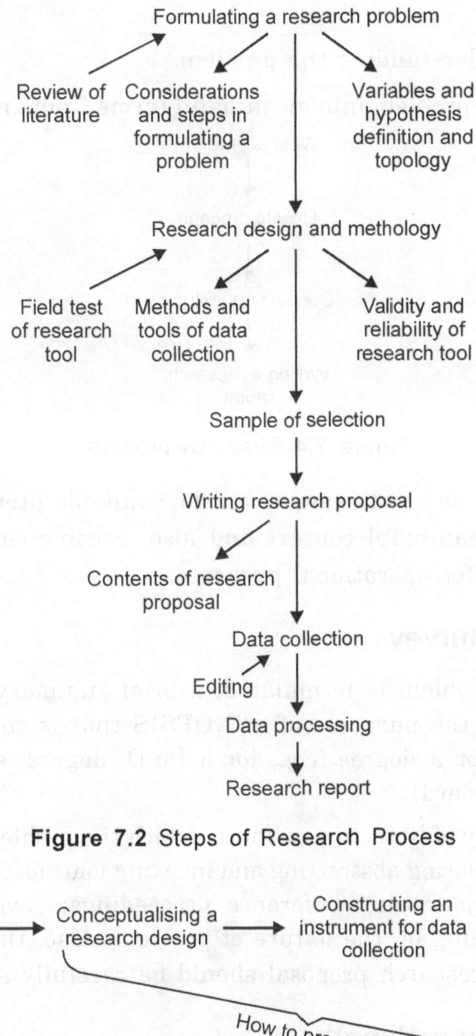

Figure 7.2 Steps of Research Process

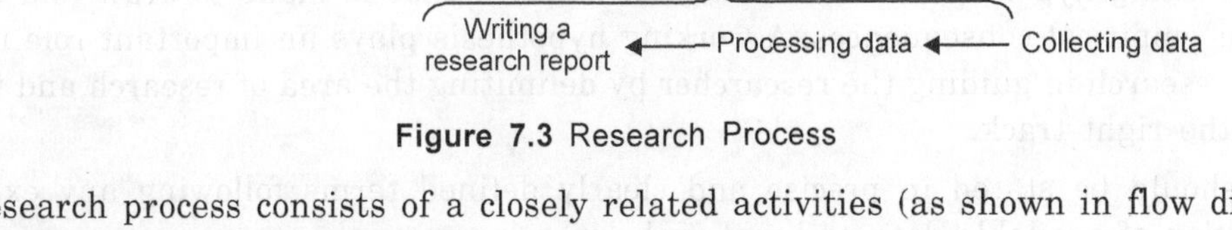

Figure 7.3 Research Process

Research process consists of a closely related activities (as shown in flow diagram) and brief description of the various steps is as under:

Formulating Research Problem

The task of formulating defining a research problem is a step of greatest importance in the entire research process. At the very begining, researcher must single out the problem he wants to study, then, he should consider feasibility of a particular solution before setting up the formulation of the problem. Thus the 2 steps involved in formulating research problem are:

(*i*) thoroughly understanding the problem.

(*ii*) rephrasing the problem into meaningful terms from an analytical point of view.

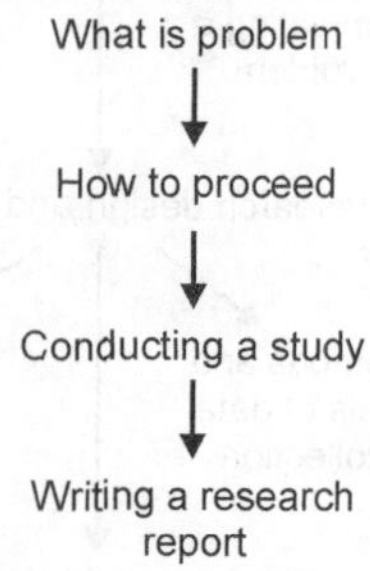

Figure 7.4 Research process

To achieve the above, he must examine all the available literature to specify his own research problem in a meaningful context and also, become conversant with data and other materials available for operational purposes.

Extensive Literature Survey

Once the research problem is formulated, a brief summary of the same should be written down that serves the purposes of SYNOPSIS that is compulsory for a research worker writing a thesis for a degree (*e.g.*, for a Ph.D. degree, synopsis is submitted to Research Committee or Board).

Thus, extensive survey of literature connected with the problem should be undertaken. This can be achieved by exploring abstracting and indexing journals; published or unpublished bibliographies; Academic journals, conference proceedings; government reports; books; internet databases depending on the nature of problem. Also, the earlier studies, if any, which are similar to the research proposal should be carefully studied.

Development of Working Hypothesis

A working hypothesis is a tentative assumption that is made to draw and test its logical or empirical consequences. A working hypothesis plays an important role in most types of research in guiding the researcher by delimiting the area of research and to keep him on the right track.

It should be stated in precise and clearly defined terms following any extensive examination of available data and material.

Preparing the Research Design

The researcher is required to prepare a research design for the research problem *i.e.*, he will have to state the conceptual structure within which research will be conducted. The following points are important preparing research design:

(*i*) availability of information.

(*ii*) availability and skills of researcher and his staff.

(*iii*) explanation of the ways in which selected means of obtaining information will be organised and reasoning leading to the selection.

(*iv*) time frame period available for research.

(*v*) finance available for the purpose.

(*vi*) need of funding if any.

Determining Sample Design

Research must decide the way of selecting a sample. The different sample designs are:

(*i*) Deliberate sampling—This involves purposive or deliberate selection of particular units of universe population for constituting a sample.

(*ii*) Simple random sampling (or chance or probability sampling)—This gives each item an equal probability of being selected.

(*iii*) Systematic sampling—An element of randomness is introduced in this and by starting with some random point, every *n*th element is selected until the desired number is secured.

(*iv*) Stratified random sampling—If the sample is drawn from a non-homogenous group, where population is stratified in a non-overlapping one.

(*v*) Quota sampling—Quotas are filled from different strata by non-probability sampling.

(*vi*) Cluster sampling—It involves grouping the population and selecting the groups as samples.

(*vii*) Multistage sampling—Involves big inquiries extending to considerably large geographical areas.

(*viii*) Sequential sample—Here the ultimate size is determined according to mathematical decisions.

Thus, by taking into consideration about nature of inquiry and related factors, sample designs should be described.

Data Collection

Primary data collection can be done through experiment by using some quantitative measurements to examine the truth contained in his hypothesis.

Execution of Project

If the project proceeded or correct line, data would be adequate and dependable.

Data Analysis

Following collection of data, researcher turns to the task of analysing the data and application of raw data to coding, tabulation and then drawing statistical inferences mechanically or by computers. Also, analysis of variance can be applied to analyse level of significance between various groups.

Testing the Hypothesis

Now, after analysing the population, the researcher is in a position to test the hypothesis, if any, he had formulated earlier. Usual important question to be answered is : "Do facts support the hypothesis or they happen to be contrary?"

By using various statistical tests such as Chi-square test, *t*-test, F-test etc., hypothesis may be tested.

Hypothesis can thus be accepted or rejecting following the analysis and if the researcher had no hypothesis to start with, then generalization based on this data may be stated as hypothesis to be tested by subsequent researchers in future.

Interpretation

If a hypothesis is tested and upheld several times, then, a research can arrive at a generalization, *i.e.*, BUILDS A THEORY.

The real value of a research lies in its ability to arrive at certain generalizations.

If initially there was no hypothesis to start with, then a research might seek to explain his findings on the basis of some theory and is known as INTERPRETATION. Usually, interpretation process may trigger off new questions that may lead to further researches.

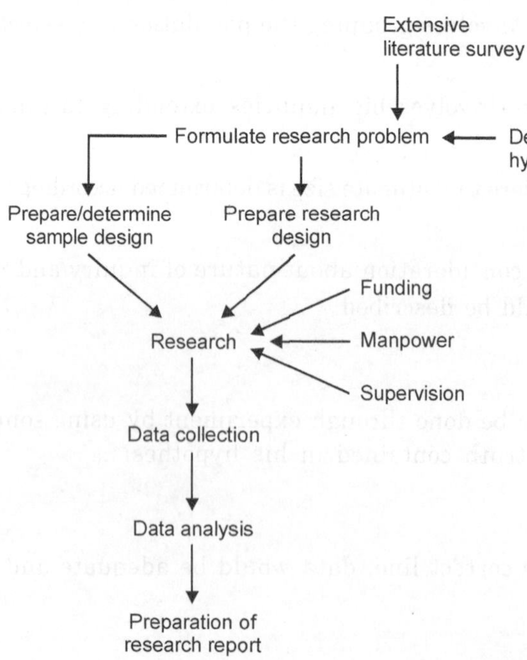

Figure 7.5 Steps in Research Process

Preparation of Report or Thesis

Finally, the researcher prepares the report of his project and the following points should be considered while writing the report:

1. Firstly, layout of report should have:
   (*a*) preliminary pages.
   (*b*) main text.
   (*c*) end matter.
   (*a*) **Preliminary pages**—Carrying title, date, acknowledgement and forward, Followed by table of contents, list of table, graph, charts etc. given the report.
   (*b*) **Main text**—It should have the following parts:
   (*i*) *Introduction*—Introduction should contain a clear statement of objective of research, an explanation of methodology adopted, scope of study alongwith limitations of study.
   (*ii*) *Summary of findings*—Summary of findings and recommendations should be given in non-technical language after introduction.
   (*iii*) *Main report*—This should be presented in logical sequence and broken down into readily identifiable sections.
   (*iv*) *Conclusion*—It is the final summing up.
   (*c*) **At the end of the report**—It should have appendices, bibliography *i.e.*, list of books, journals, reports, etc. consulted given in the end.
2. The report should be in a concise manner and objective style in simple language.
3. Charts and illustrations showing clear information should be incorporated in main report.
4. Also, 'confidence limits', constraints experienced in conducting research operations may be stated.

Qualities of Good Research

A good research is:

(*i*) systematic.
(*ii*) logical.
(*iii*) empirical.
(*iv*) replicable.

(*i*) *Systematic*—It implies that research is structured with specific (sequence of) steps to be taken in accordance with well-defined set of rules.

(*ii*) *Logical*—It should be guided by rules of logical reasoning making it more meaningfull in the context of decision making.

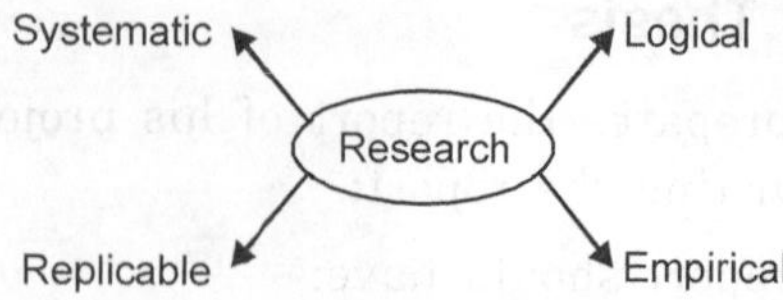

Figure 7.6 Qualities of a good research

(*iii*) *Empirical*—It implies that research is related to one or more aspects of a real situation and dealing with data which provides basis of external validity to research results.

(*iv*) *Replicable*—That is the research results can be verified by replicating the study.

CRITERIA FOR THE SELECTION OF A RESEARCH PROBLEM

The researcher must identify a problematic situation and evaluate it properly. Selection of a problem followed by its analysis and formulation is half the research work accomplished. At master's level, the students are generally not so well acquainted with subject and research methodology and here comes the sole of supervisor to guide them. At doctoral level, the student has acquired training in methodology and has sufficient time to devote to the selection of the problem. The researcher must look into following aspects so that he has not to abandon the topic at a later stage:

1. Research problem should be in area or field of specialization of research.
2. Researcher should have sufficient time and adequate funds available to him for completion of the research project.
3. The research problem should be able to advance knowledge in the field or present a solution to a practical problem.
4. The subjects or sources of data should be accessible and their willingness ascertained.
5. Funding, sponsorship and support-staff should be available.

All the above considerations will help researcher to select a significant and researchable problem. Also, research should follow norms and standards prescribed for them for pursuing their research.

TYPES OF RESEARCH

There are two broad categories of research:

1. Pure research.
2. Applied research.

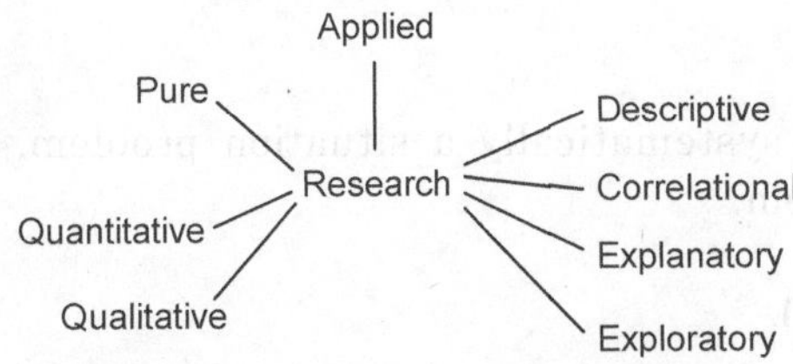

Figure 7.7 Types of research

Pure Research

It is concerned with development, examination, verification, and refined of research methods, procedures, techniques, and tools for research. *e.g.*, developing a sampling technique, to assess validity of a procedure, developing an instrument, R and D.

Applied Research

Research techniques, procedures and methods that form the body of research methodology are applied to collection of information about various aspects of a situation, issue, problem for policy formulation, administration and enhancement of understanding of a phenomenon.

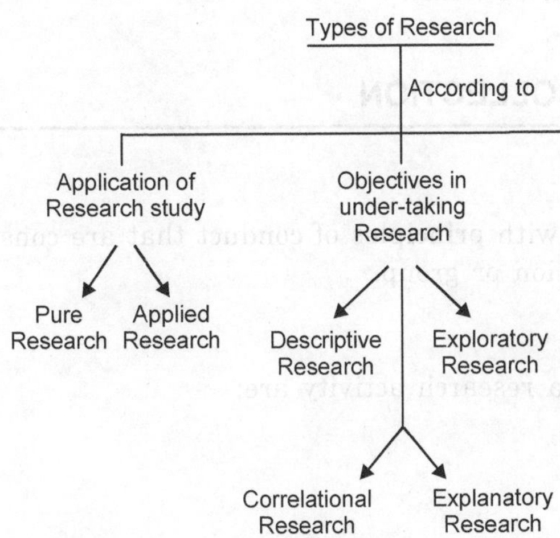

Figure 7.8 Types of Research

AIMS AND OBJECTIVES OF RESEARCH PROJECTS

The objectives of research project can be:

1. descriptive.
2. correlational.
3. explanatory.
4. exploratory.

Descriptive Research

Attempts to describe systematically a situation problem, phenomenon or provides information about a problem.

Correlational Research

Here, main emphasis is to discover or establish existence of a relationship between two or more aspects of a situation.

Explanatory Research

It attempts to clarify why and how there is a relationship between two aspects of a phenomenon.

Exploratory Research

Also termed as pilot study or feasibility study. This is carried out to investigate the possibilities of undertaking a particular research study.

Most commonly used electronic databases are:

Medline, Embase, healthroom, CINAHL.

ETHICAL ISSUES IN DATA COLLECTION

Ethics

Ethical means in accordance with principles of conduct that are considered correct, especially those of a given profession or group.

Stakeholders in Research

The various stakeholders in a research activity are:

(*i*) participants or subjects.

(*ii*) researcher.

(*iii*) funding body.

Participants or subjects (patients) are stakeholders in fields of medicine, public health, epidemiology, biotechnology and pharmacology.

Information collection exercise, experiment or drug trial and service managers and planners contribute information for a research study.

The researcher is one who collects information for a specific purpose, adhering to accepted code.

Funding

The body funding a research activity falls into the third category of stakeholders. Most research is carried out using funds provided by business organizations, service institutions—government, semi-government or voluntary—research bodies, and/or academic institutions. These funds are provided for specific purposes. The funding body may have a vested interest in the research it is sponsoring, and this could affect the way, the research is being conducted or the way of writing reports.

Thus, each category of stakeholders in a research activity may have different interests, perspectives, purposes, aims and motivations that could affect the process and way of conducting research activity and communication and usage of results. It is very important to ensure that self-interest of any party is not affecting the research, and research is not carried out in a way that harms any party.

Ethical Issues Concerning Research Participants

Figure 7.9 Ethical issues of research

Collecting Information

It should be kept in mind that requesting information from an individual may create anxiety or put pressure on him.

Is this ethical?

When researcher considers relevance and usefulness of research and is able to convince others of this also, then collection of information is ethical. However, if researcher cannot justify relevance of research he is conducting and wasting his respondent's time, then it is unethical.

Seeking Consent

It is unethical to collect information without the knowledge of participant, their informed willingness and expressed consent. In medical research, informed consent is seeked by making subjects aware of type of information a researcher wants from them, why information is being sought, what purpose it will put to, how they are expected to participate in the study, and how it will directly or indirectly affect them. Consent should be voluntary and without pressure of any kind.

If a research project has received adequate funding, then incentives can be provided to respondents to share information with you. Many pharmaceutical firms provide incentives for carrying out drug trials.

Ethics of providing incentive are equivocal : some label it as ethical, while others label it as unethical.

Seeking Sensitive Information

It can pose an ethical dilemma in research.

The Possibility of Causing Harm to Participants

Harm includes not only hazardous medical experiments but also discomfort, anxiety, harassment, invasion of privacy or demeaning or dehumanising procedures.

Maintaining Confidentiality

It is unethical to share information about a respondent with others for purposes other than research.

Ethical Issues Concerned with Researcher

1. *Avoid bias:* Bias is a deliberate attempt to hide what you have found in your study or highlight something disproportionately to its true existence.
2. *Provision or deprivation of a treatment:* It can pose an ethical dilemma for a researcher.
3. Use appropriate research methodology for conducting a study.
4. Report the findings correctly.
5. Use information obtained from respondents in an ethical manner.

Ethical Issues Regarding Sponsoring Organisation

1. *Restrictions imposed by sponsoring organisation:* The funds may be given to develop a program or evaluate it, to examine its efficiency or effectiveness, to test a product. The sponsors may select the methodology prohibit publication of findings or impose other restrictions on research which are unethical.
2. Use of information by sponsoring organisation on pretext for obtaining management's agenda in unethical.

SUMMARY

The research process is formulation of a research problem, design and methodology, writing research proposal, data collection and editing, data processing and writing a research report. While conducting a research issues of ethics, funding with respect to research participants, researcher and sponsor arise that should be carefully addressed.

REVIEW QUESTIONS

1. Describe research project.
2. What do you understand by team of biotechnology project?
3. What is organization?
4. What should be the focus areas of a research organization?

5. What is teamwork?
6. Discuss models of teamwork.
7. What is outsourcing?
8. Discuss the characteristics of a successful team.
9. What is a research process?
10. What is the logic behind research? Discuss.
11. What are various steps of research process?
12. How a research problem can be formulated?
13. Describe research methodology.
14. How a working hypothesis is developed?
15. How the task of formulating a research problem is accomplished?
16. How to prepare a research design?
17. What are different sample designs?
18. How will you collect and analyze data?
19. How a hypothesis is tested?
20. How data is collected analyzed and intepreted?
21. What are the criteria for selection of a research problem?
22. What should be the aims of objectives of research project?
23. Why a pilot study is carried out?
24. Describe the interests and motivations of different stakeholders in a research activity.
25. What is ethics? Discuss the ethical issues in data collection.
26. Discuss the ethics of collection of information for research.
27. How will you seek consent from a participant of study?
28. How to enforce ethics in research?
29. What are different models teamwork?
30. What is the goal of a insourcing?
31. Outline the steps of research problem.
32. Give an outline for preparing a research design "to find novel genomic marker of cardiovascular disease".
33. Give outline for preparing a report.
34. Enumerate qualities of a good research.
35. How will you propose, plan and define a research problem?
36. Create an outline of proposed team for a biotech research project.
37. How will you organize a research project? Discuss.
38. Describe focus areas of an organization.
39. Outline the characteristics of a successful team.
40. Debate: who is superior: team or leader?
41. Outline how a research problem is organized into a project?
42. What is the purpose of research?

43. Formulate a working hypothesis.
44. Enumerate important points for research design.
45. Give an outline for data collection analysis and interpretation.
46. How will your test a hypothesis?
47. Enlist the important criteria for selecting a research problem.
48. What are the objectives of research project?
49. What is a plot study?
50. When you are collecting information from any individual for genetic counselling, it may create anxiety on him. Is it ethical?
51. Prepare a list concerning ethics of data collection.
52. How will you avoid bias in data?
53. Prepare a table showing ethical issues concerned with research participants, researcher and sponsor.

Chapter 8

BIOLOGICAL RESOURCE CENTRES & BIORESOURCES

INTRODUCTION

"Biological resource centres BRCs are an essential part of the infrastructure underpinning life sciences and biotechnology. They consist of service providers and repositories of the living cells, genomes of organism, and information relating to heredity and the functions of biological systems. BRCs contain collections of culturable organisms (e.g., micro-organisms, plant, animal and human cells), replicable parts of these (e.g., genomes, plasmids, viruses, cDNAs), viable but not yet culturable organisms, cells and tissues, as well as databases containing molecular, physiological and structural information relevant to these collections and related bioinformatics".

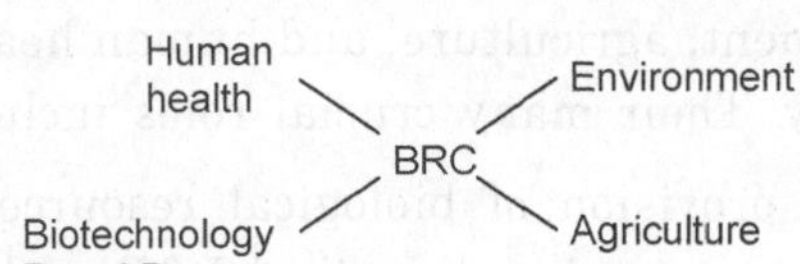

Figure 8.1 Essential fields linked to BRC

(Definition based on the one adopted at the 1999 Tokyo Workshop on Biological Resource Centres, where the concept of BRCs as an outgrowth of conventional pre-genomics ex situ collections of biological materials was developed–and incorporating scientific developments since 1999.) *BRCs must meet the high standards of quality and expertise demanded by the international community of scientists and industry for the delivery of biological information and materials. They must provide access to biological resources on which R&D in the life sciences and the advancement of biotechnology depends.*

Table 8.1 BRCs

Constituents of BRC
Culturable organisms:
Microbes
Plant cell
Animal cell
cDNA
Replicable parts:
Genome
Plasmid
Virus
cDNA
Database:
Molecular information
Physiological information
Structural information

Role of BRCs

Biological resource centres are essential for R&D in the life sciences, for advances in the quality of the environment, agriculture, and human health, and for the commercial development of biotechnology. Their many crucial roles include:

- Preservation and provision of biological resources for scientific, industrial, agricultural, environmental and medical R&D and applications.
- Performance of R&D on these biological resources.
- Conservation of biodiversity.
- Repositories of biological resources for protection of intellectual property.
- Resources for public information and policy formulation.

BIOLOGICAL RESOURCES

Biological resources–living organisms, cells, genes, and the related information–are the essential raw materials for the advancement of biotechnology, human health, and research and development in the life sciences. The revolution in molecular biology has given us greatly increased ability to obtain and to modify these biological resources and to use them for the benefit of all humankind. The sequencing and the associated analysis of gene functions for a growing number of genomes will have an unprecedented effect on the uses of biological resources and the need for access to them. Governments and industry are making large investments in recovering biological resources from nature and in exploring and engineering these resources. Their efforts include the human genome. These investments must not be lost and their results must remain accessible so as to reap scientific, economic and medical benefits.

THE NEED FOR BIOLOGICAL RESOURCE CENTRES

Access to biological resources will require repositories and distribution nodes, collectively called biological resource centres (BRCs), which will be responsible for preserving and distributing biological materials and information.

The growing worldwide demand for biological resources provides good reasons for greatly increasing the number and quality of BRCs. Only a very few large national centres are able currently to perform a comprehensive role and to provide access to diverse organisms, such as bacterial, fungal, plant and animal cells, including human genes and cells. (See Box 8.1 for a description of one of these multifunctional centres.) Other centres play much narrower, yet important, roles, supplying limited but crucial specialised resources.

Challenges Faced by BRCs

The development, expansion and survival of these BRCs face many challenges. These include:

(*i*) those posed by the molecular revolution (genomics and the information revealed by DNA sequencing),

(*ii*) accelerating efforts to conserve biodiversity, funding uncertainties that threaten stability,

(*iii*) the need for adequate quality assurance and constraints on access to biological resources within countries and across international borders resulting from private industry's protection of investments and industrial secrecy,

(*iv*) import/export regulations,

(*v*) intellectual property rights,

(*vi*) safety issues and ethical concerns about the uses of genes and other biological resources.

This chapter reviews the policy, organisational and economic challenges faced by BRCs and recommendations made by various parties and working groups on biotechnology to governments for national and international solutions.

Box 8.1. The Deutsche Sammlung von Mikro-organismen und Zellkulturen GmbH (German Collection of Micro-organisms and Cell Cultures) (DSMZ): A comprehensive centre with multiple functions

The DSMZ is an independent service and research organisation dedicated to the acquisition, characterisation and identification, preservation and distribution of bacteria, archaea, fungi, yeasts, plasmids, phages, human and animal cell lines, plant cell cultures and plant viruses. It is a non-profit, scientific institution and a centre of national importance located in Braunschweig. It is financed by the federal government (40%), the federal states (40%) and income (20%).

The DSMZ is the most comprehensive resource centre of micro-organisms, cell lines and plant viruses in Europe. As the national depository of patented biological material of this kind, it is an IDA (International Depository Authority) as defined in the Budapest Treaty and offers industry and academic research authentic, state-of-the-art preserved biological material. Its functions include:

- Collection and maintenance of the biological diversity of micro-organisms, cell lines and plant viruses.
- Worldwide shipment of cultures.
- Research relevant to the needs of the collections and on issues of biodiversity and ecology.
- Identification, characterisation and certification, including molecular approaches.
- Patent and safe deposits.
- Databases, catalogues and brochures covering each of the collections in electronic and printed format.
- Individual training.

The DSMZ currently has a collection of more than 8 700 strains of bacteria and archaea of almost all described species, 100 bacteriophages, 2 300 filamentous fungi, 500 yeasts, 740 plant cell cultures, 700 plant viruses and 400 human and animal cell lines, which is accessible to the scientific community. The breadth and depth of its collections of archaea and extremophiles (organisms growing under the most extreme conditions where life can exist, the conditions which also characterise many industrial processes where biotechnology may be applied) make it a unique biological resource.

The DSMZ culture collections and scientific services are used not only in basic research but also for elucidating and solving environmental problems, for industrial production processes and for ecological development.

Functions of Biological Resource Centres

Few Important Questions

Why are BRCs needed?

What are their essential functions?

Why should governments and the private sector care about them and take steps to ensure their survival?

Why are the current repositories of biological resources, including ex situ culture collections of micro-organisms and other living cells, housed in many countries in institutions that are often not connected to each other and are inadequate to meet the world's needs for biological resources?

The answers to these questions lie in the many roles played by BRCs:

- Preservation and provision of biological resources for scientific, industrial, agricultural, environmental and medical R&D and applications.
- Performance of R&D on these biological resources.
- Conservation of biodiversity.
- Repositories of biological resources for protection of intellectual property.
- Resources for public information and policy formulation.

Preservation and Provision of Biological Resources for Scientific, Industrial, Agricultural, Environmental and Medical R&D and Applications

By making available biological materials and information of guaranteed identity and quality, BRCs serve an essential infrastructural function for scientific investigation and R&D. Scientific enquiry requires reproducibility: experiments performed in one laboratory by one set of investigators must be replicable in another laboratory. The reliability of biological resources is as important as the purity of chemical reagents and the precision of equipment used to conduct scientific research. The availability of known, validated and precisely identified biological resources is essential for research.

BRCs are also essential sources of information and materials for industrial and many other practical uses. Given that enormous sums are invested in extracting organisms and their genes from nature and elucidating the genetic and functional molecular elements of those living resources, it is essential for these biological resources not only to be preserved but also to be used. BRCs provide the genetic elements, organisms and information used in biotechnological, agricultural, environmental and medical applications. Without them, every user would have to "reinvent the wheel" and invest innumerable hours in the costly recovery of organisms and genes and their characterisation.

Performance of R&D on these Biological Resources

BRCs have opportunities to carry out R&D on the biological resources they house. They often have the expertise needed to further the identification, characterisation and preservation of biological resources. Their R&D activities can contribute to the advancement of the life sciences and may result in valuable products that can help generate income to support the BRCs' broader functions. However, BRCs must balance this R&D function with their service function, providing and preserving biological resources for the wider scientific, industrial, agro-food and medical communities.

Conservation of Biodiversity

Microbial culture collections, viral repositories, herbaria, botanical gardens, zoos and *ex situ* plant and animal genetic resource collections all help preserve biodiversity, which is threatened by unsustainable economic development, natural disasters and global change. The benefits of the conservation of biological resources are emphasised by the *Convention on Biological Diversity (CBD)*, which highlights the need for BRCs as *ex situ* conservatories of biodiversity. Under the terms of the CBD, biological resources include genetic resources, organisms or parts thereof, populations or any other biotic component of ecosystems with actual or potential value for humanity. A number of factors link the CBD to BRCs as conservatories of biodiversity, including:

- The intrinsic ecological, genetic, social, economic, scientific, educational, cultural, recreational and aesthetic values of biological diversity and its components.
- The importance of biological diversity for evolution and the life-sustaining systems of the biosphere.
- The conservation and sustainable use of biological diversity for meeting the crucial food, health and other needs of the growing world population, which requires access to and sharing of both genetic resources and technologies.

Repositories of Biological Resources for Protection of Intellectual Property

Several collections, called International Depository Authorities (IDAs) in the Budapest Treaty (Budapest Treaty on the International Recognition of the Deposit of Micro-organisms for the Purposes of Patent Procedures), serve as legally mandated repositories of biological resources for the purpose of implementing IPR agreements. For micro-organisms, other cells and genetic elements, these are defined by the Budapest Treaty; for plant varieties, a service is defined by the International Union for the Protection of New Varieties of Plants (UPOV) treaty; such deposits are also defined in the EU Directive on the protection of biotechnological inventions. Since 1981, the Budapest Treaty has harmonised deposition procedures and patent applications. In accordance with the Budapest Treaty, IDAs maintain secrecy about the deposited resources but must furnish samples of deposited micro-organisms to entitled third parties on application to the national patent authorities.

Some culture collections also provide a special service for long-term preservation of micro-organisms whose distribution may be restricted at the discretion of the depositor. Such "safe deposits" of biological resources are a way to ensure long-term preservation without loss of ownership. This method does not comply with the requirements of a patent deposit but provides the equivalent of the protection of a "trade secret".

Resources for Public Information and Policy Formulation

BRCs provide essential expertise for formulation of government policies on biological resources and for information and assurance to the public. They can thus serve as an important interface between government, industry and the public and can help the public understand the value of conserving biological resources. They are bodies which the public and policy makers can call upon for objective help in developing regulations and guidelines for the safe and ethical use of biological resources, including those derived from human genes. Countries' laws and regulations governing access to biological resources and their exchange differ and international efforts for harmonisation should increase. Ethical issues (especially for human genetic material and the need for confidentiality and prior informed consent) are increasingly crucial public issues which policy makers must address. Much assistance from BRCs will be needed to develop and implement policies on the uses of biological resources in the age of molecular biology heralded by the genomics revolution.

NATIONAL & INTERNATIONAL BRCs

Global Network of Biological Resource Centres

The challenges and proposals presented in the preceding chapters highlight a number of needs which governments and the scientific community will have to address at national and international level if BRCs are to fulfil their mission in the 21st century. These need include the establishment of:

- National BRCs.
- An accreditation system based on scientifically acceptable objective international criteria.
- International linkages.
- Internationally co-ordinated and harmonised operational parameters.
- A global BRC network.

While the need for national BRCs could be satisfied at national level alone, the other needs can only be addressed at international level and call for the establishment or strengthening of international frameworks. Various international frameworks and organisations already link resource centres into networks and allow them to reach specific goals more efficiently than they could by acting alone. All these frameworks (examples of which are given in Boxes 8.2, 8.3, 8.4) are very useful and will not be weakened by moving towards a global network of BRCs.

National BRCs

The establishment of national BRCs can help identify and address existing gaps and take advantage of opportunities not currently met by existing *ex situ* collections. They can then improve the quality of services offered and achieve efficiencies and cost savings. Achieving co-ordination between collections of bioresources through national BRCs should add value and enhance accessibility, both nationally and internationally. National BRCs will also be needed as the nodes in the network if a global system linking BRCs is to be realised. Countries could have more than one national BRC and/or could link multiple resource centres into a national BRC. National strategies will be needed to provide adequate financial support to ensure sustainability of BRCs.

An Accreditation System Based on International Criteria

International co-operation among national BRCs requires a system for ensuring quality. This suggests the need for a system of accreditation based on international criteria with guidelines on techniques and procedures for reaching a minimum standard of quality that is transparent to the user and acceptable to the scientific community. In addition, such a system would provide emerging collections/databases a blueprint for achieving a standard that would allow them to participate in the larger network and thereby benefit a wider constituency.

Different countries have set-up National BRCs. Box 8.2 represents an example of Japan's approach to establish national BRCs.

> **Box 8.2. Towards the establishment of national BRCs in Japan**
>
> Japan maintains several collections of micro-organisms and other biological resources that could become national BRCs. In addition to the existing culture collections, Japan is establishing a new national biological resource centre of industrially useful microorganisms to meet the requirements of the life sciences and biotechnology in the 21st century.
>
> This new centre belongs to the National Institute of Technology and Evaluation. It was created to implement a basic plan agreed by five ministries (names of ministries as of December 2000): the Ministry of International Trade and Industry, the Ministry of Agriculture, Forestry and Fisheries, the Ministry of Education, Science, Sports and Culture, the Ministry of Health and Welfare and the Science and Technology Agency. In addition, funding for the centre's infrastructure is provided by the Japan Millennium Project, which is directed by the Prime Minister. The centre will be located in Chiba Prefecture. It will be one of Japan's main national BRCs.

It is possible to build this accreditation system on the model of existing guidelines, such as those published by the World Federation of Culture Collections (WFCC). (Box 8.3 describes the WFCC and its quality guidelines.) Although the WFCC has global reach and includes culture collections, it is not an official regulatory authority. It focuses on scientific rather than government policy issues and as such would not be the appropriate body to take this initiative forward.

> **Box 8.3. The World Federation of Culture Collections (WFCC): Quality guidelines**
>
> The World Federation of Culture Collections (WFCC), created in 1971, has more than 500 members, including culture collections in more than 60 countries. The WFCC is a member of international scientific organisations affiliated to the International Council of Scientific Unions (ICSU). It played an instrumental role in creating

the regulatory framework under which the Budapest Treaty was implemented. It promotes the activities of traditional microbial culture collections by providing venues for the exchange of information about microbial collections and taxonomy. It holds plenary meetings every four years and scientific workshops and training courses once a year on average. It plays an important role in developing scientific guidelines aimed at enhancing the quality and functions of those collections and in seeking financial support for them. Quality guidelines for members of the WFCC can be found at http://wdcm.nig.ac.jp/wfcc/ GuideFinal.html.

As part of its efforts to promote activities that support the interests of culture collections and their users, the WFCC pioneered the development of an international database on culture resources worldwide, the WFCC-MIRCEN World Data Centre for Micro-organisms (WDCM). The WDCM provides a comprehensive directory of culture collections, databases on microbes and cell lines as well as a gateway to biodiversity, molecular biology and genome projects. The WDCM is maintained at the National Institute of Genetics (NIG) in Japan and has records of 489 culture collections in 60 countries that serve a variety of functions. The records contain data on the organisation, management, services and scientific interest of the various collections and are linked to a second record containing the list of species held.

The WDCM database forms an important information resource for microbiological activity and acts as a focus for data activities among WFCC members.

International Linkages

International linkages are essential for providing enhanced worldwide accessibility to information and biological material [Box 8.3] describes a European network linking BRCs,]. For networking of BRCs to be truly successful, technology for co-ordinating and combining catalogues and databases to meet the requirements of science in the post-genomics era will have to be implemented. It also will be important to co-ordinate curation, as well as development and networking of informatics tools for data analysis, comparison and visualisation. From the user's viewpoint, international linkages must meet the demand for standards of similar quality with respect to biological resources and data. Through these linkages, associated databases in various disciplines (genetics, biochemistry, etc.) could be integrated and provide rapid access to expertise. Linkage of BRCs can open up opportunities for collaborative research and technology transfer and foster education and training. Some regional networks have already been established and are moving in this direction. CABRI, a European network of BRCs, for example, links a wide range of culture collections, databases and post-genomics BRCs. It has regulatory and policy functions that go beyond scientific exchanges but its reach is limited to EU Member States. A network with truly global linkages on the model of CABRI could eliminate the limitations on information flows and provide one-stop access to pertinent information and biomaterials for all countries.

Box 8.4. Common Access to Biological Resources and Information (CABRI): A European network

Common Access to Biological Resources and Information (CABRI) is a regional network linking the major European *ex situ* collections. It provides a federated database system accessible through the World Wide Web (http://www.cabri.org) and is funded in part by a grant from DGXII of the European Commission.

The project defines the tools and tests the operation of an integrated resource centre linking catalogue databases of different types of organisms, genetic materials and other "biologicals" in Europe so that, during a single search session, users worldwide can access relevant catalogues through a common gateway (and mirror sites) and request/order products. CABRI allows individual centres to maintain their own identity while sharing a single gateway for their electronic catalogues.

The centres taking part in this project currently hold 21 collections covering human and animal cells, bacteria, fungi, yeasts, plasmids, animal and plant viruses and DNA probes. Instead of having to examine a large number of databases, catalogues and other sources of information, users worldwide can check simultaneously the availability of a particular type of organism or genetic resource in many locations and order the required items once located. The quality of CABRI's service has been assessed by a technical committee and each member resource centre has contributed to defining the specifications and procedures that determine how each resource type should be handled. Entry to the network is regulated and each potential partner is evaluated against these guidelines.

The overall structure is co-ordinated by a central secretariat based in the United Kingdom.

A Global BRC Network

A global BRC network would connect national BRCs and provide the framework within which co-ordination, harmonisation and quality assurance could be provided. This would enhance the services provided to the global community by BRCs beyond what the existing international frameworks could achieve.

Specifically a global BRC network would add value by achieving the following:

- *Linkage between scientific needs and government policies.*
- *Provision of an international framework for regulatory initiatives.* Directly or through the appropriate national and international authorities.
- *Provision of a linking mechanism for countries lacking national BRCs.* Countries that cannot create their own BRCs would be able to link up with a global system that would help them solve at least some of their problems.
- *Enhanced efficiency.* A global BRC network would reduce redundancies and improve transparency and efficiency and thus, over time, help participants to harness resources.

FINANCIAL SUPPORT FOR BRC

The long-term stability of BRCs requires adequate and reliable sources of funding. But how much core support must come from governments? How can other sectors contribute to the functioning of BRCs? What models of funding or partnerships can be used to ensure the sustainability of BRCs? What constitutes an adequate support base for the sustainability of a national BRC? Can costs be lowered through international co-operation? Is there a threat that some valuable biological resources will be lost to the global community owing to lack of funding? Many biological resources that have been maintained by single individuals, institutions or companies are at risk of becoming "orphan collections" and appear to face uncertain futures. High-quality BRCs that meet the needs of industry and the scientific community require long-term guaranteed financial support to maintain their mission and infrastructure. A serious problem will arise if BRCs reach an agreement to form a network aimed at eliminating duplication and sharing biological resources should one of the members or nodes in that network fail for lack of support. Furthermore, as an important part of the richness of biodiversity is deposited in BRCs, the need for new and creative sources of funding will become more critical. The promise of biotechnology is inextricably linked to appropriate support of BRCs.

Financial Costs of BRCs

The cost of incorporating biological resources into BRCs has escalated, limiting the functioning of BRCs. The DSMZ (see Box 8.1) estimates that it costs USD 2 500-3 000 to add a bacterial culture to its collection. Given that an estimated three million bacteria remain to be isolated from nature, their acquisition and incorporation into BRCs would cost USD 9 billion. The American Type Culture Collection (ATCC) estimates that it costs between USD 5 000 and USD 10 000 (depending on the type and quality of the material - tissue cultures, organisms, databases, etc.) to add new items to its collection when the costs of quality control, validation, long-term preservation and global distribution are taken into consideration. Funding such huge costs and ensuring continuous support for maintenance and functioning of BRCs will creative international financing arrangements.

If, for financial reasons, BRCs are unable to perform their tasks under conditions that meet the demands of scientific research and the requirements of industry, countries will inevitably see high value-added products being transferred into a strictly commercial environment with at least two consequences:

- Blockage of access to these products or requiring payment of an exorbitant price (without taking into account the initial government research investment required to develop them).
- Definitive loss of products and elimination of technology transfer of those products for the foreseeable future.

While BRCs should be accessible to the broad scientific community, access need not be free of charge. Many collections currently charge fees to those who want to obtain biological materials and gain access to associated databases. Varying fee structures can be applied for access depending on the nature of the biological material (microbial, plant or animal resources), the status and constraints of the institution holding the resources and its relationship with the public and private sectors, national policies and relevant international frameworks. Varying fee structures and appropriate material transfer agreements can allow for the inclusion of private industrial collections of biological resources into a co-operative system of BRCs. Fee structures should take into account public investment in the development and maintenance of BRCs.

Sources of Financial Support

There is no single satisfactory system of funding current culture collections that could be used as a model for global support of BRCs. A variety of funding sources that include income generation and core funding may be used to support BRCs:

(*i*) Government support.

(*ii*) Private industrial support for or participation in the functioning of BRCs.

(*iii*) Private industrial support for internal restricted BRCs.

(*iv*) Public and private foundation support.

(*v*) Public fundraising.

(*vi*) Sale of biological resources and technical materials.

(*vii*) Provision of specialist services and technical consulting expertise.

(*viii*) Research income (*e.g.*, grants and contracts).

(*ix*) Fees for repository services (*e.g.*, for patent strain maintenance and safe deposits).

(*x*) Provision of technical courses.

The relative proportion of funding is likely to vary greatly. Current examples of funding range from little or no public support, the case of the American Type Culture Collection which receives only 9% of its budget from the United States government, to almost complete public subsidy, the case of Germany's DSMZ which receives about 80% of its budget from the government and only about 20% from sales of materials and services. As a result, fee structures are also likely to vary widely among BRCs, as those with little government funding will be forced to transfer the bulk of their costs to users. This can create obstacles to the exchange of cultures and harmonisation and give an advantage to users who can afford to pay for expensive strains and penalising those who cannot, particularly those in developing countries. While a uniform structure of funding is not critical, considering the different situation of public-private relations with regard to conservation and utilisation of diverse biological resources, most BRCs will require a significant government funding component, and some guarantee of continuing funding to ensure that their essential functions remain reliable for R&D and support of biotechnology.

The functional BRCs of the future are likely to require a mixture of core funding and varied sources of income and participation. Novel solutions may be needed, especially to keep biological resources in developing countries. (Box 8.5 discusses novel financing arrangements in Costa Rica.) Basing BRCs on commercial services alone will not suffice, because this would reduce the scope for collaboration at international level. Too much emphasis would be placed on income generation and maximisation of the local or global market share.

Box 8.5. INBio: Financing a centre for biodiversity conservation in Costa Rica through core funding and commercial contracts for bioprospecting

Bioprospecting, the search for valuable substances for practical uses in medicine and other fields to be found from living natural resources, is one of the oldest of human activities. Costa Rica, a developing biodiversity-rich country, has recognised the opportunities offered by the link between bioprospecting and biodiversity. It has developed new ways of exploiting this linkage which have turned it into a world leader in this field. Operating on the premise that conserving natural resources into perpetuity in a tropical developing country depends in great measure upon existing knowledge of this resource, and upon society's rational use of this resource, Costa Rica launched in 1989 an innovative and pioneering project: the National Biodiversity Institute (INBio) (*Institute National de Biodiversidad*). INBio, a non-profit organisation which seeks to maintain an *ex situ* reference collection representative of the country's biological diversity to supplement *in situ* conservation activities, receives core funding from the government and has also entered into commercial agreements to search for potentially valuable biodiversity products. INBio's strategy for commercialisation of biodiversity has focused on the development of a diversified portfolio of bioprospecting research agreements that foster innovation, learning and local capacity building. Bioprospecting agreements stipulate that 10% of research budgets for the bioprospecting activities and 50% of any future royalties be awarded to the Ministry of the Environment and Energy for reinvestment in conservation. The remaining 90% of the research budget supports national scientific and processing infrastructure and value-added activities, also oriented to conservation and the sustainable use of biodiversity. The best known achievement of INBio, which is also its most widely publicised project linking biodiversity conservation to a commercial enterprise, is a 1991 agreement signed with Merck, a pharmaceutical company, to search for naturally occurring therapeutic agents produced by plants, animals and microbes from Costa Rica's ecosystems.

Meeting the Financial Challenges

To meet the challenges of financing BRCs:

- BRCs should be encouraged to co-ordinate their activities so as to best serve their essential functions in response to the needs of sectors that depend on their biological resources.
- Governments must be encouraged to provide a baseline of long-term, core funding, to centres that qualify as BRCs, to encourage high standards of quality and to promote research, development, technology transfer and commercial exploitation.
- Various foundations and philanthropic/charitable organisations, such as the Wellcome Trust (United Kingdom) which contributes to many biomedical and biological efforts including resource centres, the Gates Foundation (United States) and the Howard Hughes Foundation (United States), which provide

support for health-related technological advances, should be asked to extend the level of support given to BRCs.

- Marketable products and services may be developed within BRCs, including those aimed at meeting regulatory demands and for sale to specialised customers, as long as they do not divert capacity from the core activities of BRCs.
- Industry should be persuaded to take a long-term view of its interests and to offer some core support for BRCs, either through funding or through direct participation in the functioning of BRCs, provided the latter maintain their independence.
- Efforts should be made to harmonise fee structures in situations where fees are usually charged and to see that charges are affordable for users.

RESPONSIBILITIES OF BRC

BRCs need to provide greater quality assurance than is currently ensured by collections and databases. What can be done to ensure the quality of national BRCs and to establish quality assurance measures? Why is quality so important for international co-operation among BRCs? How can we deal with the shortage of personnel qualified to provide the expertise BRCs require? Transforming a collection into a national BRCs that can serve both national and international needs for materials and services requires raising the level of quality to an international standard that has yet to be defined in detail.

Quality Assurance

Users of BRCs must be guaranteed reliable, high-quality biological resources and information. They must receive the same level of service irrespective of the source of the materials or information requested. Today, however, the quality of collections of biological resources is disparate. Adequate common standards of practice which constitute "good practices" for BRCs are lacking. Although efforts to achieve internationally acceptable standards of quality are under way (Box 8.6 describes a centre that provides quality biological resources), ensuring that BRCs have the same high levels of quality remains a major task that has yet to be accomplished.

BRCs must provide access to living materials, genes and genetic elements, as well as accurate information about these biological resources. The task becomes more and more difficult as the amount and diversity of living materials to be incorporated into BRCs expands. Long-term preservation of living resources is a crucial function of BRCs. It is necessary to improve the infrastructure and to develop techniques for storing DNA samples from diverse ecosystems in which "molecular signatures" are found but the organisms themselves have yet to be cultured. Ensuring the accuracy of the genetic data associated with these living resources is a further crucial function of BRCs.

A major challenge facing BRCs is to achieve consistent naming and definitions. This is essential for communication and comparability, for assuring quality and avoiding unnecessary duplication. Consistent naming and definition are indispensable if all listings and catalogues of collections of the diversity of biological resources are to be available electronically. Guidelines, however, are lacking that would establish common platforms for communication and exchange of the data and biological materials available in BRCs. Currently, informal associations and links are provided by a number of highly specialised organisations that operate informative Web sites. The improvement of data handling and enhancement of cross-referencing will require the transformation of existing catalogues into new interconnected data structures. Maintaining the quality of data and materials and their validation will require harmonised coordination between BRCs and bioinformatics databases so as to provide the range of services required by the international community of life scientists and the global biotechnology industry.

Box 8.6. The MR4: A source of quality-assured biological resources

The Malaria Research and Reference Reagent Resource Center (MR4) was developed by the National Institute of Allergy and Infectious Diseases (NIAID) of the United States as an outgrowth of the Multilateral Initiative on Malaria, a federation of agencies involved in malaria research, control and development assistance. MR4 was implemented to meet the quality resource needs of the world scientific community engaged in R&D on malaria. The purpose of MR4 is to provide reagents to the scientific community which can be used as reference standards or to generate new renewable reagents. It provides improved access to parasite, vector and human reagents and standardisation of assays using well-characterised and renewable reagents. MR4 acquires, authenticates, preserves, produces and distributes all materials except live mosquito vectors to qualified users. These include but are not limited to parasites, antigens, antibodies, DNA constructs, RNA extracts, purified proteins and human biological materials. MR4 benefits the global community of malaria researchers by easing the burden of distribution and quality analysis of reagents and by increasing access to renewable reagents by the malaria research community worldwide. Besides reagents, MR4 provides an electronic bulletin board for users, workshops and training programmes, comprehensive online databases and printed catalogues describing the available reagents. The US government funds MR4, which is operated by the American Type Culture Collection (ATCC). There is no charge for reagents but shipping costs must be covered by the recipient. MR4 demonstrates the importance of a resource centre able to meet the quality requirements of the international scientific community.

Expertise

The accelerating loss of the world's biological diversity through habitat destruction, pollution and ecosystem fragmentation has been accompanied by a loss of taxonomic experts trained to discover, identify, describe and classify the world's biodiversity. Retirement of taxonomic specialists, shifts in academic recruitment and staffing and reductions in graduate training have combined to impede biodiversity research and conservation, particularly for large but poorly known groups such as bacteria and fungi. Vast numbers of species in understudied "invisible" groups constitute critical elements of food chains and ecosystems, both aquatic and terrestrial, but the high proportion of unrecognised species in these groups limits research and progress in many areas of biology and conservation.

Few experts in the fields of bioinformatics and genomics have been trained or would be available for employment by BRCs. Hence, BRCs will need to be actively involved in training and education programmes. In the 21st century, taxonomy will be strongly affected by bioinformatics and genomics, and BRCs should foster a new generation of taxonomists able to utilise informatics and molecular techniques fully. It will be very advantageous if BRCs can share expertise as well as materials and information through an integrated network (Box 8.7 describes an effort by the United Kingdom to improve co-ordination and networking at national level). Academia will also have to respond to the training needs for future staffing of modern BRCs.

Box 8.7. The Consortium of United Kingdom National Culture Collections (UKNCC): A strategy to enhance expertise at national level

A network of UK national collections was first established in 1947. It located collections of living organisms at centres of expertise to provide a resource for research and development. Over the years, the collections have increased their holdings to more than 70 000 microbes and cell lines and play a vital role in preserving the output of research programmes and in contributing basic materials for biotechnological development. During the late 1980s, it became clear that the conditions under which the culture collections were operating no longer fully met user demands. Among several issues of concern was the growing shortage of human resources with appropriate skills. Taxonomy and genomics, and the molecular biology relevant to both were identified as critical areas requiring development. As no single member of the network of national collections was able to address the emerging skill shortages on its own, the UK government recommended the establishment of the UKNCC as a central co-ordination mechanism for the collections in 1996. The UKNCC is co-ordinating some of the activities of the nine national collections, including collaboration among scientists working in the collections and sharing of technology and the associated human expertise. While this has met some of the initial needs, shortages of skilled manpower and expertise persist, and further efforts will be necessary to address these.

Challenges of BRC

To achieve quality assurance, common standards of practice must be implemented that deal with the following major issues:

- Quality management/quality assurance systems that are unified across international borders.
- Authenticity of biological materials, databases and bioinformatics and accuracy of labelling.
- Processing of cultures, cell lines, and genetic constructs, including procedures and standards for ensuring their long-term stability and quality control.
- Accuracy of the data collected and supplied.

- Expertise and training of human resources, particularly of a new generation of taxonomists able to use molecular techniques and informatics.
- Sharing of expertise among centres through co-ordination and networking.
- Use of undocumented materials and lack of citation in publications.

Restriction to access BRCs

A number of factors including financial limitations restrict access to holdings of collections of biological resources and include the following categories:

Protection of Human, Animal, Plant and Environmental Health and Safety

Many countries have specific requirements governing the shipment, handling and possession of living resources so as to protect human, animal, plant and environmental health. Access to biological resources requires the safeguards necessary to prevent untoward consequences. This necessitates a regulatory framework that restricts access so as to ensure safety. The International Air Transport Association (IATA) regulations on the shipment and carriage of biological materials provide the overall framework governing movement of biological materials to and from BRCs. However, the myriad of non-harmonised local and national regulations presents obstacles to international exchange and the advancement of science and biotechnology and could severely handicap the role of BRCs at international level.

Particular concerns have been raised about exchanges of certain biological agents and toxins which can be misused as agents in biological warfare or bioterrorism. Some organisations have taken the precautionary step of halting exchange of biological resources that may be listed as agents for potential use in bioterrorism. The Australia Group, an informal group of 30 countries formed in 1984, develops lists of hazardous micro-organisms, toxins and equipment that could be used in biological warfare programmes, so that export controls can target specific suspect countries. Some OECD countries, such as the United States, have developed additional regulations concerning the exchange of listed agents that are considered to be dangerous pathogens and toxins that might be misused. These regulations may be affecting legitimate access by the scientific community. Ongoing negotiations in Geneva for a protocol under the Biological Weapons Convention for an international accord that may include provisions for reporting activities relative to specific agents of concern could further restrict access to BRCs. Uncertainty about which agents are already included on restrictive lists of agents, and which may be added to or deleted from such lists, makes it difficult to ensure exchanges that will allow for continued scientific research on dangerous pathogens while maintaining national and international security. The potential for lawsuits involving alleged damage to health and safety is also causing some BRCs to restrict access to certain biological materials.

Ethical Protection of the Rights of Individuals and Patients

The exponential growth of samples from humans for medical research and genetic testing has created new challenges for BRCs. Over the last two decades, medical research has begun to make extensive use of products of human origin in therapeutics, oncology and most recently, genetic disease. This has raised many ethical issues involving protection of confidentiality and patient rights, including issues of consent. BRCs have to be prepared for their role in transactions involving human materials and ensure appropriate expertise to guarantee protection of the rights of individuals and patients. At present, there is no agreed international system to control access to human biological resource data and biological materials of human origin and derived products that can be exchanged by BRCs and made available for wider use.

Samples and data from genetic testing challenge the technological capacities of BRCs and their ability to deal ethically with protection of the rights of individuals and patients. BRCs must be able to control access to sensitive patient data and biological samples. They must ensure that there is correct patient consent and that the identity and civil rights of donors and relatives are safeguarded. Additionally, it is essential to provide stringent quality assurance and traceability controls. Computerisation of the data must be implemented in a very strict technical and organisational environment, including cryptographic techniques.

Commercial genetic testing is offered internationally, and human samples and related data are being exchanged across national borders, particularly for research purposes, not always with the knowledge of donors. Such samples and the related genetic information can be stored in BRCs, which currently operate in the absence of clearly established international frameworks for quality assurance and the protection of security, privacy and confidentiality of such human bioresources. R&D and applied services related to genetic testing have outpaced regulatory frameworks. International harmonisation is essential to protect patient rights and provide the necessary ethical guidelines for BRCs.

Private Industrial Investment and Industrial Secrecy

Many biological resources are held exclusively in industrial collections. Generally, such private industrial collections are withheld from public access to protect financial investments and industrial secrets. Private industrial biological resources typically are made accessible to the wider scientific community only when patents protect them or when they are no longer deemed to be of specific economic value. This can lead to conflict between the public and private sector when there is a perceived need to provide access for the advancement of science and the betterment of humankind, as exemplified by the race to sequence the human genome. In that case, agreement to provide access to private and public sequence data was reached between CELERA - a private industrial company - and the human genome project sponsored by the US government only after difficult negotiations and a call for full access to the data made in 2000, by President Clinton of the United States and Prime Minister Blair of the United Kingdom. The negotiations involved in reaching the agreement to public release of the human genome sequence data highlight the challenge to be faced in trying to co-ordinate and harmonise BRCs, with the aim of providing access to biological resources in both the private and public sectors. The CELERA case points to the possibility of making some biological resources available to the public through BRCs that are not currently accessible to the wider scientific community.

Import/Export Regulations

In response to economic as well as the health and safety concerns already discussed, many countries have established import and export regulations that control exchanges of specific biological materials across international borders. These regulations include requirements for licensing and quarantine that strongly affect the operations of BRCs and their ability to provide ready access to biological resources. Compliance with import/export regulations is especially complicated owing to differing national regulatory frameworks and a lack of international harmonisation. The import/export regulations can limit international exchange among BRCs and their users.

IPR Protection

Proposals to institutionalise and link BRCs internationally require close examination in terms of national and international legal requirements for ownership and protection of IPR. Any international effort to co-ordinate BRCs must recognise that intellectual property rights are primarily defined by national laws and that ownership is mainly governed by property laws. Rules and regulations governing access and exchange of biological resources are complex and depend upon the nature of the material, national legislation, the positions of countries with regard to relevant international legal agreements, such as the Budapest Treaty, and patenting and licensing policies.

The G8 Heads of State and Government at their Summit in Okinawa (July 2000), recognising IPR as a major issue for biotechnology in the post-genomics era, called for "a system of balanced and equitable intellectual property protection for gene-based inventions, based wherever possible on common practices and policies" and encouraged efforts to achieve broad harmonisation of patenting policies for biotechnological inventions.

Prior to the genomics revolution, patents and IPR protection were not a major problem for *ex situ* collections. Micro-organisms that have been patented to protect IPR are made accessible through collections under the terms of the Budapest Treaty. Without such IPR protection, both individual scientists and industry would have withheld these biological resources as "trade secrets". However, the patenting of genes and gene sequences has created an IPR-related access problem owing to uncertainties about copyright protection for databases and the implementation of stringent licensing agreements for patented genes/gene fragments.

This may greatly limit access to patented genes. Limitation of access to such biological materials and processes, which are indispensable for biomedical research, has been criticised in the United States and other countries.

Material Transfer Agreements

As current national and international regimes are not sufficient to address all issues relevant to access to material, intellectual property rights and safety, institutions - including BRCs - have developed material transfer agreements (MTAs) which are legal instruments for establishing contractual relationships to define liability and to specify allowed uses of biological resources. MTAs eliminate ambiguities about the rights of use of biological materials deposited in collections. They rely on local laws to control the assignment of IPR and to specify allowable uses of biological materials and data. Because MTAs establish customised contractual relationships, they provide flexibility regarding assignment of IPR, conditions of access and permissible use. In some cases, MTAs contain provisions that would lead BRCs to restrict access.

Ways to Enhance Access to Biological Resources

To enhance access to biological resources, the following ways can be considered:

- BRCs should be accessible to all legitimate users worldwide and serve as international gateways to facilitate access to biological resources in the framework of international laws and regulations.
- Countries should increase their efforts to achieve greater international harmonisation of the laws, rules and practices governing access. Legal and regulatory differences among countries, particularly with regard to health and safety, use of human materials and IPR, can lead to unnecessary restriction of access to and exchange of biological materials.
- Private companies should be encouraged to open to the public parts of their collections that are not critical for their competitive position, either directly or through recognised BRCs.
- Governments must remain alert to possible negative long-term consequences of restrictive gene licensing practices on biological research and biotechnology and on the rights of BRCs to provide access to genetic biological resources, and must be prepared to address these negative consequences when they can be documented.
- Governments need to work towards international harmonisation of the broad variety of laws, regulations and practices aimed at protecting the health and safety of humans, animals, plants and the environment from potentially hazardous biological materials. This will discourage inappropriate uses of biological resources.
- Governments need to develop internationally compatible laws, standards and practices regarding human materials and data, in order to protect individual and patient rights and confidentiality, so that the ethical handling of biological materials and data from humans can be guaranteed.

A CALL FOR ACTION FOR BIOLOGICAL RESOURCES

If the government scientific community and the private sectors work together, then the following goals for global expansion of biotechnology:

(*i*) Establishment of national BRCs.

(*ii*) Development of an accreditation system for BRCs based on international criteria.

(*iii*) Creation of international linkages among BRCs to facilitate international co-ordination among nations BRCs.

(*iv*) Co-ordination and establishment of standards, rules and regulations for national and international BRCs.

(*v*) Establishment of global BRC network

The establishment of a global BRC network would greatly improve the conditions under which biological materials and informations are preserved and exchanged. This challenge calls for full support of governments, scientific community and the private sector for allow BRC to grow with the global expansion of biotechnology.

SUMMARY

- Biological resource centres BRCs are an essential part of the infrastructure underpinning life sciences and biotechnology. They consist of service providers and repositories of the living cells, genomes of organism, and information relating to heredity and the functions of biological systems.
- The growing worldwide demand for biological resources provides good reasons for greatly increasing the number and quality of BRCs.
- BRCs provide essential expertise for formulation of government policies on biological resources and for information and assurance to the public.
- The establishment of national BRCs can help identify and address existing gaps and take advantage of opportunities not currently met by existing *ex situ* collections. They can then improve the quality of services offered and achieve efficiencies and cost savings.
- A global BRC network would connect national BRCs and provide the framework within which co-ordination, harmonisation and quality assurance could be provided.
- BRCs need to provide greater quality assurance than is currently ensured by collections and databases.

REVIEW QUESTIONS

1. What are Biological resource centres?
2. What are the roles of BRCs?
3. What are the challenges faced by BRCs?
4. Give functions of Biological Resources Centres.
5. Why are BRCs needed and explain their essential functions?
6. Explain in detail about the sources for financial support to BRCs.
7. Give detail descussion for the Responsibilities of BRCs.
8. What are the ways to Enhance Access to Biological Resources?

Chapter 9

CAPITAL INVESTMENT

COMMERCIAL POTENTIAL OF BIOTECHNOLOGY

Biotechnology has unlimited potential due to its capability to generate unlimited range of and useful products/services concerned with virtually every aspect of human existence. *e.g.*, in mid-90s, over 130 biotechnologically derived pharmaceuticals aimed at everything from hemophilia to AIDS, and from anaemia to leukaemia, were under regulatory review in USA. The contribution of biotechnological products to global market is rising rapidly and is expected to increase from US $ 100 billion/year in 2000 to further higher.

Also, the biotechnology industry in India is growing rapidly in the wake of liberalization of the economy that fostered alliances between India companies and multinationals. The demand for biotechnological products in India has been estimated at around Rs. 55 billion (US $ 1.85 billion) in 2000 and may double up by 2007 year end. The major share of this demand would be in the areas of human and animal health (72%), followed by that for industrial products (27%), agricultural sectors account for a very small portion (7%) of the demand.

The new biotechnology clearly demands very high expertise and skill and continued heavy funding coupled with dedicated effort. Therefore, highly industrialized countries have a edge over less indistrialized ones and more so, over the developing countries both with regard to research and development (R and D) activities, and the exploitation of market potential. This becomes evident when list of biotechnological products originating from developed countries are compared with those from developing countries : almost all the products are coming from developed countries. Thus, the world trade would become increasingly concentrated in the already highly industrialized and affluent countries, leaving the other countries at a considerable disadvantage. This problem would further aggravate as companies have started to exploit plant genetics to modify 'third world crops'.

The biotechnology research is both public and private funded and private sector is increasingly interested in biotechnological research with aim of making profits. The essence of any biotechnological process is the recovery of the concerned product in a useful form. The efficiency of product recovery is reflected in product cost. Sometimes process of product recovery may be either in efficient or costly preventing the commercial exploitation of the biotechnological process, *e.g.*, recovery of insulin, interferon etc. This operative derives inputs from chemistry, chemical engineering, biochemistry and biochemical engineering.

Important areas where biotechnology is making marked contributions.
Human health
Medicine
Animal Health
Chemicals and Biochemicals
Forensic
Forestry, horticulture
Renewable energy and fuel
Mining
Fisheries

Biotechnology Entrepreneurship

Over last two decades biotechnology has also been used for commercial gains and has attracted investments in the stock market, which resulted in closure, merger and acquisition of existing biotechnology companies. This was because the scientists who started the biotechnology companies lacked experience in business. Also, the businessman who tried to use biotechnology to make money also failed because they did not have the knowledge of biotechnology. Therefore it gave rise to a new terminology BIOTECHNOLOGY ENTREPRENEURSHIP, which has become a specialized subject. This subject needs attention of those aspiring to enter biotechnology company and for sustaining it for commercial gains. To be successful, a variety of skills are also needed apart from research experience, degrees. He should possess adaptability, intelligence, confidence, ability to interact with others, humility, flexibility and patience to be successful. Also, he should have good communication skills, should be persuasive and creative. Also, he should have the basic knowledge of capital investment, product-based life cycle. He should be able to interpret market surveillance and plan product design, cost estimation and analysis to make appropriate fruitful decisions of capital investment.

Scientific disciplines contributing to molecular biotechnology which generates a wide range of commercial products

The ultimate objective of all biotechnology research is the development of commercial products. Consequently, molecular biotechnology is driven to a great extent by economics. Not only does financial investment currently sustain molecular biotechnology, but clearly the expectations of financial gain was responsible for the considerable interest and excitement during its development. Tracing down the history of commercialisation, the unprecedented enthusiastic public response to Genetic encouraged others to follow. Between 1980 and 83, 200 small biotechnology industries were founded in USA with the help of tax incentives and funding from both stock market speculation and private investment. Herbert Boyer was first research scientist at University of California at San Francisco and then a Vice President of Genetic, University professors started many of the early companies. During 1980s, rapid profileration of biotechnology business occurred and small companies were absorbed by the large ones, strategic merger took place and joint ventures were undertaken.

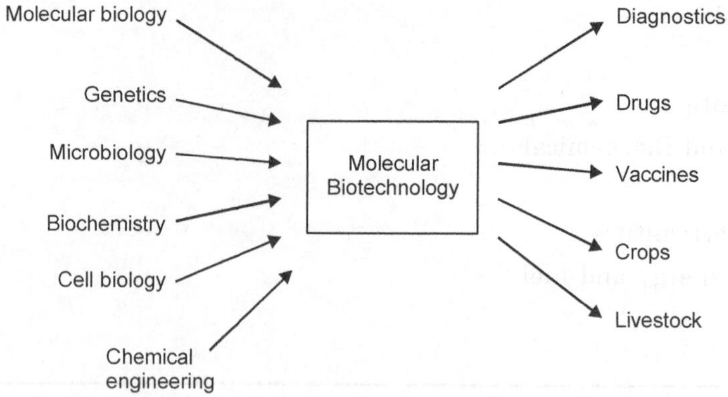

Figure 9.1. Inputs and outputs of molecular biotechnology

By mid-1990s, more than a dozen new drugs produced recombinant DNA technology had been certified for use in humans. By 2000, product sales for molecular biotechnology commodities was US $ 100 billion per year. However, profits, for biotechnology companies have been elusive still the continuing enthusiasm of investors for biotechnology indicates, at least in their estimation, that molecular biotechnology will have a pervasive impact on society.

New independent molecular biotechnology companies have always been specialized and tend to stress the use of a particular aspect of recombinant DNA technology that is often reflection their names such as Immunes, ImmunoGen, MedImmune, ImmuLogic were formed to produce genetically engineered antibodies for treating infectious diseases, cancer and other disorders in humans.

Most of the commercial development has been centred in USA. In other countries where investment capital is not readily available and where there is less emphasis on entrepreneurial activity, large corporations and governments have taken an active role in creating indigenous molecular biotechnology initiatives.

In Japan, biotechnology has been declared a **"strategic industry"** and made a national priority by the government. In Japan, researchers have acquired necessary expertise by collaborating with US companies and universities and now major Japanese corporations are more directly involved in molecular biotechnology research and product development.

The commercial molecular biology will be exciting in coming years. Although the specific predictions are risky because new technological innovations rapidly replace existing technologies.

Capital Investment

Genetic (San Francisco, USA) was the first ever company to be launched in field of biotechnology and made an initial public offering (IPO) of $ 35 million at the rate of $35 per share that soared to $ 88 per share and closed at $ 56 per share at the end of the day, giving a valuation of $ 400 million.

Success of a biotechnology company depends on its patent portfolio and licensing revenue; successful deal with pharmaceutical selection of right partner estimation of capital investment and manufacturing and profitability and cost analysis for decision making.

COST ESTIMATION OF THE PROJECT

Estimating costs

Demand sets a ceiling on the price the company can charge for its product.

The company wants to charge a price that covers its cost of producing, distributing, and selling the product, including a fair return for its effort and risk. Net result is not always profitability when companies price products to over full costs.

The costs are of two forms < fixed / variable.

Fixed costs include rent, heat, interest, salaries etc. variable costs vary directly with level of production, and their costs tend to be constant per unit produced.

Pricing

While setting pricing policy, the following six-step procedure are followed by the companies:

1. It selects its pricing objective.
2. It estimates demand curve.
3. It estimates how its costs vary at different levels of output.
4. It examines competitors' costs, price and offers.
5. It selects a pricing method.
6. It selects the final price.

Pricing Structure

Companies do not usually set a single price, but rather a pricing structure varies according to geographical demand, market segment requirements etc.

Changing Price

After developing pricing strategies, firms often face situations where they need to change prices in response to declining market share, desire to dominate the market, in response to competitor's price change.

Profitability

Market strategies for biotechnological products.

BIOTECH PRODUCT-BASED LIFE CYCLE

In the life cycle of a product, nine steps have been identified where Biotechnology ethics are applied:

1. Frame work setting, proposal, funding, communication.
2. Early research and patenting.
3. Product design, development and testing.
4. Product assessment, regulation, registration, communication.
5. Market launch (including labels and communication)
6. Market surveillance, enforcement, communication, user education.
7. Product re-evaluation.
8. Evaluate performance of ethics evaluation.
9. Improve governance of ethics evaluation.

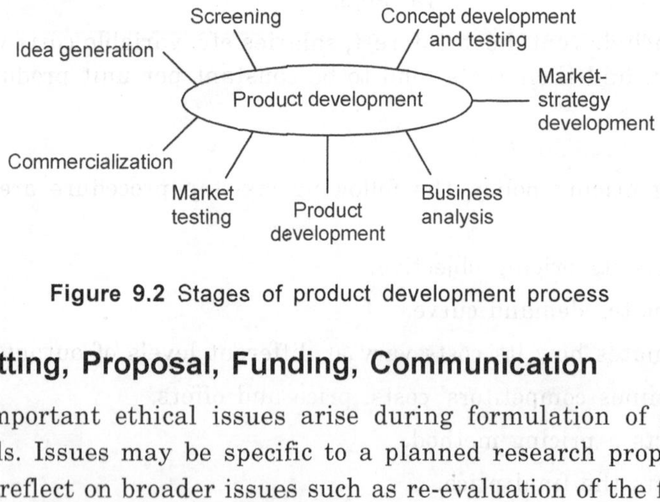

Figure 9.2 Stages of product development process

Framework Setting, Proposal, Funding, Communication

The most important ethical issues arise during formulation of ideas, goals, and research proposals. Issues may be specific to a planned research proposal or they may open the need to reflect on broader issues such as re-evaluation of the framework within which funding is taking place. *e.g.,* "Broad" issue-type would be research using embryonic stem-cells in terms of ethics, political philosophy, and governance issues.

Key issues

- How should researchers and society deal with projects that are described as "playing God" by some observers? Is it sufficient for a researcher to announce, "I will be able to create such-and-such (*e.g.,* artificial life, cloned humans, etc.)—society should have a debate about it"?

Agencies regulating these issues

- International Organizations e.g.,

  FAO.

  HUGO.

  COMEST.

  IBC.

- National and International Agencies of:

  Funding.

  Environmental and International Development Groups.

  Industry Associations.

  Parliament.

  Patent.

Early Research and Patenting

Early research in the laboratory or in confined conditions is important for later research or even full blown industrial production in the biotech context. Since biological research is based on samples, and the ownership and control over these living samples is an issue in both the health and environmental sectors.

Key Issues

High research poses its own ethical issues. Aside from the obvious cases of biological weapons research, research into xenoplantation and other methods that may cause the transmission of diseases from animals into the human population can be considered from an ethical viewpoint. The threat to biodiversity arising from certain environmental uses of biotechnology also falls in this category.

Biotechnology has led to an increase in the use of laboratory animals (*e.g.*, for immunological methods). This is not a biotech specific ethical issue but, because of the scale, it should be considered. Further, biotechnology also allows the creation of animals that may suffer "by design".

The origin and use of living materials poses an array of ethical issues. Key topics are practice of bioprospecting (searching for useful biological materials) and the ownership of human issues. The related issues are ethics of breadth of patent claims, licencing schemes, farmer's privileges and the idea of benefit sharing.

Product Design, Development and Testing

In the biotech ethics and bioproducts context, issue of the efficacy of biotechnology products arises. Biotechnology may allow use of the materials currently considered "waste", improve the efficiency of production, and produce outputs that are less harmful than alternatives.

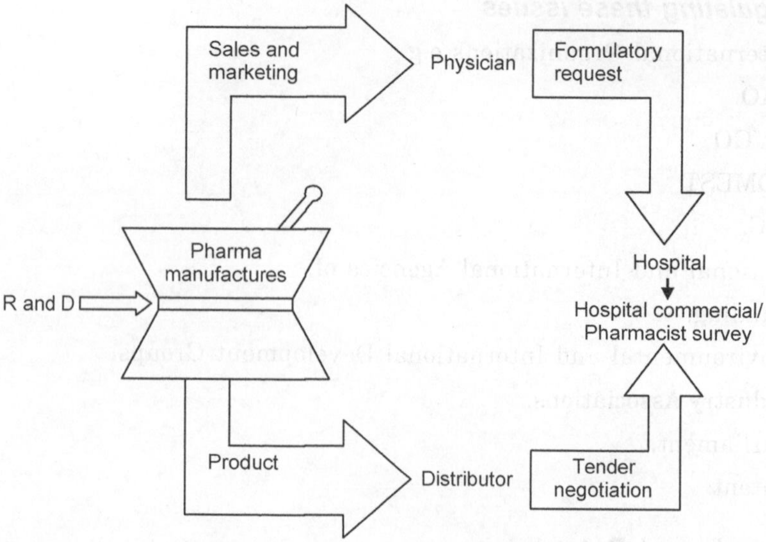

Figure 9.3 Productivity and R and D activity of pharma industry

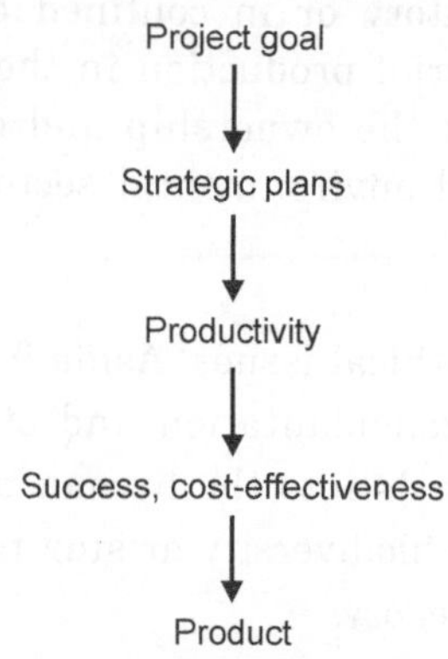

Figure 9.4 Project management

Product Assessment, Regulation, Registration, Communication

When the products are fully developed, then need for evaluating its physical risks and benefits and international co-operation is advisable for products used in trade and products that may move across borders unintentionally.

Market Launch

Net all products entering the consumer's market undergo the same regulator oversight—the use pattern and product claims influence the regulatory approval required.

The labeling of biotech product draws attention to the process by which the product was generated.

Market Surveillance, Enforcement, Communication User Education

The arrival of increasing numbers of genetic tests raises ethical issues over their potential misuse by doctors and patients and over potential donors by advertisers. Also, banking of DNA raises privacy concerns. Advent of gene therapy and genetic counselling gives rise to a number of technical and ethical issues.

Product Re-evaluation

Industry monitors its products and may decide to re-evaluate label claims, use, user information, etc.

Evaluate Performance of Ethics Evaluation

This includes re-evaluation based on data and external audits or advice to evaluate performance of ethics.

Improve Governance of Ethics Evaluation

The ultimate goal should be to enact change following re-evaluation to reflect on how pervasive and transformative biotechnology may be.

Thus product evaluation process is a good model to approach ethical issues surrounding biotechnology.

SUMMARY

Biotechnology has unlimited commercial potential. However, it demands very high expertise and skill and continued heavy funding coupled with dedicated effort to plan and launch a biotechnology company or product. For this, a fair knowledge of economics in terms of capital investment and product life cycle is required.

REVIEW QUESTIONS

1. Discuss about commercial potential of biotechnology.
2. Describe biotechnology entrepreneurship.
3. What are important areas where biotechnology is making marked contributions?
4. Which scientific disciplines contribute for generation of commercial biotechnology products?
5. Give an account of biotech product-based life cycle.
6. What is bioprospecting and ownership of biological materials?
7. Discuss the commercialization of biotechnology.
8. What should be the skills of biotechnology entrepreneurship?
9. Chart out a plan for estimating cost of a proposed biotechnology project.
10. Discuss the pricing policy of a product.
11. Describe biotech product based life cycle.
12. Discuss strategies of product launch.

Chapter 10

MARKETING STRATEGIES FOR BIOTECHNOLOGICAL PRODUCTS

The key survival of pharmaceutical and biotechnology companies is to place successful products on the market place. Project managers are becoming an increasingly integral part of that strategy.

Biotechnology and pharmaceutical companies face constant challenges in the course of developing new pharmaceuticals or other products.

WHAT IS PROJECT MANAGEMENT

Project management is application of knowledge, skills, tools and techniques to a broad range of activities in order to meet the requirements of the particular project. These results are defined in terms of four factors : cost, schedule, performance and scope.

Factors Affecting Project Management

Cost — budget allocated to the project.

Schedule — timeline for the project's deliverables.

Scope — magnitude of the job.

Performance — how well the team members do their work.

Project management of a project in pharmaceutical companies.

It focusses on the following points:

1. Setting project goal.
2. Putting strategic plans into practice.
3. Increasing productivity and efficiency of staff.
4. Establishing measures of success.
5. Quantifying value commensurate with cost.
6. Optimizing the use of organizational resources.

7. Incorporating quality principles.
8. Overcoming technical challenges.
9. Standardizing routine tasks.
10. Ensuring that available resources are used in the most effective and efficient manner.
11. Planning and executing for clinical evaluation.
12. Managing communications.
13. Successfully scaling up the discovery to market introduction.
14. Ensuring fast time to market.

NEW PRODUCT DEVELOPMENT

Marketers play a key role in the new-product process by identifying and evaluating new-product ideas and working with R&D and others in every stage of development.

A company can add new products through acquisition or development. The acquisition route can take three forms—

(*i*) company can buy other companies.
(*ii*) it can buy a license or franchise from another company.
(*iii*) it can acquire patents from other companies.

The development route can take two forms—

(*i*) company can develop new products in its own laboratories or
(*ii*) it can contract with independent researchers or new-product development firms to develop specific new products.

Categories of New Products

1. New to the world products.
2. New product lines.
3. Additions to existing product links.
4. Improvements and revisions of existing products.
5. Repositioning of existing products.
6. Cost reductions.

Stages of Product Development Process

Eight Stages are involved in Product Development Process:

1. Idea generation,
2. Screening,
3. Concept development and testing,
4. Marketing—strategy development,

5. Business analysis,
6. Product development,
7. Market testing, and
8. Commercialization.

At each stage, the company must determine whether the idea should be dropped or moved to the next stage.

Launching New Products

Launching new products as brand extensions into related product categories is one means of broadening the brand meaning.

Companies should have routine innovation process companies that fail to develop new products are putting themselves at risk.

New product-development can be risky. New products can fail for many reasons: ignoring or misinterpreting market research, overestimating market size, high development costs, poor design, incorrect positioning, ineffective advertising or wrong price, insufficient distribution support.

To develop successful new products, company carefully defines and assesses the target market, product requirements, and benefits before proceeding.

Budgeting for New-Product Development

Senior management must decide how much to budget for new-product development. R&D outcomes are so uncertain that it is difficult to use normal investment criteria.

Organizing New-Product Development

Many companies assign responsibility for new-product ideas to *idea managers.* But, product managers are often so busy managing existing lines that they give little thought to new products other than line extensions.

A large number of biotechnology companies into existence during last decade. In 2001, 1379 biotechnology companies in USA and 2104 biotechnology companies in Europe were registered. Due to anticipated growth of biotechnology industry, these companies are attracted huge investments in the stock market. On the other hand, many companies have met with failures and closures. In the past, many scientists started biotechnology companies for commercial gains who had no familiarity with business world. On the other hand, business experts unfamiliar with biotechnology started biotechnology companies. These people faced failures and consequently learnt by their mistakes.

In view of this, a student of biotechnology should have the knowledge of factors that influence success of a biotechnology company. They should be familiar with management of projects and marketing of biotechnological inventions. An effort is being made in this chapter to familiarize students with various aspects of biotechnology that have a bearing on the success of biotechnology business.

Capital Investment

Genentech (San Francisco, USA) was the first biotechnology company in USA to make an initial public offering (IPO) of $ 35 million at the rate of $ 35 per share which soared to $ 88 per share within the first 20 minutes and closed at $ 56 per share at the end of the day, giving a valuation of $ 400 million.

The average IPO raised by individual companies in last two decades did not exceed $ 20-30 million per year, although the total capital was raised. The capital raised by biotechnology industry steadily improved over the years towards the end of 20th century.

Number of new biotechnology companies have been floated in area of genomics research, and most of them may not be able to sustain and therefore merger and acquisition of companies occurred.

The last decade witnessed merger and/or acquisition of biotechnology companies which happened in most of the cases due to inability of several companies to retain their independent existence. *e.g.*, Celer a Genomics acquired Axy Pharmaceuticals and Lexicon Genetics purchased Coelacanth. Also, many companies merged in 21st century *e.g.*, Sequinom and Gemini Genomics who specialized in information mining for the Human Genome Project merged towards the end of 2001. The purpose of this merger was to combine mass spectrometry-based genetic analysis system of sequenom with clinical population genomics of Gemini Genomics. Thus, this merger combined the human genetic resources with rapid analytic system to generate a more powerful data generating machine. This raised $ 250 million in IPO and this merger was seen as a synergistic effort following a well planned and thoughtout strategy.

Success of a biotechnology company depends on its patent portfolio and licensing revenue. The issues of patents in biotechnology will be discussed in subsequent chapters.

Survival of biotechnology companies sometimes depends upon successful deals with pharmaceutical and other companies and selection of right partner in biotechnology industry involves—

1. designing of search criteria, which should include both science and business skills. *i.e.*, scientific skills and R&D competence and geographic proximity of partners and market.
2. Knowledge of large and diverse database about biotechnology companies that could be prospective partners.
3. Screening process—which involves negotiation of the terms of deal.

Once a deal has been materialised following the above three steps, good business relationships are required to boost the business. *e.g.*, Pfizer and Neurogen had a fruitful collaboration for licensing drug NGD-91 for Alzheimer disease.

WHAT SHOULD A NEW COMPANY HAVE?

A new company should have a focus.

It is not always easy to transform an important discovery or brilliant idea into a commercial opportunity. Many of young biotechnology companies have done it successfully.

Thus, one of the basic questions, a new company would have to address is to announce or display its focus to **launch** its product into market. Some companies have succeeded in getting its product to the market due to its superb early product selection. *e.g.,* Amgen (USA), Sugen (USA), Vertex (UK). On the other hand, such a focus can also meet failure when selected product fails in clinical trials. *e.g.,* British Biotechnology's (UK) matrix metalloproteinase inhibitor program failed indeed.

So, young companies should be careful in focusing their attention on product development and/or R&D programs. A company may have skill for drug discovery, but may not be equipped for drug development. Such a company if enters into drug discovery or clinical trials without estimating cost and risk may face failure. One should also assess the treatment for the drug in question being developed.

Because cost-factor is also involved in this. *e.g.*, a single phase III trial of drug for stroke may be ten times costlier than that for migraine.

Thus, planning is essential to avoid fatal surprises for the company.

BIOENTREPRENEUR

Bioentrepreneur—This term has been coined for students of biotechnology aspiring to become future entrepreneurs.

Skills of Bioentrepreneur

A bioentrepreneur should possess a variety of skills to be successful apart from having research experience, degrees, publication. A successful bioentrepreneur should have intangible attributes for coping with complex ambiguous situations. He should have the following qualities to be successful:

— confidence.

— ability to adapt.

— patience.

— intelligence.

— ability to interact with others.

— persistence.

— ability to take risks.

— humility.

— flexibility.

Also, he should have good communication skills: he should be able to write and speak clearly and confidently.

Also, he should be persuasive and creative. If one really aspires to become bioentrepreneur, one can learn these attributes by attending conferences and/or taking bioentrepreneurial training and educational courses offered by various universities in different countries. To name a few : Entrepreneurial Management Center (SanDiego, USA),

Entrepreneurship Program (Brown University),

MBA Entrepreneurship Oxford Brookes, (UK),

Entrepreneurship Courses (Entrepreneurship Development Institute of India, Gujarat).

Finally, these attributes are learnt by experience. This guidance based on wisdom of those who have learnt the art of bioentrepreneurship, either the hard way by making mistakes themselves or else spent time observing others doing it, may benefit students of biotechnology aspiring to become future entrepreneurs.

MARKETING STRATEGIES FOR BIOTECHNOLOGY PRODUCTS

Marketing planning begins with formulating an offering to meet target customer's needs or wants.

Marketing Strategies

Since it takes time to roll out a new product, work out the project, fill dealer pipelines and gain consumer acceptance, sales growth tends to be slow at this stage. Also, sometimes due to product complexity and fewer potential buyers, sale of an expensive product are slowed.

Life-Cycle of Product

It is divided into four stages:

(*i*) introduction.

(*ii*) growth.

(*iii*) maturity.

(*iv*) decline.

(*i*) *Introduction stage*: Companies that plan to introduce a new product must decide when to enter the market. To be first can be rewarding, but risky and expensive. To come in later makes sense if the firm can bring superior technology, quality or brand strength.

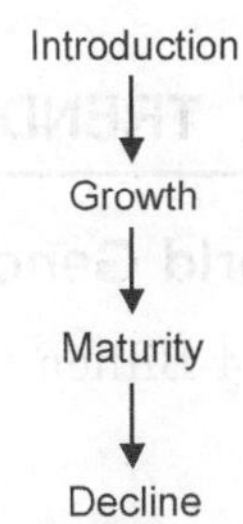

Figure 10.1 Life-cycle of product, stage

(*ii*) *Growth stage*: It is marked by rapid climb in sales and the firms use several strategies to sustain rapid market growth namely, improvement in quality of product and addition of new products; increase in its distribution coverage, lowering of price to attract next layer of price-sensitive buyers and product-preference advertising.

(*iii*) *Maturity stage*: In this stage, sale growth slows and profits stabilize. This indicates overcapacity in the industry. Thus, companies increase advertising and trade and consumer promotion. They increase R&D budgets to develop product improvements and line extensions. Also, weaker products are abandoned by companies and they concentrate more profitable products and on new products.

(iv) *Decline stage*: Sales decline for a number of reasons, including technological advances, shift in consumer tastes, and increased domestic and foreign competition. As sales and profits decline, some firms withdraw from the market, others may reduce the number of products they offer. Unfortunately, most companies have not developed a policy for handling aging products. The appropriate strategy depends on industry's relative attractiveness and the company's competitive strength in that industry.

ADVERTISING

Advertising can be used to build up a long-term image for a product or trigger quick sales. Advertising can efficiently reach geographically dispersed buyers. Certain forms of advertising can require a large budget, whereas other forms do not.

Qualities of Advertising

(i) *Pervasiveness*—advertising permits the seller to repeat a message many times. It also allows the buyers to receive and compare the messages of various competitors.

(ii) *Amplified expressiveness*—advertising provides opportunities for dramatizing the company and its products through artful use of print, sound and color.

(iii) *Impersonality*—advertising is a monologue in front of, not a dialogue with, the audience.

MARKET TRENDS

Total World Genomic Market

USD 4 Billion (2005)

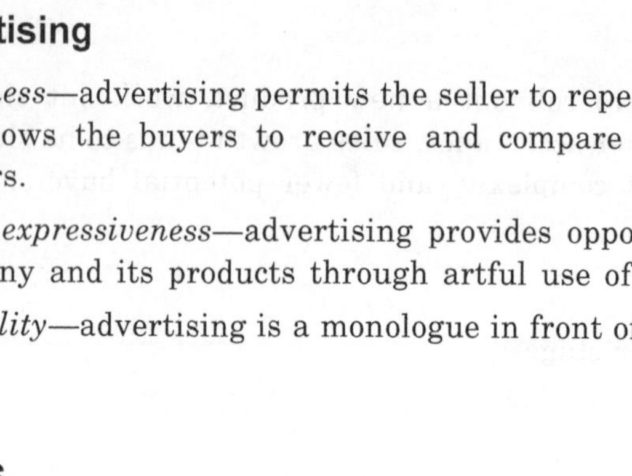

Figure 10.2 Total world wide genomics market : USD 4 Billion (2005)

Market Segments

- Array
- Molecular cloning
  - PCR
  - Hybridization

    - Labelling
    - Detection
- Sample preparation and synthesis
    - Nucleic acid sample preparation
    - Purification
    - Synthesis
- Sequencing
    - Sequencing
    - Resequencing/comparative genotyping
- SNP genotyping

Market Trends

The life science tools industry consists of a broad range of companies providing technology solutions that form basis of drug discovery, applied market testing (*e.g.*, biodefense, food, forensics, environment etc.), and basic scientific and medical research.

Eight key sub-segments of life science tool sectors are:

- genomics.
- proteomics.
- cell biology.
- cloning.
- combinatorial chemistry.
- small animal *invivo* analysis.
- bioinformatics.
- general lab ware.

The market survey indicates that life science tools sector will be approximately $ 25 billion in sales in 2006 and will grow at a 7% compounded annual growth.

The life science tools sector is a very complex market with its sub-segments at various stages in their growth cycle. The '90s saw the growth of genomics-oriented markets, resulting in the sequencing of human genome. Today, the growth is fueled by cell biology and small animal invivo analysis, thereby providing better data, leading to development of safer drugs.

Although the proteomics space has been adversely affected by the slow down in Pharma spending, mass spectrometry has been the major contributor to growth. This has been fueled by the technology advances, sales to applied markets, and increased utility as a clinical diagnostic.

In the case of cell biology, drug discovery will accelerate future growth, by high through-put and high-content analysis, functional cell-based assays, and RNAi-base applications.

Noticeable shifts are also emerging among consumers and buyers of these products. As pharma shifts from a one-size-fits all approach to individually tailored therapeutics, the impact on the tools segment will be significant. Academic spending will due to budget cutbacks in US and EU.

The slowdown in customer spending has been offset by explosive growth in applied markets and home-brew testing both in US and overseas. Companies are trying to extend their are competancy as tools and reagent providers for home-brew tests to main stream the clinical diagnostic players. Eventual market penetration and success will depend on their ability to understand market dynamics, develop commercial and regulatory expertise and provide accurate and reliable tests.

Geographically, North America and Europe dominate the life science tools market. Growth is estimated to be flat in North America due to NIH cutbacks and slow down in Pharma. Europe will exhibit moderate growth due to decrease in CRO/CMO and applied market testing. Significant growth opportunities are expected in India and China.

The quest for leadership in this market has spurned a flurry of M and A activity, none of which necessarily predicts market leadership.

The underlying theme of "Biotech 2006 NJ/PA" symposia was immediate need for innovative solutions to reduce the cost and increase the speed and productivity of all phases of R and D required to being safe and effective drug to market.

Productivity in the pharma industry is down and costs are up and outsourcing schemes to be a better option for US and EU.

Outsourcing certain R and D activities overseas can stream line operations. Offshoring R and D in terms of access to study subjects, trained personnel, lower-cost infrastructure, and labour pools. But care should be taken, and it is advised to keep a close eye on contract and licencing terms, quality control measures, regulatory issues, and time lines.

Biotech's Changing Competitive Landscape

Biotechnology companies, especially those profitable today, face a coming decade that may be even painful than the past decade was for global pharma, when many saw their valuations cut in half, not to mention all restructuring, and management havoc.

A couple of dozen companies accounted for over 95% of the sector valuation of the early 90s. Today, that figure is downed to 70% as their multiples have been halved, exceeding even the most bearish predictions.

This is despite the fact that their contributions to industry sales is still at the same level, or around 84% (down from 89%). The cash flow share also has eroded only modestly from 90% to 86%.

Most biotech companies achieved their success behind just one or two block busting drugs that are priced boldly and marketed aggressively.

Unfortunately, as happened with large pharma, billions in R and D have failed to produce much in the way of a next round of innovations.

Managers of these companies have successfully put into practice two lesson's from large pharma text book—well-time life-cycle management strategies.

Remember, things are about to change on two fronts:

Next generation competitive innovations are in last stages of development and the FOB pathway is being defined, which will begin the flow of lower cost bigenerics by the end of this decade, first in Europe and soon there after in the U.S., Europeans patents on many of the big biologic blockbusters have expired or will expire over the next several years, where as the US patents begin to lapse into the next decade.

Likely to be facing competition from next-generation innovations, and soon, are Epogen (Roche's) Herceptin (GSK) and Avastin (Sanofi's). Even a modest improvement destroys the first mover advantage, as Lucentis did to Macugen in AMD sales; Macugen went from $50 million in quarterly sales to $9 million in just two quarters.

Another development that is only slightly less painful is the aggressive price competition, most Asian biogeneric competitors are confident of selling biologics at half the brand price and still achieving 30% operating margins.

It seems increasing clear that once a biotechnology company reaches a certain size, it, like its large pharma brethren, becomes unable to get much out of its heavy R and D spending. Everyone is looking for ways to fill their empty larders, as the new science is taking longer to mature and needs another decade or more. So, for the time being, it is a zero-sum game, and only a lucky few are able to overpay and bring in one of the few exciting late stage products.

The new science will bring innovative therapeutics with predictable productivity within a generation. Their impact on the quality of our lives is going to be even greater than the impact 'IT' (Information Technology) has had over the last generation.

Such targetted products aimed at well-diagnosed sub-patient populations will need much smaller trials of short duration (supported by extensive on-market, monitoring with IT tools), requiring focussed marketing with little sales effort.

Firstly industry will have to survive another decade of painful transition where analysis of the industry pipeline shows only incremental life-cycle management types of new products. M and As may be the only effective near-term answer. Since there are only few companies with timely innovative products and good deals are hard to find, with keen competition and bidding wars bringing final prices well above the fair values.

To conclude, like pharma, the life science, biotechnology and supply industry needs to understand its customers. It is becoming increasingly important to be realistic that as competition is intersifying and acquisitions are leading suppliers into new, unfamiliar markets.

Also, life science product life cycles are short, so companies should extract as much value from their products as possible. By identifying how scientists choose products, the companies can better understand how to impact this process using market research.

SUMMARY

It takes time to roll out a new product successfully and gain consumer acceptance and make profits. It is not always easy to transform a brilliant idea or important discovery into a commercial opportunity and many of entrepreneurs have done it successfully. Care should be taken to manage project and marketing of biotechnological inventions.

Also, budgeting is important for managing a project.

REVIEW QUESTIONS

1. What do you mean by marketing strategies?
2. Discuss launch of product?
3. What is life cycle of a product?
4. Describe the stages of product development.
5. What is project management. Discuss?
6. Describe bioentrepreneurship of a product.
7. What is the role of advertising in marketing?
8. How a product is evaluated for its success and consumer acceptance?
9. What are the factors that affect project management?
10. Prepare a list of important points for project management.
11. Chalk out the plan to develop new product.
12. List out stages of product development.
13. Discuss the launching of new products.
14. How to plan budget for developing a new project?
15. Give an account of what a new company should have.
16. Discuss cost factor involved in product development.
17. What is bioentrepreneur?
18. Describe the qualities of successful entrepreneur.
19. Describe the life-cycle of product.
20. Discuss marketing strategies.
21. Discuss role of advertising in marketing a product.
22. Enlist the qualities of advertising.
23. Discuss market trends for biotechnology.
24. Discuss the changing scenario of biotech industry.

Chapter 11

Intellectual Property Rights Concepts and Relevance

INTELLECTUAL PROPERTY (IP)

IP arises from an application of intellect and ingenuity and is usually in the form of an idea, concept, design, process etc. to generate a product ultimately. With emergence of modern technology, intellectual property is legal characterization and treatment of trade-related biotechnological processes and products.

Under biotechnology, important examples of intellectual property is processes and products that result from development of genetic engineering techniques (using restriction enzymes) to create recombinant DNA. These IPs can be copied and used by others, thereby reducing the benefits of original inventors.

The right of an individual to derive from intellectual property and to exclude others from doing so is referred to as INTELLECTUAL PROPERTY RIGHTS.

UTILITY PATENTS for genetic materials (both plants and animals) have been allowed in some countries so that patented material cannot be used for further breeding or cultivation (in case of seeds) without paying a fees to the patent holder.

These IPRs affect (both favourably as well as unfavourably) the conservation, availability and use of Plant and Animal Genetic Resources (PGR and AGR).

Also, IPRs may adversely affect:

- food security.
- use of evolved agricultural practices.
- biological diversity.
- ecological balance.

BENEFITS OF IPR

Biotechnological products can be protected by any of 4 IPRs (Patent, trade secret, copyright, and trademark).

These properties can be bought, sold and licenced like any property.

Factors Affecting Selection of Most Appropriate of Mode of Protection

1. *Pace of Technological Development*—In case of rapid technological growth, trade secret approach may be preferred.
2. *Cost-Effectiveness of Obtaining a Patent*—One has to decide between cost of secrecy (trade secret) and cost of obtaining and enforcing patent.
3. *Security*—If it is impossible to prevent disclosure of a trade secret, one may prefer rights other than secrecy.
4. *Need to show Patents to Investors*—For the purpose of showing invention to investors, patents may have to be shown.

Also, need of protection depends on the nature of subject matter that needs to be protected. *e.g.*, an instruction manual can be subjected to copyright or protected as trade secret, but cannot be protected as a patent.

CATEGORIES OF IPR

1. Trade Secret.
2. Copyright.
3. Trademark.
4. Patent.

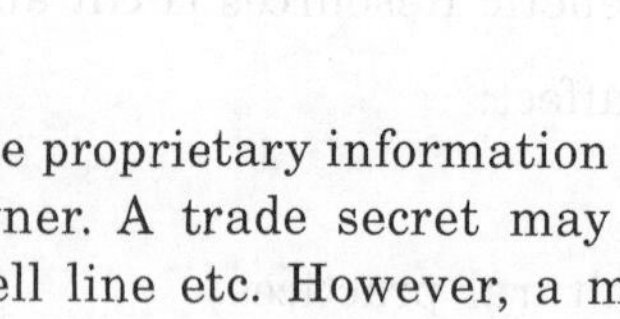

Figure 11.1 Categories of IPR

Trade Secret

Trade secret includes private proprietary information or physical material that allows a definite advantage to the owner. A trade secret may protect a formula, production process, a microbial strain or cell line etc. However, a manuscript, design, product etc. cannot be protected as a trade secret.

Trade secret in biotechnology includes:

- cell lines.
- hybridization condition.

- merchandising (corporate) plans.
- customer lists.

Duration

Trade secrets have unlimited duration and the process is simpler as compared to patents.

Disclosure of Trade Secret

Disclosure and unauthorised use of a disclosure of a trade secret is punishable by law and owner may be allowed compensation.

Advantages of Trade Secret

1. Unlimited duration.
2. Easy to obtain—lack of legal formalities and requirements while patent is granted 2 years after the application is filed.
3. Involve reduced risk of someone improving upon the process/formulation etc.
4. Does not require filing of application.
5. Contesting and enforcing IPR.

Limitations

1. Its maintenance is costly.
2. It has no protection from independent innovation/invention.
3. It cannot be applied to many IPs.
4. Since it involves nondisclosure, this delays and hampers scientific/technological progress and further innovations.

Copyright

Certain IP that are not patentable, are protected by copyright. These IPs include books (authored and edited), audio and video cassettes. A copyright cannot be reproduced in part or total without the permission of the person holding the copyright (author, editor, publisher, producer).

Copyright is possible only on expressed material (printed, pained, tape/video/computer recorded or expressed in any other form).

Copyrights rules are modified from time to time. In case of biotechnology, copyright, may cover DNA sequence, computer databases, DNA instruction manuals. However, protection of copyright is limited *e.g.*, ideas given in print can be used for any purpose though photocopy of book may not be allowed.

Trademark

It is symbol or word used by a manufacturer or an agent to identify and distinguish his goods from those produced by others.

e.g., in biotechnology, laboratory equipments bear trademarks, certain vectors used in recombinant research are known by their trademarks.

Patents

A patent is a grant of right to exclude others from making, using or selling on invention for a limited period (in USA it is 20 years, in India, it is 5 years). A patent is valid in a country that has granted it, but, one can apply for the same in 2 or more countries and the process is cumbersome.

Patents are granted for—invention, improvement/innovation in an invention, process of producing a product and, a concept.

Requirements for Award or a Patent

1. Novelty.
2. Inventiveness.
3. Industrial application and usefulness.
4. Patentability.
5. Disclosure.

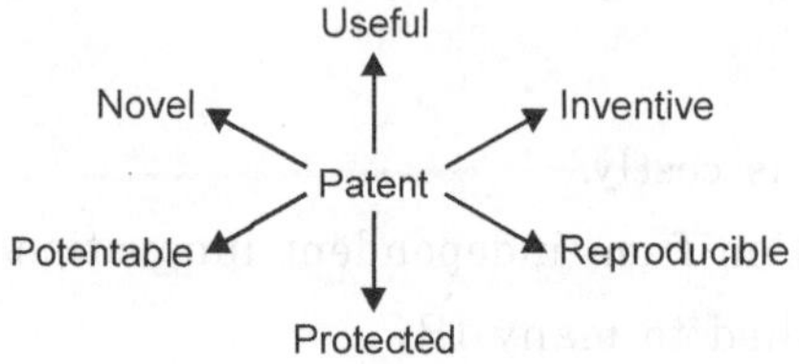

Figure 11.2 Criteria for patenting

Procedure

The details of patent requirements will be discussed in next chapter.

1. Preparation of an application for a patent according to prescribed proforma.
2. Filing of application with Patents Office of the country.
3. Scrutiny of application by competent person and if found suitable for patenting is published for information of all concerned.
4. Objections—can he raised by patenting authority or anyone who challenges application file. Appeals and challenges are decided by competent authorities.
5. Grant/award of patent to the applicant.

MANAGEMENT OF IPR

IPR is acquired by IP owners for anticipated profits on commercialization of concerned IP. This further requires R and D efforts which involves:

1. Transfer of IPR to generate maximum profit from IP.
2. Collaborations with business establishments to facilitate commercialization of IPRs.

3. Monitoring of infringements of IPRs.
4. Renewal of patents and designs periodically.
5. Evaluation of Royalty for further periodic renewal in country of interest.

BENEFITS OF IPR

1. IPR encourages and safeguards intellectual and artistic creations.
2. It promotes quick spread of newer ideas and technologies widely by disclosure of patents.
3. It encourages investment in R and D efforts and funding.
4. It leads to overall economic development.

PROBLEMS OF IPR

1. IPR encourages monopoly and industrial rivalry and takeovers.
2. In case of broad patents, IPR will work only for financially powerful corporations/ nations. This will be detrimental to scientific and technological progress and would pose a threat for global food security. Also, it will further increase the gap between developing and developed countries in terms of economic status and quantum of innovations (IPR holdings).
3. It may adversely affect biological diversity and ecological balance.

Developing countries should undertake well planned programmes to promote innovations and inventions to boost their IPR holdings for their overall economic and scientific growth and development.

SUMMARY

One of the most important issues that has come up after emergence of modern biotechnology is legal characterization and treatment of trade related biotechnological processes and products termed as **intellectual property.** One needs to be conversant about the intellectual property rights and patent system to protect, licence, trade and market his research and inventions.

REVIEW QUESTIONS

1. What is intellectual property and what are the rights available to protect it?
2. Short notes:
   (*i*) Process of patent.
   (*ii*) GATT.
   (*iii*) Benefits of IPR.
   (*iv*) Utility patents for genetic material.

3. How IP can be protected?
4. Enlist advantages and limitations of trade secret.
5. What is copy right?
6. What is a patent?
7. How IPR is managed?
8. What are the benefits and problem of IPR?
9. How will you exercise your choice to protect an intellectual property?
10. How IP differs from patents?
11. Make a list of benefits of IPR.
12. Make a list of mode of IP protection.
13. What is concept of trade secret in biotechnology?
14. Make a list of advantages of trade secret.
15. Prepare a list of items coming under copyright.
16. Prepare a list for requirement for awarding a patent.
17. List the benefits of IPR.
18. Enumerate the problems of IPR.

Chapter 12

BIOTECHNOLOGICAL PATENTS

INTRODUCTION

The principal objective of biotechnology is to produce commercial products for economic gain.

No company would, initiate high-risk, long-term projects with out knowing that results of its research efforts can be legally protected from competitors. Also, society is also encouraging industrial innovation. It is for the government to grant exclusive rights to inventors for novel products and processes they develop. These sanctioned privileges are collectively termed as INTELLECTUAL PROPERTY RIGHTS.

IPR

Intellectual Property Rights

They include:

1. trade secrets.
2. copyrights.
3. trademarks and
4. patents.

Trade Secrets

It comprises of private information about specific technical procedures and formulations that a company wishes to protect from others.

Copyrights

Protected authorship of published work from its unauthorized use.

Trademarks

It can be either symbols or words that identify a particular process or product of a company.

Patents

For biotechnology, patents form most important part of intellectual property. Patent is a legal document that provides exclusive rights to the patent holder for implementing the invention commercially.

PATENT

Features of Patent

1. On the basis of the extent of claims of patent, patent holder can develop other products derived from their original invention.
2. Also, they can sell right to use their invention to their competitors for developing a product based on it.
3. Patent is a public document containing a detailed description of invention.
4. It also informs about nature and limits of invention, allowing people to start to continue working in a particular direction.

Patent decisions and law vary from country to country:

(*i*) In US, the duration of exclusion rights of a patent was 17 years after it was officially awarded.

(*ii*) In Canada, and many European countries it is 20 years from the date of filing the patent application.

Now there is an International Agreement, life of a patent is limited to 20 years from date of filing. It usually takes 2 to 5 years following the filing of the initial patent application before it is granted.

Four Fundamental Requirements for Patenting

1. The invention after having been shown to work must be "novel".
2. Invention must contain an innol.
3. Invention must useful in some way.
4. Every **patent application** must contain a description of the invention to show that a person is knowledgeable in the same field capable of implementing his invention.

Issues that are not Patentable

Certain inventions and discoveries are not patentable namely:

(*i*) scientific theories.

(*ii*) mathematical methods.

(*iii*) aesthetic creations.

(*iv*) therapeutic treatments of humans or animals.

Also, a patent cannot be granted for anything that is a "product of nature".

Applying for a Patent

There is no simple, immediate system for the grant of a patent. The application must be prepared by an expert and organized in a definite pattern.

The application must have:

- a title.
- an abstract.
- selection on background of invention.
- description of current "state of art" in the field of invention.
- comprehensive summary of invention with relevant figures, schematic representations.
- account of nature of invention.
- how it works.
- list of claims about the invention.
- and how invention may be used.

Then application is submitted to Patent and Trademark Office, where it is reviewed for novelty, utility, acceptability non-obviousness, feasibility of invention. The application is examined by examiner and if it meets all the criteria for patentability, then a patent is awarded.

PROTECTION OF PATENT RIGHTS is the responsibility of patent holder.

If a patent application is rejected by an examiner, applicant can appeal the decision with Patent Appeals Board and further can challenge legally.

Table 12.1 Patent Application

Application
Title
Abstract
Background of invention
"State of Art" infield of invention
Summary of invention
Working of invention
List of claims
Proposed use/application of invention

Major Categories of Patent

1. Product Patents.
2. Process Patents.

Table 12.2 Categories of patent

Categories	*Example*
1. *Product Patents:*	
Substance	Cloned genes, recombinant proteins, monoclonal Ab, plasmid, vectors.
Composition of matter	Vaccines, pharmaceutical, mixtures, microorganisms and transgenic organisms.
Devices	DNA sequence, pulsed-field gel electrophoresis.
2. *Process Patents:*	
Process of preparation	DNA isolation, PCR applications, purification of recombinant protein, vector-insert construction.
Methodologies	Nucleic acid hybridization assay, diagnostic assays, PCR based detection systems.
Actual use	Non-therapeutic animal treatment systems, fermentation of genetically modified organisms.

With the development of molecular biotechnology, questions about whether private industries should be allowed to own or patent genetically engineered organisms have been raised.

Patenting Multicellular Organisms

The patenting of multicellular organisms continues to raise ethical and social concerns. To date, a transgenic mouse (on co mouse) carrying an activable gene that makes it susceptible to tumour formation has been patented in both US and Europe. Also, genetically manipulated plants have been accepted as patentable inventions.

Patenting transgenic animals will be the challenge on moral grounds. Danish Parliament has passed a statute that exempts animals from becoming intellectual property. Therefore they are not subject to patent protection.

Patenting and Fundamental Research

Patenting has an impact on how University-based biotechnology research is conducted. Traditionally, science, especially university-based research, has been an open system with a free exchange of ideas and materials through publication and personal communications. However, scientific community has begun to feel that integrity of traditional scientific inquiry has become secondary to self-interest, where public recognition and financial gain from primary innovations are the prime motivations for conducting scientific research. Now scientists are advised by patent lawyers to keep their work secret until a patent is filed. Consequently, the lure of patenting has made a large number of scientists reluctant to talk about their work, until the patent has been filed.

Also, due to shortage of funds available to researchers, licensing fees and royalities from patents can be source of new income. Massachusetts Institute of Technology files more than 100 patents annually in all research fields, generating $ 5.5 millions per year from licencing patent rights.

To sum up, due to enthusiasm for patenting and patent protection, traditional science may become hostage to patent holdings and research will become less fruitful. On the otherhand, traditional way of doing science is an out modelled inefficient and indulgent exercise and drive patent ownership will spur new discoveries. With the development of molecular biotechnology question arises regarding allowing the private industries to own or patent genetically engineered organisms.

BIOTECHNOLOGICAL PATENTS

Patent

Patent is a legal document issued by government (patent office) that safeguards the privileges and rights of an invention/inventor. It allows holder the right to manufacture, sell or use an invention for a defined period of 20 years usually.

Patenting in Biotechnology

Patent is most important form of Intellectual Property Rights (IPRs) in biotechnology.

Under biotechnology, processes and products resulting from genetic engineering techniques. (using restriction enzymes for creating recombinant DNA) are examples of Intellectual Property (IP). Also, this biotechnological IP encourage creation of Research and Development (R&D) units, raising of funds, and commercial production of marketable items. Many legal and public policies of biotechnological research have been challenged and modified.

Need of the hour is to make research scientists, University/Institute administrators will increase the pace of research for development of technologies in biotechnology.

International Harmonization of Patent Laws

Patent laws of different countries are quite variable.

Properties of Patent

1. Patents are valid only in the country of awards.
2. Patents are granted only to new inventions.
3. Obtaining patent is a costly affair.
4. However, patents are obtained from two or more countries.

Criteria for Patenting

1. Invention must be novel : NOVELTY
2. Invention must useful : UTILITY
3. Invention must be inventive : INVENTIVE
4. Invention must be disclosed in such a way that it is reproducible easily by other researchers : DISCLOSURE
5. It should be granted a SCOPE OF PROTECTION
6. It must relate to a technology where patents are permitted : PATENTABLE

Fundamental Requirement of Patent Law

Inventor should describe the invention fully in the application.

Making Patent Application

Patenting is a commercial decision, assisted by legal advice.

It must contain detailed information about the invention:

- background.
- description of nature of invention by using illustrations, figures.
- description of its utility.

The patent application with its accompanying description and deposited material is kept confidential till its publication.

Time Period

In many European countries, the process of grant patent starts 18 months after publication of the application. In Japan and USA public access to deposited material is allowed after granted some enforceable right to the applicant.

Treaties

International Treaties

1. Paris Convention Treaty (PCT).
2. World Intellectual Property Organization (WIPO).
3. European Patent Convention (EPC).
4. Trade Related Intellectual Property Rights (TRIPs).
5. World Trade Organisation (WTO).

India and TRIPS

TRIPs forms a part of General Agreement on Tariffs and Trade (GATT) which is most comprehensive multilateral agreement on IPR.

TRIPS cover a variety of intellectual properties including patents and plant variety protection. Member countries have to frame their patent laws within broad framework of GATT.

India is a signatory of GATT and amended Patents Bill in 1999.

Categories of Biotechnological Inventions that are Patentable

1. Methods/processes that generate useful products.
2. Production of biologicals *e.g.*, antibiotics, antibodies, vitamins.
3. Application of various processes/products : *e.g.*, using promoter sequence for regulating action of gene.
4. To obtain strains of microorganisms, cell lines.
5. DNA sequences.
6. Methods of genetic modification of organisms.

PATENTING OF GENES AND DNA SEQUENCES

Artificially synthesized genes normally fullfill the requirements of patent and are patentable. In USA, requirement of practical applicability of a gene is relaxed. *e.g.*, in case of isolated genes, vectors, transformed cells expressing hormone, angiogenesis factor (AGF) *e.g.*, gene aroA (confers glycophosate resistance isolated from mutant bacterium was patented in USA. On the other hand, in UK and India, isolated natural genes are not patentable.

Gene Patents and Genetic Resources

Development countries are technology rich but gene poor. On the other hand, developing countries are technology poor, but they are gene rich. Developed countries have made extensive collections of germplasms of all important crops of developing countries and are using them to develop superior variety which are sold to developing countries to generate huge profits.

Patenting of Life Forms

Life forms are not patentable in India. In developed countries naturally occurring microorganisms are not patentable, however, modified microorganisms by employing more ingenious techniques such as genetic engineering are now patentable. USA and Japan allow patents on non-naturally occurring, non-human multicellular organisms. European Union allows patents on genetically modified microorganisms, plants and animals. Such patents are not allowed in India. So far, patents have not been granted for genes owing to the reason that genes are natural, universal, inherent biological function units of all life forms.

Issues Related to Patenting Life Forms

Points Favouring

Points favouring patenting genetically modified life forms:

1. Their production requires large financial, technical and innovative inputs.
2. They perform novel and useful function.
3. They generate economic benefits for nation.
4. They provide financial returns to inventor.
5. Assured returns from inventions promote R&D and thus inventiveness.

Main Objections

They are based on moral, ethical, religious grounds:

1. Life forms are products of nature.
2. Their genetic modification does not mean their invention.
3. Biotechnological innovation cause cruelty to animals.

BROAD PATENTS IN BIOTECHNOLOGY

Broad patents granted in USA for plant traits and technology processes are as follows:

1. For technology

(*a*) Antisense RNA technology : Enzo Biochem Inc.

(*b*) Gene gun method of genetic engg. of soyabean : WR Grace & Co.

2. For specific traits

(*a*) Transgenic plants : with increased lysine: Pioneer Hi-Bred

(*b*) Sunflower with low saturated FA : Dekalb Genetic Corp.

3. For plants

(*a*) All Transgenic

(*i*) Cotton : WR Grace & Co.

(*ii*) All Transgenic Soyabean : WR Grace & Co.

(*b*) All Transgenic Brassica : Calgene Inc.

However, patent for transgenic cotton has been challenged in USA and revoked. These broad patents are morally unacceptable and fundamentally inequitable. If such protection are allowed, IPR will work only for financially powerful corporations/nations leading to their monopoly control over biotechnological modifications which would be determental to scientific and technological progress.

Current Issues in Patenting

The most current issue is "when can live forms be patented?"

The human genomic project have elucidated almost the entire sequence of human genome, besides identifying the genes.

Patenting of DNA sequences and genes has become a debatable issue. So far, no patents have been granted for genes.

Patent law makes a distinction between invention and discovery and does not allow patent for a discovery. However, if a natural substance has been first isolated, then the process developed to isolated this may be patentable. Similarly antibiotics, and other microbial metabolites are patentable substances.

Other examples are:

(*i*) pure vitamin B_{12}.

(*ii*) E-coli in which human genes have been incorporated for production of : human insulin, human GH, human tissue plasminogen activator (tPA) have been recognized for patent.

Cases Dealing with Patents of Products of Nature Contested in USA

1. Factor VIII

Protein VIII C was purified by Scripps Clinic and Research Foundation (USA). Genentech later produced VIII : C by recombinant method and was sued by Scripps for infringement of their reissue patent.

2. Erythropoietin

Amgen Inc held a US patent for preparing erythropoietin. However, Genetics Institute Inc. obtained a broad product claim for erythropoietin.

3. tPA

UK patent claim for recombinant tPA was allowed to Genentech which later failed on legal grounds to US patent.

4. Human nerve growth factor (βNGF)

Patent application for recombinant βNGF was rejected by US Patent Office, based on absence of evidence that recombinant product was significantly different from natural material or has any novel properties.

5. Hybridoma Technology

Wistar Institute's application to US Patent Office for producing viral antibodies by hybridoma technology was turned down. But, use of monoclonal antibodies was later allowed by High Court of Appeals in USA.

INDIAN RESPONSE TO PATENT UPHEAVAL

Patent activity is greatly concentrated in EU, USA and Japan and account for over 90% of patent applications filed worldwide.

It is feared that high technologies like biotechnology, (which demand huge financial and high technological inputs) would further increase economic and IPR holdings gap between developing and developed countries.

India must undertake well planned programmes to overhaul their social, scientific, legal and political environments to promote innovations and inventions. India has developed its own (Plant Breeder's Rights) PBR system. Also, India has amended its patent laws as per provisions of GATT and TRIPS suggestions. But, natural genes are not patentable in India.

Patenting and Biotechnology Research

The biotechnological research might not have progressed to the same extent as it is today without the dreams of getting the patents by scientists and research funding organisations.

BASICS OF PATENT LICENSING

Patent License

A license is a document or agreement giving permission to do something.

However, a patent is only a right to exclude others from making, using or selling ones invention. A patent does not give its owner the affirmative right to make, use or sell the patent invention.

The license must always be aware that there may be other patents that cover the product. So, license agreement should be a clear, unambiguous document that accurately describes the transaction.

SUMMARY

Due to enthusiasm for patenting and patent protection, tradition science may become hostage to patent holding and research will be less fruitful. With the development of molecular technology, fundamental issues are arising regarding what to patent, how to patent and how to derive benefits from patent. A biotechnologist needs to be conversant with IPR and patenting laws and ethical issues related to it.

REVIEW QUESTIONS

1. What is intellectual property right? List its components.
2. What are the important features of patent?
3. How one can apply for a patent?
4. What are major categories of patent, give examples?
5. Discuss patenting and fundamental research.
6. Should the genetic material be patented?
7. What the current issues in patenting?
8. What are broad patents granted in biotechnology?
9. Give an account of cases dealing with patents for producing natural products.
10. What is IP and what are IPRs?
11. Make a list of features of patent.

12. Give an account of patent laws in various countries.
13. What are categories of IPRs?
14. What are treaties regarding patenting?
15. Make a list of products patented under two categories of patents.
16. Give an account of patenting and fundamental research.
17. Prepare a list of issues that can be patented and those who cannot be patented.
18. How to apply for a patent?
19. Enumerate patenting of gene and genetic resources.
20. Debate: patenting of genetic material: whether it should be or it should not be allowed.
21. Make a list of current issues in patenting.
22. Give an account of Indian scene of patenting.
23. Explore the basics of patent license.
24. What is GATT?